Moving to the Cloud Corporation

Moving to the Cloud Corporation

How to face the challenges
and harness the potential of
cloud computing

Leslie Willcocks
*Professor of Technology Work and Globalization, London School of
Economics and Political Science, London, U.K.*

Will Venters
*Lecturer in Information Systems, London School of Economics and
Political Science, London, U.K.*

Edgar A. Whitley
*Reader in Information Systems, London School of Economics and
Political Science, London, U.K.*

First published 2014 by
PALGRAVE MACMILLAN

Palgrave Macmillan in the UK is an imprint of Macmillan Publishers Limited, registered in England, company number 785998, of Houndmills, Basingstoke, Hampshire RG21 6XS.

Palgrave Macmillan in the US is a division of St Martin's Press LLC, 175 Fifth Avenue, New York, NY 10010.

Palgrave Macmillan is the global academic imprint of the above companies and has companies and representatives throughout the world.

Palgrave® and Macmillan® are registered trademarks in the United States, the United Kingdom, Europe and other countries.

ISBN 978–1–137–34746–6   hardback

This book is printed on paper suitable for recycling and made from fully managed and sustained forest sources. Logging, pulping and manufacturing processes are expected to conform to the environmental regulations of the country of origin.

A catalogue record for this book is available from the British Library.

A catalog record for this book is available from the Library of Congress.

DEDICATION

To Angela and Hannah – both are an inspiration.

CONTENTS

LIST OF TABLES AND FIGURES

About the Authors

Dr Leslie Willcocks is Professor of Technology Work and Globalization at the London School of Economics and Political Science and Director of the Outsourcing Unit there. He is known for his work on global sourcing, information management, IT evaluation, e-business, and organizational transformation as well as for his practitioner contributions to many corporations and government agencies. He is an Associate Fellow at Green-Templeton College, University of Oxford. He has been Editor-in-Chief of the *Journal of Information Technology* for the last 25 years, and is joint series editor, with Mary C. Lacity, of the Palgrave book series *Technology Work and Globalization.*

He has co-authored 37 books, including most recently *Advanced Outsourcing: Rethinking ITO, BPO and Cloud Services* (Palgrave, London, 2013), *The Rise of Legal Services Outsourcing* (Bloomsbury Press, London, 2014), and *Global Business Management Foundations* (Steve Brookes Publishing, Stratford, 2014). He has published over 230 refereed papers in journals such as *Harvard Business Review, Sloan Management Review, MIS Quarterly, MISQ Executive, Journal of Management Studies, Communications of The ACM*, and *Journal of Strategic Information Systems*. He writes a regular column on outsourcing called 'Admissible Evidence' for *Professional Outsourcing* magazine and is a regular keynote speaker at international practitioner and academic conferences. With extensive consulting experience, he is regularly retained as adviser and expert witness by major corporations and government institutions. Contact: l.p.willcocks@lse.ac.uk

Dr Will Venters is a lecturer within the Information Systems and Innovation Group, part of the Department of Management at the London School of Economics, and an associate of the Outsourcing Unit there. His research focuses on the development of widely distributed computing systems. His recent research has focused on grid computing, cloud computing, and knowledge management systems. He has researched distributed work and systems in various organizations including government-related bodies, the construction industry, and the financial services and health sectors, and most recently among particle physicists at the Large Hadron Collider at CERN. He has undertaken consultancy for a wide range of companies and has published articles in journals including the *Journal of Management Studies*, *Information Systems Journal*, *Journal of Information Technology*, *Information Technology & People* (where he is also an associate editor), and *Journal of Knowledge Management Research & Practice*. Until recently he was a member of the board of Youthnet, the UK's first online charity, and was the former chair of a national volunteering charity. He writes a blog on cloud computing at http://utilitycomputing.wordpress.com and regularly speaks at both academic and practitioner conferences on this topic. Contact: w.venters@lse.ac.uk

Dr Edgar A. Whitley is a reader in Information Systems in the Information Systems and Innovation Group at the London School of Economics (LSE). He has a B.Sc. (Econ.) and a Ph.D. in Information Systems, both from the LSE. Edgar is the co-editor of *Information Technology & People*. He has recently completed the EnCoRe project (www.encore-project.info), which addressed the role of consent (and the revocation of consent) as a mechanism for providing control over the use of personal data. Together with Gus Hosein, he has recently published *Global Challenges for Identity Policies* (Palgrave, 2010). He has published a number of refereed journals on cloud and is an expert on data privacy and security in the context of the Internet. He is co-author of several studies of cloud and the future of business and regularly presents on this subject to practitioner audiences. Contact: e.a.whitley@lse.ac.uk

ACKNOWLEDGMENTS

First and foremost, as ever, we thank the now over 4,000 executives across the globe who have participated in our survey and interview research on information and communications technology, outsourcing, innovation, and now cloud computing, over the last 23 years. Without them our work, including the present volume, just would not have been possible. For the present research project we interviewed over 120 practitioners on their cloud experiences and perspectives, as well as surveying over 1,300 in two surveys. We would like to thank them all for their wonderful illustrative stories, the hard-won knowledge they bring to bear on the issues, and their kindness, responsiveness, and openness when it comes to research access, despite their intensely globalized work patterns. Due to the sensitive nature of cloud computing and sourcing, many participants requested anonymity and cannot be publicly acknowledged. Participants who did not request anonymity are acknowledged in the appropriate places throughout the book. We are very grateful to all our colleagues at the London School of Economics for their tolerance and support, especially over the last three years, when this book was in incubation. Thanks also to the great team we are now part of in following through on the cloud research. They are Peter Reynolds of MIT, Mary Lacity of the University of Missouri, and Alan Thorogood and Daniel Schlagwein of the University of New South Wales. We would also particularly like to acknowledge the great support of Accenture throughout, and specifically in the 2011–2012 round of interviewing, and with the most recent, 2013–2014, global survey and interview work we have been doing in Europe, Asia Pacific, North America, and Europe. Thanks in particular to John Hindle, Matthew Coates, and Gabi Custodio of Accenture for all the great introductions, for the time you spent with us, and for giving us a much smoother passage toward our goals than we could have ever hoped for. Special thanks from us and the team to Gabi Custodio for having faith in us and supporting the 2013 research project.

On personal notes, Leslie would like to thank his circle of family and friends for their forbearance and humor, and especially Damaris,

George, Catherine, Chrisanthi, Andrew, and Christine for the getaway times at the opera, beach, theatre, galleries, tennis, whatever. As ever, he thanks his beloved wife Damaris for making life exactly what it should be. Will would like to thank his wonderful wife Angela and daughter Hannah, to whom this book is dedicated, who show him that love is above all. Edgar would like to thank his family and friends for all their support over the years, and Vivien – who has been there for him on the journey to the cloud.

We are also hugely grateful to all at Palgrave for commissioning the book, and for seeing it through to the bookshops – physical and otherwise – so professionally and speedily. We would like to thank in particular Tamsine O'Riordan, Karen Beaulah, Emma Ross, Joseph Laredo, and the excellent design and proofreading team.

Preface – Toward the Cloud-enabled Business

INTRODUCTION

As more organizations harness the low costs, elastic processing power, and high flexibility of cloud computing services, the cloud-enabled business is progressing from theoretical blueprint to reality. No business executive today can ignore cloud computing. Many global organizations are already using it, and more and more cloud services are becoming available. The promise is immense. But along with offering promise, cloud computing generates challenging questions. While it promises to deliver a wide and powerful range of capabilities, its potential uses are exceptionally broad and difficult to foretell. Further, it will affect how computing is done and managed, how information is controlled, and the economics of business technology. The technology's novelty and the hype found in some media stories make it even harder to evaluate its potential, costs, and risks. With so many issues to explore, decision makers can easily succumb to 'analysis paralysis' or the temptation to abandon their inquiry to the IT department. But cloud computing is too important for such missteps.

Senior executives must come to a timely, focused, and productive evaluation of cloud computing. They also need to revisit that assessment regularly, for, as this book details, cloud computing is already enabling strategic transformations. Some time ago at Accenture we identified six key business questions that decision makers new to the cloud computing phenomenon should ask.[1] The questions still have huge relevance. By focusing on these questions, executives can narrow their inquiry without succumbing to superficiality, and start to identify opportunities and risks for themselves. The questions are: first, what is cloud, and how does it work? Second, what specific benefits can cloud bring to my organization? Third, can I depend on cloud to save my organization money? Fourth, how will cloud affect the way my organization competes? Fifth, what risks must my organization manage? And last, what are my next steps? You will find thoughtful answers to these questions throughout this book.

You will also find in chapter 6 a detailed answer to the other key question that cloud computing raises, and on which I will spend some time here, both because of its importance and also because of the many misunderstandings around the subject. That question is: What are the implications of cloud computing for the IT function? In my view, cloud brings a precious opportunity to redefine and reshape IT's relationship with the business. This change can transform agility, speed, and cost not only in IT, but also for the business as a whole – creating a new type of high-agility, high-growth organization that Accenture calls the 'cloud-enabled business.' All senior executives in a cloud-enabled organization will need to manage, organize, and resource the IT function in a very different way. Here at Accenture we see this shift having several dimensions.

CLOUD – CHANGING BUSINESS AND IT RELATIONSHIPS

First, IT must evolve to secure its future in a cloud-enabled business. The migration to cloud services brings profound implications for all the value drivers in an organization, ranging from speed to market, to operational agility, to strategic options. If the IT function does not reflect these impacts by evolving the way it works and interacts with the business, it risks being sidelined and ultimately even becoming redundant in the eyes of its customers within the organization.

In the cloud era, a business unit leader has the option of bypassing IT and buying services direct from cloud providers. Given the speed at which the sophistication, range, and take-up of cloud solutions are gaining momentum, there is a risk that this scenario is already happening. In cases where customers bypass IT in this way, the outcome, we find, is usually highly damaging, with negative impacts on IT costs, standardization, interoperability, and integration. To reduce these risks and remain relevant in the cloud era, IT must demonstrate the tangible value it provides to the business.

To remain relevant, IT needs to evolve its capabilities and processes at pace, particularly, as this book makes clear, in the areas of supplier selection and management, risk management, and governance. Specifically, it will need the ability to team and collaborate more closely with business customers, understand their needs more deeply, and then meet those needs more responsively by sourcing, managing, and integrating a diverse mix of cloud-based, on-premise, and legacy services. What will these changes mean for the IT function?

IT must shift its focus from building bespoke systems to selecting and managing pre-configured components. In a cloud-enabled world, organizations will gain competitive advantage in the marketplace less from systems developed and built in house, and more from the ability to procure and piece together the right cloud components to meet the right customer needs at the right price. This requires a fundamental shift of focus for many IT organizations, which have traditionally served their customers in the business largely by building, operating, and maintaining bespoke systems.

This change has major implications for talent. IT's legacy role means that its core skills base has been primarily concentrated around the technical capabilities needed to take business requirements, develop systems that deliver against them, and then run those systems to continue to meet those needs. While technical skills will still be important going forward, they will need to be balanced with more highly developed capabilities in areas such as understanding business needs and managing relationships with business customers and cloud suppliers. We will say more about the impact on skills later. IT functions that move early, driving a radical reshaping of the IT operating model to reflect the implications of cloud, will have the best chance of avoiding the threat of obsolescence in the fast emerging cloud-driven environment in which we already find ourselves.

IT must become the 'data custodian' for the entire business. As more business and personal interactions, processes, and transactions – from invoicing and payment to customer relationship management (CRM) – migrate from physical to digital platforms, a deluge of data is being generated, both structured and unstructured. The ability to collect, manage, protect, and analyze these data is becoming a critical differentiator for businesses across all sectors. In a cloud environment, corporate, customer, and transactional data will be shared, processed, and communicated across a wide range of cloud-based services. As a result, a critical need exists for a 'data custodian' that looks across the entire business and acts as the protector of data integrity, security, and consistency throughout all systems and processes. IT needs to seize this role as its own. The pivotal importance of data was underlined by the findings of the *Accenture 2012 Technology Vision*.[2] Of the six key themes it highlighted, two focus on data. One is 'converging data architectures,' which successfully rebalance an organization's data architecture portfolio and blend the structured with the unstructured to turn data into new streams of value. The other is 'industrialized data services,' which manage data differently to make them more valuable. IT needs to position itself to capitalize on both themes, again reinforcing its value to the business. Our *2013 Technology Vision* adds in the importance of design for analytics and data velocity as two of the seven key developments for every business in becoming a digital business.[3]

IT must evolve into a role as a 'service director and integrator.' In shifting its focus away from system builds and toward preconfigured components, IT must also begin to act as a director and integrator of a widening range of internally and externally sourced IT services, both legacy and cloud. This role will require the ability to identify, source, and rapidly mesh pre-configured third-party cloud-based offerings into business-relevant service bundles. This is about more than monitoring compliance with technical standards. IT needs to demonstrate proficiency in managing operational complexity, as external cloud providers service a growing array of needs across the business, and as service outages or issues arise across multiple external components and suppliers. IT also has an important role to play in developing a deep understanding of the rapidly changing supplier landscape, thus helping the organization to provide architectural integrity, access the most appropriate and cost-effective services, and reduce commercial risk.

In moving to this new role of service director and integrator, IT functions will be helped by developments on the supply side. Currently, there is a trend toward more generic IT services – such as infrastructure, application platforms, e-mail, and collaboration – being offered by larger cloud providers. These big players can easily integrate their offerings with existing technologies, leverage their economies of scale to offer low costs, and function as trusted providers due to the high stability and security levels of their services.

At the same time, smaller niche cloud players are making inroads in more business-specific areas, as their highly specialized services compete ever more effectively with costly bespoke development solutions.

As cloud providers increasingly meet both of these needs by delivering processes, applications, or services based on shorter-term, pay-per-use contracts, the IT organization's ongoing shift from traditional service provider to service director and integrator – which began in the outsourcing era – will increase in both pace and scope. We believe that the IT role will consist of the following three integral elements:

a) **Selection of services** – In the dynamic cloud marketplace, high performers will be differentiated by their ability to identify and seize opportunities as soon as they arise. To excel in the selection of services, IT organizations will not only need to be up to speed with changes and opportunities in the market, but will also need to look ahead in both the IT and business domains, and identify future business possibilities and demands.

b) **Integration of services** – With success depending on the cost-effective reuse of standard services together with best practices offered both inside and outside the organization's boundaries, the integration of business processes, technology, applications, and data will become key. Additional challenges will include the varying maturity levels of vendors, and the variations between different providers' terms of service, service level agreements (SLAs), and technical integration capabilities, all of which are often non-negotiable.

c) **Operational excellence and security** – The continuity and ongoing optimization of all IT services – whether procured from the cloud or from a non-cloud outsourcing supplier or provided in house – will remain of critical importance. IT needs to assume responsibility for these aspects. With confidential business data and personally identifiable information moving outside the organization's borders, IT security will need to respond rapidly, progressively, and appositely – a need that links to IT's related role as data custodian.

IT must adopt a new operating model for the cloud era. To lock in place all the changes highlighted above and make the benefits permanent, IT will need to adopt a new operating model that reflects the distinct opportunities and risks of cloud-based provisioning. This new model must empower IT to team closely with business customers to understand and meet their changing needs, using a skillfully integrated blend of cloud and legacy/on-premise technologies. It is a model where process maturity is key – and which brings significant implications for the IT organization's workforce and skills. In its new role as IT service director and integrator, IT will need a different focus on capabilities, functions, and roles from the days when it was a traditional IT service provider. The migration to the new cloud operating model will impact every area in IT – but an overarching imperative across the whole IT function will be to shift the skills mix toward higher-value activities. This will mean placing less emphasis on skills in IT service development and service delivery, and more on skills in IT management, service strategy, and business/supplier and vendor management processes. It will also be vital to invest in continuous skills development across all areas. In the future, the quality of an organization's IT capability will depend increasingly on its ability to make effective use of the latest cloud innovations. IT employees in all areas of the IT function will need continuous skill and knowledge development to ensure that they stay fully up to speed with market trends, capabilities, and best practices.

There will need to be profound change in the all main areas of the IT function. Consider **business relationship management**. With the adoption of cloud, the IT organization now has a major opportunity to step up the value chain by acting as a true business enabler rather than a reactive delivery organization. For IT to succeed in making this change, it will be more important than ever for the IT function to understand business priorities and support strategic and innovative thinking by articulating how it can help. In an environment where the business can procure cloud computing solutions directly using a credit card, the IT organization must bring solutions proactively, rather than being seen as an obstacle. For business relationship management this means: faster decision cycles; improved provider and customer management capabilities; well defined SLAs and operational level agreements (OLAs).

Meanwhile, **service strategy** will be more closely intertwined with the business strategy to help confirm that the organization can act on new opportunities the moment they arise. As cloud drives a shift from server-based to service-based architectures, IT needs to maintain a strong focus on enterprise architecture, and an end-to-end overview of the relationships between business initiatives, business processes, underlying IT, and data. Integration and data architecture will become vitally important, covering fundamental topics such as decoupling and master data management. This again underlines the importance of IT's role as the organization's data custodian. These changes bring a number of imperatives in the area of service strategy: more holistic security architecture; market-aware enterprise architecture and design; increased investment flexibility and accountability; and faster decision cycles.

Service development will also need to change. In a cloud environment, the IT organization's project and program management function is likely to provide the highest value when staffed with talent from the IT organization and the business. In a service-based architecture, functional requirements and service levels are becoming more important than pure technical requirements. However, the IT organization still is responsible for – among other things – integration, designs, and security mechanisms. These impacts on service development will require two key changes in this area: integration and testing must become the backbone of IT; testing and automation must be enhanced.

Cloud also implies big shifts in how **service management** is delivered. The service operations, service delivery, and continuous service improvement functions are responsible for the delivery of reliable IT services to the business, while continuously improving quality – irrespective of whether these services are offered in house, by outsourcing partners, or from the cloud. These services will be offered to the business through a transparent service catalog that includes both pricing and SLAs. Simultaneously, support will need to be provided for the services of many different vendors with varying maturity levels, using the service desk and on-site support functions as a single point of contact for customers in the business. Proactive capacity planning becomes key to scaling services up and down in accordance with business requirements. IT leadership should focus particular attention on the maturity, automation, and quality of the following service management processes: mature incident management capability; consistent definition and monitoring of SLAs; well defined SLAs/OLAs; and metrics-driven internal goals.

IT management also changes with cloud. In many organizations, IT budgets are currently revised yearly, and high fixed costs are charged to different business units based on metrics such as size or number of servers. One of the biggest benefits of cloud computing is the pay-per-use model. Leveraging this model demands the implementation of service-based metering and billing. This in turn requires IT finance personnel to be able to price services correctly and charge them to the business in an accurate and timely manner. Again, skills are an issue in IT management, since a service director and integrator needs a different skill set from a traditional service provider. To fulfill the role of service director and integrator effectively, IT organizations will need to focus less than before on task-based technical abilities. Instead, IT organizations will require resources competent in areas like business process integration, vendor management, and communication. So the IT HR function will need to attract and retain talent and skills to provide these new capabilities. These changes bring several implications for IT management: closer integration of operations and finance; an increased role of security management and policy setting; a new approach to disaster recovery and the related policy setting; more mature and holistic risk management; more accurate charge-back models; and increased investment flexibility and accountability.

Finally, and more obviously, **vendor management** will shift. In a cloud environment, the number and criticality of the services provided by external parties increase, making it more important than ever for IT to have an up-to-date overview of the IT marketplace and upcoming trends. This requirement also increases the importance of the vendor management function. In order for vendors to stay closely aligned with the organization's IT ecosystem, the IT function should hold regular meetings with important vendors to identify opportunities, discuss issues, and build trusting relationships. To improve its vendor management and control capabilities – while also reflecting its increased focus on higher-value activities and reduced span of control over suppliers in the cloud – the IT function may decide to recruit specific domain experts who can manage providers more rigorously and effectively.

NEXT STEPS: TOWARD THE CLOUD-ENABLED BUSINESS

I have focused on the IT function, but, as we believe, and as this book makes clear, cloud computing is far too important a technology to leave entirely, or even primarily, to technologists. While the work of migrating from conventional to cloud computing is likely to fall on the shoulders of the CIO, other senior executives have important, indeed key, roles to play. To make sure that an organization maximizes benefits and minimizes risks, senior business executives need to do the following:

Ask hard questions and demand data-based analyses regarding cost savings. Do not assume that there will be automatic and substantial cost savings. Do a return on investment analysis. Consider conversion and ongoing costs as well as savings. Do not be intimidated by the jargon. Experiment or pilot on low-hanging fruit such as workgroup applications, or on a non-mission-critical, non-integrated application. Then be ready to scale up once you have proved that the benefits are worth it.

Establish a clear governance structure for cloud computing. Many organizations have rules and structures in place that govern how IT decisions are shared between line and IT executives. Use them (and if they do not exist, create them) to decide who inside and outside the IT organization should be engaged in decisions on cloud computing, and what decision-making rights and responsibilities they have.

Keep cloud efforts on track. Make sure that cloud computing receives the focused thinking, planning, and follow-up it requires. Use the answers to the six questions outlined above to identify and address immediate business needs that lend themselves to cloud computing and longer-term opportunities for cloud, to develop a plan for using public and private clouds, and to gain the capabilities the plan requires. Make sure that the organization senses and responds appropriately to the impact cloud is having on its industry and competitive environment.

Set the standards for success. Provide the necessary oversight to the IT organization. Make sure goals and deliverables are well understood, and projects are well aligned with business needs. Clarify how the value from cloud computing is to be determined: what quantitative and qualitative benefits are sought? And consider what else constitutes success besides value achieved and projects completed: skills developed, partnerships established, and risks addressed.

Provide the necessary support. Besides financial resources and technical talent, support other activities that will underpin the success of cloud initiatives. For example, organizations may benefit from a community of practice or a cloud program office to develop the skills and share the experiences of people engaged in cloud projects.

Buy cautiously, appraise frequently. It is still a little early to predict who the major cloud providers will be in a few years, what capabilities they will deliver, when they will deliver them, and how well. So when selecting cloud providers, carefully consider whether they have the potential to be a desirable partner in the future. Even after they are chosen, evaluate your partners on their financial stability, as well as on their ability to improve functionality and service levels, to integrate data across different technology platforms and cloud services, and to deliver on their promises.

It will take time for organizations to transition to cloud computing. Most executives are still grappling with its risks and possibilities, and the cost of writing off current IT investments. Still, a massive transition to a hybrid of cloud and conventional computing is under way. The capabilities and potential savings from cloud are too great to ignore.

In addition, software developers and venture capitalists will be drawn to this new market. The low development cost, short development cycle, and quick return on cloud services are irresistible. This means that future IT advances and innovations are much more likely to be based on cloud technologies than on conventional computing. The critical issue is not whether cloud computing will become a fundamental technology in the next decade. What is critical is how companies will make money from the capabilities it offers.

CONCLUSION: THIS BOOK

The migration to a cloud-enabled business is a journey of intense change and discovery both for IT and for the business as a whole. It is one that all parties must undertake together and in close alignment or risk missing out on the full benefits that cloud offers. This book is a welcome, vital, and timely guide. The authors from the highly respected London School of Economics and Political Science – Leslie Willcocks, Edgar Whitley, and Will Venters – have intensively researched the cloud phenomenon over the last three years in its period of early take-off. At Accenture we have been pleased to contribute to and partly support their research work. With their long-standing backgrounds in the study and practice of information technology, outsourcing, and digital innovation, they are able to give a long-run view of the convergence of advanced information and communications technologies to the present point. In their first chapter, then throughout the book, they show cloud computing developing as part of a much broader, increasingly interrelated set of technologies that need to be shaped and managed to realize the potential for business, individuals, societies, and economies. The early chapters spell out the promise of cloud technologies, and what their research shows to be the likely technological and service trajectories of cloud. They alert us to the real challenges and most likely impacts, and suggest a longer time frame than many have suggested for enduring organizational, societal, and business innovations to come through. Innovation is a complex set of processes, and cloud is actually 'clouds' – that is, a complex, ever-evolving set of technologies. While much cannot be anticipated, in its later chapters this book provides some valuable insights into likely developments. The book also focuses directly on the skills and capabilities, and role, of the future IT function – the main issue I have addressed in this Preface.

Readers of this volume will gain rich insight into the cloud phenomenon – into the future and how it can be shaped – and better understand how cloud technologies will influence and inform our business, social, and economic lives, on an increasingly global basis.

Matthew Coates
Managing Director, Cloud, Global Sales and Strategy
Accenture

Introduction

Cloud computing is a service-based perspective on the provision of computing through the exploitation of technical innovations such as virtualization, high-performance networks, and data-center automation. The topic has seen an explosion of interest in the popular media and in business circles as well as registering tremendous take-up in the academic and technical literatures. As early as 2010, Amazon's annual revenue from cloud services was estimated at between $500m and $700m. At much the same time Forrester, the research analysts, predicted a global market for cloud computing worth $61bn for 2012 and they believed this would grow to $241bn by 2020. Benefits would not be restricted to private sector supplier revenues; the U.K. government, for example, aimed to save £1.4bn over four years (2011–2015), in part by launching its own cloud service, while a recent Centre for Economics and Business Research (CEBR) study predicted that the adoption of cloud computing had the potential to generate €763bn of cumulative economic benefits over the period 2010–2015 across the five European economies of France, Germany, U.K., Italy, and Spain. The benefits would come from business development opportunities, business creation, net cost savings, and indirect gross value added (GVA). The study also suggested an additional direct and indirect job creation impact of nearly 2.4 million jobs.

However, these have been predictions, and predicting technological trajectories and their social, economic, and business impacts has always been a difficult and fraught affair, despite the air of certainty and precision often associated with such numbers. Our research shows that despite the widespread interest in the potential benefits of cloud, the enterprise impacts of cloud appear to be emerging more slowly and over a much longer time horizon than many commentators have been suggesting. It is widely recognized that diffusion of new technologies rarely takes place at a steady rate. Instead, it tends to follow an S-shaped curve, starting quite slowly, needing to demonstrate many attributes, and passing through several phases before being fully adopted. The developers and users of cloud computing are on this curve and it will take time before the anticipated organizational benefits of cloud actually materialize. What is less clear, however, is the range of antecedent factors that influence the rate of adoption. Is cloud computing a technology whose technological features will enable fairly rapid adoption and innovation or does cloud computing have characteristics of a 'slow train coming' whereby adoption and subsequent innovation will be limited by other factors?

The objective of this book is to draw on detailed empirical research to better understand the cloud phenomenon and the drivers and inhibitors of cloud adoption and innovation. We also identify how cloud computing is being, and is likely to be, used – in business and other organizations. In doing so, we uncover practices and lessons useful to those embarking on the journey of harnessing the potential of cloud computing and allied advanced technologies. From this foundation we then tread more lightly and speculatively in looking at the shape of the future for organizations and the impact cloud computing could have on our personal, social, and wider economic lives.

Throughout, we see it as important to differentiate the short-term from the long-term possible impacts of cloud technologies and not to conflate the two into too immediate a timeline. Our respondents, especially those working closely with existing systems and technological infrastructures, invariably warned us against assuming that full cloud functionality would be delivered very quickly. Business executives, on the other hand, understandably wanted the significant benefits that cloud could bring within much shorter time horizons – an all-too-familiar story in the IT field. The impact of major innovation, especially technological innovation, has frequently been delayed. On past experience some have offered the rule of 10/10. This means it takes ten years to develop fully the technology set and another ten for it to be implemented, accepted, institutionalized, and exploited in a society. Recently, social networking has perhaps broken this rule dramatically, but cloud, as a convergence of a range of technologies, looks like a 10/10 transformation. This does not mean that we are starting from the beginning, as many aspects of cloud computing are already quite far along this technology development timeline.

We describe in this book the challenges cloud presents, the major impacts that will have to be worked through and the management, organizational, and sectoral changes that will need to occur if the more dramatic innovations in service, business operations and the way businesses compete and government agencies run themselves, are to be realized within the next ten years.

THE RESEARCH BASE

To assess the impact that cloud computing may have on enterprises it is important to evaluate the claims made in the existing literature and critically review these claims against empirical evidence from the field. This book draws on several main sources: an interview base in two research interventions covering 2010–2011 and 2012–2013, industry and academic reports, the LSE Outsourcing Unit 1600 organization sourcing database, a large-scale survey, and a follow-up survey in 2013. We undertook 35 initial interviews with leading industry players across the cloud supply chain. These were added to during 2011–2012, following the procedures outlined below. By late 2012 we had interviewed a total of 56 providers of cloud infrastructures and services, system integrators, analysts, and users of cloud services. During 2013 we interviewed a further 35 case participants and also carried out a cloud survey at the February 2013 Outsourcing World Summit,[1] covering 133 respondents. In terms of roles, we spoke to CEOs, CIOs, marketing and operational managers, strategists, consultants, analysts, and service directors. Interviews were normally undertaken by one person and were held over the phone. They typically lasted at least one hour, some running to over two hours.

In addition to a review of the academic literature and associated industry reports, a distinctive feature of the work reported is the inclusion of results from a large-scale survey of IT industry practitioners. The survey was undertaken by HfS Research[2] in conjunction with the LSE Outsourcing Unit. HfS Research is the foremost research analysis firm and social-networking community focused on helping enterprises make complex global sourcing decisions. It has 120,000 monthly visitors and 37,000 subscribers and leverages this community of sourcing professionals to deliver rapid insights into the global sourcing industry. The first survey ran between October and November 2010. Many of the key results from the survey are presented. Other views on the data and an updated survey for October

2011 are available on the HfS site.[3] The survey was conducted online and disseminated across a broad number of networks and media to collect a large sample of business (non-IT) executives, IT executives and technology vendors, advisors/consultants, and providers of cloud-based services. A total of 1035 responses were collected: 214 from IT executives; 414 from business executives, 407 from technology vendors, advisors/consultants, and providers of cloud-based services.

Our second survey ran in February 2013. The survey sample of 133 delegates captured a range of firm sizes as measured by number of employees worldwide. The average size of firm for customer respondents was 50,751 employees, for provider firms 32,494 employees, and for advisor firms 4201 employees. The sizes ranged from a very small advisory firm with only three employees to a very large client firm with over 300,000 employees. We also asked customers to indicate the industry which best described their organizations. Financial services (34 percent) and insurance (13 percent) were the most represented industries.

These research resources have proved very rich, to the point where we have been able to construct this book out of its findings. In the next section we summarize the arguments of the book, and the topics covered.

THIS BOOK: AN OVERVIEW

The book begins by locating cloud as part of the content-centric era. This is the fourth wave of power based on advanced information and communication technologies following on from the systems-, PC- and network-centric eras, while sharing and partly being founded on these three. Chapter 1 provides a deeper look into where cloud is now, and the likely development of this content-centric era. In chapter 2, employing our Desires Framework, we look at the technological aspects and promise of cloud – what the technology does, and what it is useful for. In chapter 3 we focus on the service dimensions of cloud, pointing to three disruptions that will lead to a service-dominant logic in the IT supply industry. In chapters 4 and 5 we look at five major user challenges with cloud, focusing in detail in chapter 5 on security and privacy issues. In chapter 6 we look at the diffusion of innovation processes and how cloud can be introduced into business organizations. In chapter 7 we discuss management issues, retained capabilities, and human resources, and ways forward for delivering on the potential of cloud over the next five to ten years. In chapter 8, based on our most recent research, we give a detailed insight into the new forms of organization enabled by, and likely to result from, cloud applications. In the final chapter, we provide a broader look into the future, exploring how cloud, in combination with five other technological developments, will, over the next ten years, have profound implications for all of business and social life in both developed and emerging economies. Let us look at the arguments in more detail.

In **chapter 1** we provide a history of technology development leading to the internet and cloud, and the economic and technical challenges and opportunities turbulent technology has presented for management and business. While the subject of cloud is being discussed everywhere, there is a lack of substantive, objective evidence about not just technological trajectories but about the potentially more far-reaching business implications of cloud. We take a longer view across four eras of technological development, and locate cloud in the fourth, content-centric era. This helps us avoid buying too heavily into the language of 'all change' and radical transformation, and making unthinking responses to business hype and fashions. Cloud must be seen in the context of previous so-called 'revolutions' – particularly in technology and in service outsourcing – and can even be portrayed as a 'back to the future' phenomenon but based on superior technology. The chapter points to how organizations will become cloud corporations over the 2014–2025 period, fueled by cloud and six other major technological developments. We also establish a benchmark for where cloud adoption lies in 2013/14, finding that most, but by no means all, client organizations were low on the learning curve in terms of adoption and exploitation of the massive potential inherent in cloud computing.

In **chapter 2** we detail the fundamental technologies represented by cloud, and point out some significant differences from what has gone before – not least more powerful computing/processing capabilities, fatter transport pipes, wireless broadband access, and more open and flexible protocols. We find that cloud is in many ways (finally) delivering on the promises of the past. In a new environment, people appear more prepared to put these capabilities to work due to dynamic changes in internal and external factors: competition/innovation, globalization, user demographics, management readiness, and supplier ecosystems. The chapter discusses definitions of cloud, describes its constituent parts – in fact there are many clouds – and provides a Desires Framework as a way of evaluating cloud technologies against user requirements. We propose four technological desires, these being equivalence to the technology that was previously in place (including equivalence on security, availability, and latency dimensions), variety (ability to provide requisite variety), abstraction (ability to hide non-pertinent detail), and scalability (ability to add or remove resources quickly to match workloads). We argue here that the Desires Framework provides a very useful way of looking at cloud computing and what it offers to business and other users.

Chapter 3 shows how cloud emerges out of a distinctive service-based perspective on computing. We argue that as cloud becomes pervasive in use there will be a radical shift toward service performance, a move from IT products to business services, and a reconfiguration of the supply industry. We find that cloud escalates greatly the importance of service performance in the external IT and business services industry. We suggest four customer metrics for evaluating delivery – quantity, performance (quantity versus target), value, and quality, with the last measure answering the question: Did the customers like what we did? Cloud accelerates the existing shift from IT-based products to business services. Cloud will also lead to radical changes in the IT supply industry but this will not be on an 'all change' basis, rather a 'hybrid' scenario playing out over a ten-plus-year period. The challenge to the supply side is to reconfigure the industry to meet the demand for business services made possible by cloud. Moreover, those business services will need to relate to the customer objectives for *business* cost reduction/rationalization, agility, innovation, and consumerization. We argue for, and detail, a new stratification of the supply industry. Inherent in these major shifts is a new service-dominant logic. Key elements within this service-dominant logic are the extent to which cloud enables creative use of the technology for business purposes, the simplicity with which such innovations are enabled, and the efficiency of such enablement. We therefore argue that it makes just as much sense, in a service-focused world, to talk less of technology-as-a-service, and more of efficiency-, simplicity-, and creativity-as-a-service.

In the **chapter 4** analysis, we note that there are notable perception differences between business and IT executives on expectations and risk inherent in cloud, with IT executives tending to be the more cautious. We also point to a 'false security' that cloud adoption might engender – both on risk and on performance. We focus on the five challenges that seem particularly critical at this stage in the development of cloud use within organizations. The five challenges emerging from the research are: security and legal risks; defining the client–supplier relationship through contracting; the lock-in dilemma; managing the cloud; and the integration challenge. We discuss these challenges in detail, providing illustrative examples and also a discussion of service level agreements. For each challenge we discuss its relative importance, the likelihood of its impact changing over time and the potential responses business can make to meet the challenge. We pay particular attention to the integration challenge, as this is perhaps the most difficult to deal with for corporations. It involves building a new retained organization, aligning strategy and cloud, relating cloud developments to legacy systems and conventional (internal and external) IT services, and delivering cloud services to end-users, while fitting into the overall cloud eco-system. We provide examples, however, of organizations that have worked through these challenges and that provide lessons from their experiences and practices.

Because security and privacy concerns over cloud have received such a high profile, we devote **chapter 5** to revisiting the specific risks in more detail. Our research shows nine business security and privacy concerns introduced by cloud for client and supplier organizations. We also point to legal developments across and within a variety of jurisdictions, designed to curtail risks to security and privacy. The EU Data Protection Directive and specifically the UK's Data Protection Act are discussed as examples. At first sight these legal dimensions threaten to leave cloud computing dead in the water, but legislation is always running behind the technological impacts. Moreover, as we detail, by 2013 numerous bodies had issued advice and guidance to businesses on how to proceed. In the light of these, and of security and privacy challenges, we assess the most feasible technological and business responses. At the same time we also make explicit some challenges latent in the above that may well become apparent and come to haunt moves to cloud. These include technological challenges, tensions between centralization and decentralization within the corporation, between supplier strategies for becoming service integrators and/or primary contractors for cloud and competition, between increased commoditization of service and client demands for customized services to support business agility and differentiation.

Chapter 6 examines the speed and nature of cloud diffusion. As a set of technical innovations, cloud will go through three phases: invention, commercialization, and diffusion. At the start of 2013, cloud was still predominantly in the second phase. Moreover, diffusion will not take place at a linear rate, not least because cloud developers and users are on a learning curve that will take a considerable amount of time to climb before sizable impacts materialize. The innovation trajectory with cloud will be cumulative, starting mainly with IT-operational innovations, then gathering pace over time on business process and market innovations. We argue that speed of innovation will be shaped by four key antecedent factors – the attributes of the innovation itself; the degree of supplier collaboration; the speed with which diffusion through informal, unplanned communication and influence moves to formal, planned dissemination; and the attributes of the innovation implementation process, that is the range of factors that support or slow an innovation's progress from design to adoption, diffusion, and usage, through to exploitation. The chapter establishes that executive support for an innovation agenda with cloud is strong, although we also find that innovation has not been the immediate business imperative for cloud adoption. We discuss how cloud encourages innovations in infrastructure and service, and, pointing the way to chapter 7, show how cloud requires a changing role for the IT function. Our conclusion is that cloud, as far as the business innovation agenda is concerned, may well be a 'slow train coming.' Nevertheless, we do argue for long-term innovations accumulating into the slow building of the cloud corporation, through incremental, architectural, and radical innovations enabled by and involving cloud services. Building on chapter 3, where we spelt out the challenges the IT supply industry faces in building the foundations of the cloud corporation, in this chapter we detail the work required by the organization itself if it is to achieve such a self-transformation.

Chapter 7 addresses the realities of corporate readiness. In the face of turbulent technologies, we consistently find that an emphasis on technology and technology-related skills guarantees adoption but rarely exploitation. There is a danger that a lot of cloud offerings are, so far, technology solutions in search of business problems. To get cloud onto a more strategic agenda and identify the relatively few applications that produce disproportionate business value, the technology function has a vital role, but needs to shift from its traditional skills, roles, and values. The IT function has been on a journey for two decades from being a back-office technical function to being a service-oriented provider that delivers business value operationally. It is now managed by business and technology leaders as a strategic business resource. A much touted purpose of outsourcing, and now of cloud, has been to accelerate this process, freeing up internal staff to become more business-focused and strategic in contribution. This chapter looks to answer the fundamental questions raised for the internal IT function about managing cloud. These are: What retained capabilities will be needed to run the technology function? What specific management capability challenges and worry points are coming to the fore with cloud deployment? And how can these be dealt with? In practice, with each technology cycle, cloud being but the latest, and with ever increasing usage of the external services market, our work demonstrates that high-performing technology functions are managed by a relatively small internal team of highly capable, demand-led and primarily strategy- and business-focused people. Here we focus on the technology function, the role of which is central to cloud deployment, but the same logic applies to, for example, the human resource, finance and accounting, procurement, and administrative functions.

In **chapter 8** we build on the cloud corporation concept of chapters 3 and 6, and take a future perspective, imagining (based on current research) the impact cloud computing will have on commercial and government organizations. By moving the IT servers outside the organizational firewall, cloud computing can make it easier for organizations to innovate new collaborative arrangements. Just as logistics was completely re-invented through the adoption of shipping containers, so standardized commodity IT services may revolutionize corporate IT and business processes. Using case studies as diverse as government agencies, businesses, particle physics, and student protest movements, the chapter shows how cloud computing is enabling new forms of organization. In particular, we posit six ways in which cloud will change the organization – through requiring and facilitating increased collaboration with stakeholders, through adoption of new forms of IT systems within the organization, through blurring the socially constructed boundary between work and home, through reinterpretation of the IT role relative to the strategic direction of the corporation, through the actions of external parties harnessing the power of cloud computing, and through integration of IT with the wider value network. All this adds up to a shift toward a corporation that itself will have ill-defined, 'cloud-like' boundaries. We see these changes not affecting all organizations, nor all parts of one organization, equally. Not least because, as we argue in chapter 6, organizations will continue to aspire to be 'ambidextrous' – that is they need to balance the diametrically opposed qualities of adaptability and alignment. They need to adapt nimbly, harnessing the innovative potential of cloud, whilst simultaneously continuing to leverage their existing business models and approaches.

In **chapter 9** we turn to considering the future more broadly and imagine the impact cloud computing could have on our personal, social, organizational, and economic lives. We draw upon predictions for twelve disruptive technologies – of which cloud is one – and focus on the five that are likely to operate in combination with cloud and each other to create massive impacts. These are mobile Internet, automation of knowledge work and the role of big data, the Internet of things, robotics, and digital fabrication. For example, mobile Internet devices may well become the dominant access mode for the cloud corporation's services. Digital fabrication, linked with cloud, may well revolutionize manufacturing and enable us to 'think globally and fabricate locally.' Big data, enabled by cloud computing developments, may well enable the discovery of previously unknown patterns within business. Enabling a wide range of devices, including sensors and robots, to communicate to and through the Internet has given rise to the term 'Internet of things.' It is these devices that will provide the data for big data-type analysis and that will demand cloud computing services. From all this we conclude that cloud is going to be a key shaper of the bigger picture from now to 2025, and this will provide the environment in which the cloud corporation will need to find its home.

CHAPTER I

Cloud in Context: Managing New Waves of Power

INTRODUCTION

How to locate the cloud phenomenon? Cloud's profile has been very high in the media since 2008. On corporate radars, cloud has been rising from something to note through something we can use to something that may help us transform the business. Those new to technology watching will recognize a bandwagon and want to jump on. The old technology watchers will have seen much of this before, through waves of technological advances. When moving to cloud, they will take a more pragmatic, better informed, more granular approach to the latest gee-whizzery. This chapter is designed to support such a perspective. We take a longer-term perspective on cloud, backwards, as well as forwards. For both history and the likely future have a lot to teach us about how to act now.

An understanding of the fundamental information and communications technology shifts from the 1960s to 2025 provides a starting point for exploring cloud-based technologies and their challenges and implications for organizations. There are, of course, all too many predictions about technology futures. In this chapter we will try to focus on the more credible and objective attempts to move our understanding forward. Moschella makes much sense in positing four main eras – so far – in information and communications technology (ICT) adoption and use.[1] These are shown in figure 1.1. Each era has seen roughly a six- to seven-year cycle of investment in specific technologies. Strassmann explains that, although technology innovation cycles have shortened, computer adoption times have stayed at about seven years.[2] This arises because it takes at least that long to institutionalize related managerial, social and organizational changes. There have been some notable exceptions since, of course, but the point on institutionalization has often been overlooked, as we show when we consider cloud-based technologies and innovation in chapter 6.

Here we will first look at each era and its underlying economics. The basic shape of the argument follows Moschella, Strassmann, and Willcocks and Graeser.[3] What follows is, necessarily, a simplified overview, but note that figure 1.1 depicts eras overlapping at many points. After outlining the four eras, we will then explore in more detail the fourth era in the light of more recent reports and predictions about the direction of technologies in general and ICTs in particular.

THE SYSTEMS-CENTRIC ERA 1964–1981

It is generally accepted that what Moschella calls the system-centric era began with the IBM S/360 series – the computer industry's first broad group of steadily upgradable, compatible systems. The dominating principle through most of this period was that of Grosch's law. Arrived at in the 1940s, this stated that computer power increases as the square of the cost – that is, a computer that is twice as expensive delivers four times the computing power. This law favored large systems development. Investment decisions were fairly simple initially and involved centralized data centers. IBM dominated supply and protected its prices: 'one negotiated delivery schedules and technical support, not costs or budgets.'[4] In response to dissatisfaction with centralized control of computing by finance functions, there followed centralized time-sharing arrangements with non-finance functions, some outsourcing by scientific, engineering, and production departments to independent service suppliers and subsequently moves toward small-scale computers to achieve local independence. This led to stealthy growth in equipment costs outside official central IT budgets, but also a dawning understanding of the high life-cycle support costs of systems acquired and run locally in a de facto decentralized manner.

From about 1975 the shift from centralized to business-unit spending accelerated, aided by the availability of minicomputers. Also, in a competitive market, prices of software and peripherals fell rapidly and continuously, enabling local affordability, often outside IT budgets and embedded in other expenditures. Without centralized control, it became difficult to monitor IT costs.

FIGURE 1.1 ┃ **IT Investment Cycles 1964–2025 (adapted from Moschella, and Willcocks and Graeser)**

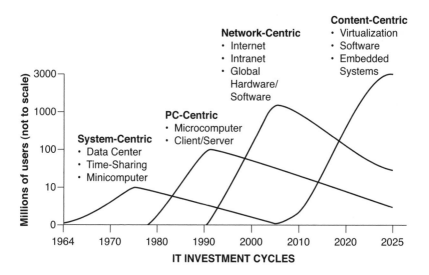

THE PC-CENTRIC ERA 1981–1994

The PC-centric era began with the arrival of the IBM PC in 1981. The sale of personal computers (PCs) went from US$2 billion in 1980 to $160 billion in 1995. This period saw Grosch's law inverted. By the mid-1980s the best price/performance was coming from PCs and other microprocessor-based systems. The underlying economics was summarized in Moore's law, named after one of the founders of Intel. Moore's law stated that semiconductor price/performance would double every two years for the foreseeable future. The prediction has remained fairly accurate into the 2000s, helped by constantly improved designs and processing volumes of market-provided rather than in-house developed microprocessor-based systems. The PC-centric era saw shifts from corporate, mostly proprietary, to individual, commodity computing. The costs of switching from one PC vendor to another were low, while many peripherals and PC software took on commodity-like characteristics. A further shift in the late 1980s seemed to be toward open systems, with the promise of common standards and high compatibility. However, it became apparent that the move was not really from proprietary to open, but from IBM to Microsoft, Intel, and Novell. Subsequently many of the open systems initiatives were scaled back significantly.

These technical advances provided business unit users with enormous access to cheap processing. ICT demand and expenditure were now coming from multiple points in organizations. One frequent tendency was a loosening of financial justification on the cost side, together with difficulties in, or lack of concern for, verifying rigorously the claimed benefits from computer spending. From 1988 onwards, technical developments in distributed computing architecture, together with organizational reactions against local, costly, frequently inefficient microcomputer-based initiatives, led to a client/server investment cycle. The economics of client/server have been much debated. The claim was that increased consolidation and control of local networks through client/server architectures would lower the costs of computing significantly. However, Dec, for example, argued that a client/server set-up for 5000 users costs 70 percent more than a comparable mainframe/terminal configuration.[5] Strassmann suggested two reasons for this: the propensity to specify the latest technologies resulting in continuous high-cost upgrades and difficulties in anticipating the high personnel support costs associated with client/server.[6] Further pressures on technology, support, and training costs also came from users demanding instant keystrokes, rapid database access times, and seamless network functionality.

The PC-centric era saw a massive explosion of personal computing, with, for example, some 63 million PCs built in 1995 alone. However, though the equipment and software was inexpensive on a price/performance calculation, it did not usher in a period of low-cost computing. Constant upgrades, rising user expectations and the knock-on costs over systems life-cycles saw to that.[7] By the mid-1990s the cost per PC seat was becoming a worrying issue in corporate computing, especially as no consistent benchmarks on cost seemed to be emerging. Published estimates ranged regularly from \$3000 to \$18,000 per seat per year, probably because of differences in technology, applications, users, workloads, and network management practices. From the late 1980s one increasing response to rising computing costs, especially mainframe, network, telecommunications, and support and maintenance was outsourcing, mostly selective, but in some cases 'total', that is handing over computing, representing over 80 percent of the IT budget, to third-party management. As Willcocks and Lacity point out, this propensity continued into 2012/13.[8]

THE NETWORK-CENTRIC ERA 1994–2005

Though the Internet has existed for over 25 years, it was the arrival of the Mosaic graphical interface in 1993 that made possible mass markets based on the Internet and World Wide Web (WWW). This era was defined by the integration of worldwide communications infrastructure and general purpose computing. Restricting as it does WWW graphical capabilities, communications bandwidth began to replace microprocessing power as the key commodity. Attention shifted from local area networks (LANs) to wide area networks, particularly Intranets. Even in the late 1990s there was already evidence of strong shifts of emphasis over time from graphical user interfaces to Internet browsers, indirect to online channels, client-server to electronic commerce, stand-alone PCs to bundled services and from individual productivity to virtual communities.[9]

Economically, the pre-eminence of Moore's law was being replaced by Metcalfe's law, named after Bob Metcalfe, the inventor of the Ethernet. Metcalfe's law states that the cost of a network rises linearly as additional nodes are added, but that the value can increase exponentially. Software economics have a similar pattern. Once software is designed, the marginal cost of producing additional copies is very low, potentially offering huge economies of scale for the supplier. Combining network and software economics produces vast opportunities for value creation. At the same time the exponential growth of the number of Internet users from 1995 suggested that innovations that reduced use costs whilst improving ease of use would shape future developments, rather than, as previously, the initial cost of IT equipment.[10]

By 1998 fundamental network-centric applications were e-mail for messaging and the World Wide Web – the great majority of traffic on the latter being information access and retrieval. Transaction processing in the forms of electronic commerce for businesses, shopping, and banking for consumers and voting and tax collection for governments were also emerging. The need to reduce transaction costs through e-commerce resulted in a further wave of computer spending. Here also there were real challenges for the Internet's ability to provide levels of reliability, response times and data integrity comparable to traditional online transaction processing expectations. Dealing with these challenges had large financial implications. Markets were also developing for audio and video applications. A key technological change throughout was that most of the existing PC software base needed to become network-enabled. Moschella also predicted a shake-out in the ways in which transmission services would be provided.

These developments and challenges depended on the number of people connected to the Internet and there were, in this era, significant national differences in this metric. However, as more people went online, the general incentive to use the Internet increased, technical limitations notwithstanding. One possibility mooted at the time was that IT investment would lead to productivity. In turn this would drive growth and further IT investments. The breakthrough would be when corporations learned to focus computing priorities externally – on reaching customers, investors, suppliers, for example – instead of the historical inclination primarily toward internal automation, partly driven by inherited evaluation criteria and practices.[11] Even so, as Moschella noted at the time:

> much of the intranet emphasis so far has been placed upon internal efficiencies, productivity and cost savings ... (and) ... has sounded like a replay of the client/server promises of the early 1990s, or even the paperless office claims of the mid-1980s.[12]

A CONTENT-CENTRIC ERA 2005–

It is notoriously difficult to predict the future of information technologies. Even technologists struggle. For example, Ken Olson, founder of DEC, predicted in 1977 that there was no reason why anyone would want a computer in their home and Bill Gates once suggested that Microsoft would never make a 32 bit operating system. For the period from 2005 we already have some strong trends to draw upon. Moschella put forward one plausible view about where these would lead and we build upon his suggestions below. He outlines shifts from electronic commerce to virtual businesses, from the wired consumer to individualized services, from communications bandwidth to software, information and services, from online channels to customer pull, and from a converged computer/communications/consumer electronics industry value chain to one of embedded systems. A content-centric era of virtual businesses and individualized services would depend on the previous era delivering an inexpensive, ubiquitous, and easy-to-use high bandwidth infrastructure. For the first time, demand for an application would define the range of technology usage rather than, as previously, also having to factor in what is technologically and economically possible. The ICT industry focus would shift from specific technological capabilities to software, content, and services. These are much less likely to be subject to diminishing investment returns. The industry driver would truly be 'information economics,' combining the nearly infinite scale economies of software with the nearly infinite variety of content.

Metcalfe's law would be superceded by the law of transformation. A fundamental consideration is the extent to which an industry or business is bit- (information-) based as opposed to atom- (product-) based. In the content-centric era the extent of an industry's subsequent transformation would be equal to the square of the percentage of that industry's value-added accounted for by bit as opposed to atom processing activity. The effect of the squared relationship would be to widen industry differentials. In all industries, but especially in the more 'bit-based' ones, describing and quantifying the full IT value chain would become as difficult an exercise as assessing the full 1990s value chain for electricity.

At the time he wrote, Moschella's was an inspired guestimate about the future. A lot has happened since to give his overall vision a great deal of plausibility. Technology has advanced at great pace in the new century, with the convergence of technologies into what has come to be called cloud computing being a major development, especially since 2008.

Let's look at more recent examinations of present and future technologies and their implications, in order to give context and a time dimension to the cloud focus of this book. In doing so, let us bear in mind that 'cloud computing' and 'cloud' are shorthand terms for a complex set of converging information- and communications-based technologies supporting and running through the World Wide Web and Internet. There is no one cloud but private, public, and hybrid clouds, together with different types of services offered through cloud including Software-as-a-Service (SaaS) Infrastructure-as-a-Service (IaaS) and Platform-as-a Service (PaaS) and hosted services. These technical issues will be dealt with in the next chapter. In this chapter, we seek to give the bigger context and time horizon for what we call moving to the cloud corporation, by which term we are referring to the increasing use of cloud technologies by organizations in the long-term pursuit of becoming digital businesses.

MOVING TO THE CLOUD CORPORATION 2008–2025

To give this context, a useful starting point is a thoughtful examination by McKinsey Global Institute of the key disruptive technologies for the 2013–2025 period.[13] The study identified twelve disruptive technologies, with cloud technology – described as hardware and software resources delivered over the Internet or network, often as a service – as one of them. On cloud technology the report provides some indicative figures on scope and economic value. For example, it may well cost three times more to own servers rather than to rent them in the cloud. Cloud can impact 2.7 billion Internet users around the world, involving the use of over 50 million servers. Cloud could impact significantly the $US1.7 trillion of GDP economic value related to the Internet and some $3 trillion of corporate spend on information and communications technologies. The report also suggested that technologies in combination could multiply impact. In chapter 9, looking at the bigger picture, we suggest this is particularly true for cloud in relation to the mobile Internet, automation of knowledge work, the role of big data, the Internet of things, robotics, and digital fabrication.

We will revisit the twelve disruptive technologies in chapter 9. If the McKinsey report provides the big picture to 2025, Accenture in 2013 offered a complementary technology vision but at a more disaggregated, business level, focusing mainly on developments in digital technologies on a shorter time horizon.[14] For the report's authors, every business will become a digital business. Here the Accenture report suggested seven major developments, with cloud amongst these:

- **Relationships at scale** – Businesses need to rethink their digital strategies to move beyond e-commerce and marketing. Digital offers a new approach to consumer engagement and loyalty, since companies can manage relationships with consumers at scale.

- **Design for analytics** – Business leaders need the right data to define the strategic direction of the enterprise. The present generation of software was designed for functionality, but the future generation must be designed for analytics as well.

- **Data velocity** – This refers to the pace at which data can be gathered, sorted, and analyzed to produce insights that managers can act on quickly. As expectations of near-instant responses become the norm, business leaders will rely heavily on higher data velocities to gain a competitive edge.

- **Seamless collaboration** – To increase productivity, enterprises must move beyond standalone social and collaboration channels and begin to directly embed those channels into their core business processes. The report expects businesses to build social, collaborative applications throughout the enterprise.

- **Software-defined networking** – Like other virtualization technologies, software-defined networking (SDN) has the ability to radically change the flexibility with which businesses and IT operate. With virtualization investments already paying off in servers and starting to pay off in storage, businesses can turn their attention to virtualizing the network in order to extend the life of their infrastructure and reap the full value of their virtualization investments.

- **Active defense** – IT departments struggle to keep pace with advances in security technology. The move to active defense/risk-based approaches to security management, analytics-driven event detection and reflex-like incident response needs to happen on a broad scale if the full potential of digital technologies are to be realized in business.

- **Beyond the cloud** – The report points out that the cloud has arrived. It has been over 14 years since Salesforce.com was founded and 5 years since it topped one million subscribers. Likewise, finance and HR cloud-services company Workday was founded in 2005. In 2006, Amazon Web Services began offering IT IaaS and has since offered PaaS. Software giants such as Microsoft, Oracle and SAP have made significant progress in cloud-enabling their applications. However, there have been delays in corporate take-up of cloud. Enterprises should increasingly view cloud as an overarching approach that considers the value of PaaS, IaaS, SaaS, and several other as-a-service technologies. Enterprises will increasingly determine how these technologies can best become a part of IT's current toolbox. From now on, what is important, say the report's authors, is to put the cloud to work and start realizing cloud's transformational impact across the business.

One can see here how cloud will increasingly interact and support the other six major developments as businesses increasingly become what we call cloud corporations. The report identifies signs of real progress towards such a vision. It estimates that by 2016, enterprises will devote 14 percent of their overall IT product and services spending to cloud, up from 5 percent in 2011. More importantly, by that same time, 46 percent of new corporate spending will be on cloud-enabled technologies. The report also records that leading enterprises are approaching new system architectures with a 'cloud-first' mentality, that is, looking at what can be achieved with the different types of cloud rather than reflexively considering in-house development or off-the-shelf solutions (see also chapter 4). We note in our own 2013/4 work in progress that Proctor and Gamble and Johnson and Johnson are just two examples of such pioneers. However, the Accenture's report also identifies, as does our own research (see chapter 6) that as at 2013, cloud opportunities remained largely underdeveloped. Their research shows where the biggest gaps lie: more than one-third of large enterprises had yet to implement any cloud technology, public or private, in their infrastructure. For platform cloud technologies, that percentage jumped to one-half. SaaS continued to lead cloud adoption in the enterprise. Of large enterprises, 43 percent were at least piloting public SaaS with nearly half of those (19 percent of the total) having committed a large percentage of their business to it. The report expected lagging areas, such as IaaS and PaaS, to accelerate between 2013 and 2018. Continuing innovation and investment would drive further improvements in areas important to the enterprise, such as cost and security. As a result, IaaS growth would pick up and PaaS, bringing cost saving, flexibility, and time to market advantages, was likely to become the primary application development and re-platforming approach for the enterprise.

The Accenture report also foresees businesses operating in a hybrid world. For the foreseeable future, traditional software systems will continue to play a crucial role in the overall IT landscape. Recognition that the hybrid world of cloud and traditional IT have to co-exist has important implications for how an enterprise prepares for the future. In many enterprises, skills have been separate and isolated. But a hybrid world requires hybrid skills, with the most valuable talent being the architect who understands the functions and roles of all the pieces and who knows how they all work together. We address such key skills issues in detail in chapter 7, together with the related governance and enterprise architecture issues raised by the Accenture report.

Parallel with our book, a report by Deutsche Bank, *Cloud Transforming IT Services*, also positions cloud computing as still in the early stages of growth.[15] Given cloud's cost-saving ability and organizations' margin pressures, the report saw budget allocations to cloud services increasing over five years, with cloud revenues also growing at 30 per cent compound annual growth rate (CAGR) to ~$20bn from 2012 to 2016. Based on Industrial Development Corporation (IDC) estimates, the Deutsche Bank report expected the total market size for cloud computing to grow from US$40bn in 2012 to $98bn in 2016, with SaaS reaching $37bn; IaaS, $30bn; system infrastructure software service, $20bn and PaaS, $10bn.

The report found cloud gaining traction in budget share and 'go-lives.' It saw enterprise customers retaining control over the vast majority of their IT workloads over the next ten years (2012–2022) and reducing expenditure on off-the-shelf enterprise resource planning (ERP) software as additional capabilities are sourced from the cloud, not from ERP integrations. However, clients would need greater functionality and automaticity from their existing ERP integrations to support their private clouds. According to IDC, 15.1 percent of the $62.7bn applications market in 2011 (~$9.2bn) came via cloud, but with the total expected to be around 20 percent by 2020. The report gives one example of where the trend might lie. In early 2013, JPMorgan Chase announced a migration of almost all its internal .NET and Java applications (2000 applications, four data centers – one of the larger PaaS migrations announced to date) to a private PaaS environment by Apprenda, doing so on top of its existing infrastructure. JPMorgan estimated improvements of nearly 700 percent in developer productivity and a 50-day reduction in go-to-market time for new applications, along with a 45 percent reduction in infrastructure costs (infrastructure jumped from 40 percent to 70 percent). The report writers suggest that JP Morgan's example makes a compelling case for other large-scale organizations to consider PaaS, especially if the increase in use was maintained.

The report also states that customers were aiming to move to cloud in five years or less. Quoting a 2012 IDC survey, 74 percent of firms with 1000 employees or more were likely to move 50 percent of their application environment to the cloud by 2016, 35 percent of firms with 1000 to 4000 employees would move half of their software application environment to the cloud by 2014/15 and just 14 percent of firms with more than 1000 employees would move their applications to the cloud beyond 2016. Smaller firms would likely shift to cloud rather quickly and larger firms would take slightly longer due to their heavy workloads and needing time to formulate migration plans.

On the service delivery side, the report highlights four major implications of cloud:

Cloud will change the delivery model. As opposed to maintaining a high-touch relationship with clients throughout project delivery lifecycles, service providers in a cloud world will lessen the degree of client interaction as cloud becomes more and more integrated within clients' enterprises. Front-end consultation will likely become more important in a cloud world (allowing providers with consulting capabilities to potentially charge premium prices for cloud engagements), while traditional implementation activities will become shorter in duration and see pricing pressure as cloud competes away their value-add by eliminating the need for manual system integration. In short, value-add will come from service providers' innovation in delivering business-relevant information more efficiently than traditional services allow. Also, two cloud services – platform as a service (PaaS) and testing-as-a-service (TaaS) – can substitute for traditional services and open up new revenue opportunities for service providers (e.g. mobility and business analytics).

Consulting will not be threatened by cloud. According to the report, Cloud has limited opportunities for substitution of management consulting as it focuses on speed of delivery, not what the report calls 'epistemic value-add.' Cloud services will likely be bundled with management consulting, allowing providers to move from a front-end consulting engagement through to cloud services delivery while maintaining client relationships (albeit more low touch). Consulting providers, however, will likely deliver different work streams as a result of cloud, with less ERP implementation (ERP engagements could become shorter and shorter as cloud affords more visibility into operations than that given by ERP). Organizational readiness, assessment, and application transformation are likely to see a rise in demand given cloud's magnitude and potential utility, possibly buoying consulting revenues as greater portions of budget are allocated to cloud.

Some suppliers will be well positioned for the cloud. This is interesting because so many commentators have suggested the demise of more traditional outsourcing suppliers as a result of cloud. In our view, expressed later in this book, this was always to underestimate the ability of such suppliers to pre-empt and adapt. The report mentions as examples Accenture, CSC, and Cognizant. By advising clients on cloud solutions best suited to their businesses and integrating cloud with existing IT structures, Accenture provides management support for cloud-integrated IT environments. Additionally, the firm holds partnerships with 25 cloud providers including Amazon, Cisco, Google, salesforce.com, and VMware, selected on the basis of security, reliability, ease of integration, and client preferences and offers firm-wide methodology that clients can adopt regardless of their orientation to public, private, or hybrid clouds. For Deutsche Bank, Accenture has a clear roadmap of how to move from traditional to cloud services with minimal business model disruption, planning to invest more than $400m to develop a cloud platform to integrate and manage cloud delivery. The firm has already built a track record that should help cultivate client relationships as the move to cloud accelerates in coming years. CSC's cloud offerings focus predominantly on infrastructure management, providing an IaaS data center service through a public multi-tenant offering in a CSC data center (its CloudCompute offering) or a private single-tenant service in either CSC's or the client's own data center (its BizCloud offering), with additional managed services available. Cognizant provides cloud consulting through its Cognizant Business Consulting practice, implements public, private, or hybrid clouds with a vendor-neutral approach, and handles post-go-live support of cloud-based processes. The firm offers SaaS, IaaS, PaaS, and business-process-as-a-service (BPaaS) services.

New opportunities, including big data, analytics, mobility, and industry-specific outsourcing, will open because of cloud, offsetting some cannibalization. Cloud computing serves as the wellspring for greater value-added from analytics, as it allows organizations to store and easily access increasing amounts of data unmanageable by in-house functions – data which can be used to better anticipate changes in the business climate. As organizations complete investments in initial analytics offerings and see value accrue as a result, they will concurrently invest in mobility offerings to expand analytics functionality to sales forces and field operators, allowing for near real-time communication of sales information and operational planning to meet resultant demand. The report sees business analytics – the use of technology to investigate drivers and past business performance and predict future performance – as a significant driver of IT investment in the next five years, something we found in our own studies and reported in other 2013 surveys.[16] To make sense of exponential growth in unstructured, qualitative data, organizations need analytic tools and services capable of making the stored information intuitively actionable – an issue we will pursue in later chapters.

Given an absence of in-house talent in analytics, the report believes that organizations will begin to shift IT budgets away from traditional core ERP and infrastructural solutions to business analytics as data become more unstructured and patterns in end-demand become increasingly difficult to interpret. As a result, IT service providers with established analytics practices will see increases in their contract opportunities. As clients become more comfortable with cloud-based services and deploy them more widely in their organizations, they will expect business process outsourcing (BPO) providers to support cloud-based environments. As clients move to a cloud-based environment, their disparate business requirements and lack of technical resources will make outsourcing more appealing, even more so with providers with whom they have previously worked. Therefore the report expects a resulting increase in outsourcing volume from migration to the cloud, although with cannibalization of traditional outsourcing work, since much would become bundled into the cloud. Thus, in theory, outsourcing providers could undergo a decoupling of revenue growth from headcount growth as services shift away from traditional labor delivery to delivery via automated systems.

These reports provide a good grounding and lots of constructive speculation on the future of cloud computing. They commonly see cloud as highly important not just to individual organizations but to whole economies. They also see the necessity to take a long time horizon when assessing the impacts of cloud. These two points are in line with our own findings and support the overall argument of this book.

BENCHMARKING CLOUD DEVELOPMENTS

To get a fix on where the evolution to cloud services had got to by 2013, we carried out our own survey of client organizations.[17] Sixty-nine percent of customers reported that their organizations had already adopted some type of cloud services. Customers also indicated the degree to which their organizations had adopted Iaas, PaaS, and SaaS. Customers reported that 55 percent of their organizations had already adopted IaaS in a private cloud but only 20 percent had adopted IaaS in a public cloud. The customer organizations clearly preferred private clouds over public clouds, with nearly 42 percent of respondents claiming their organizations had no present or future plans to adopt public cloud.

Customers reported that 55 percent of their organizations had adopted SaaS and 11 percent would adopt in the future. Only 4 percent said that their organizations had no plans to adopt SaaS, although 29 percent confessed they did not know whether their company had adopted or had plans to adopt SaaS. Customers reported that 29 percent of their organizations already had adopted PaaS and 18 percent will adopt in the future. However, given that PaaS is primarily used by software developers, it was not surprising that 36 percent of respondents said they did not know about PaaS adoption within their company.

The top-rated business objective by clients, suppliers, and analysts alike was cost efficiency, followed by scalability, rapid deployment, avoiding the complexity of managing IT, and ensuring high security. Specifically, 28 percent of respondents said cost efficiency was the number one ranked business objective, 17 percent of respondents said scalability was the number one ranked business objective, 15 percent rapid deployment and 8 per cent avoiding IT management complexity.

There are a couple of surprises in the responses. First, 55 percent of survey respondents did not rank innovation among their top five priorities despite believing in the high potential innovation value inherent in cloud services. Our research also found that where sought, cloud services were enabling significant business and IT innovation.[18] Why in 2013 was innovation not a high priority? Clients mentioned cost pressures and other demands in recessionary times and a lack of organizational readiness for innovation. In chapter 6 we discuss broader reasons to do with diffusion of innovation processes. Second, although prior research found that security concerns have been the primary barrier to cloud services adoption,[19] by 2013 61 percent of respondents did not include 'high security' and 65 percent did not include 'data protection' among their top five priorities. Survey respondents clearly acknowledged that security concerns were valid, but they also indicated that security issues were not preventing organizations from adopting cloud services. We deal in detail with security concerns in chapters 4 and 5 but our case study research[20] has actually been finding that for small-to-medium-sized enterprises (SMEs), security *improved* in the cloud. Prior to cloud adoption, some of the small-sized client firms did not have adequate data replication or business continuity in-house. One client said, for example, 'our server was in a closet over there.' After cloud adoption, SMEs often reported that their cloud providers had superior security and data protection capabilities.[21]

The other interesting finding – with 2013 as our benchmark – relates to client satisfaction with cloud services. Were clients satisfied with (a) the business value they were getting from cloud services and with (b) the overall performance of their cloud service providers? On a scale of 1–7, the average customer response was 4.90, indicating customers were only 'slightly satisfied' with the business value from their current cloud services. Pertaining to the overall performance of cloud service providers, the average customer response was 4.94, also indicating customers were 'slightly satisfied'. We will investigate in more depth the service challenges and the reasons for such assessments in chapter 3 (on service) and chapters 4 and 5 (on challenges).

As at 2013 cloud services emerged as receiving a fairly high level of take-up mainly across IaaS, PaaS, and SaaS, with a focus on private clouds. There was an increasing use of external service providers, but mainly for cost efficiency, scalability/flexibility, and rapid deployment reasons. An Everest Group survey at much the same time confirmed these primary objectives and saw an overwhelming preference for private clouds across workloads ranging from ERP finance and accounting migration, e-mail and collaboration and customized applications.[22] They attributed this to security concerns and integration challenges – issues we deal with in chapter 4. The Everest Group also noted other major challenges as: lack of talent (see chapter 7), especially for BPaaS and PaaS adoptions; lack of suitable solutions for BPaaS; and noted that cost constraints were also being flagged as a key barrier to adoption. At the same time, it noted across workloads a significant maturation in adoption, not just e-mail/collaboration and websites, but moving to critical business applications including ERP for finance and accounting, business intelligence/analytics and customer relationship, marketing automation, and e-commerce tools. The report also noted that business units and users were increasingly influencing the adoption process, with the IT function playing a strong role in physical infrastructure decisions and those not bearing on direct revenue generation, for example disaster recovery, test environments, e-mail/collaboration, and storage and archiving. The report noted that as users become more influential in the adoption process, service providers will have to adapt their orientation from unit cost reduction to ROI, from superior control to flexibility in business operations and from technological sophistication to 'how can it help my customers'? Our own surveys support these findings and in chapter 3 we show that, for the IT supply industry, cloud actually is a harbinger of and requires a transformation in, the service dimension.

In our own 2013 survey, innovation had been de-prioritized, at least for the time being. Security concerns inhibiting adoption, at least of private clouds, were not found to be as high a priority despite the findings of earlier surveys in the 2010–2012 period. Indeed, some SMEs were reporting higher security as a result of moving to cloud services. At the same time clients were not reporting high satisfaction with cloud services. These findings support the conclusion that, as at 2013/14 most client organizations were low on the learning curve in terms of adoption and exploitation of the massive potential inherent in cloud computing. This book is designed to examine that potential and the challenges cloud presents – both the temporary and the more intractable – to clients, suppliers, corporates, and government and not-for-profit agencies alike.

CONCLUSION

We position cloud, then, as a set of technological developments within the network-centric era, that with convergence and accelerated advances in ICTs, is underpinning and driving the content-centric era and allows transformation of processes, business models and strategies, management, organizations, content offerings, and dimensions of service. In chapters 8 and 9 we provide detail on how the cloud is likely to play out in changing organizations and the bigger picture to 2025, in combination with developments in mobile Internet, automation of knowledge work, the role of big data, the Internet of things, robotics, and digital fabrication.

The reports on cloud as at 2013/14 provide much food for thought. They are important for their attempts to look beyond a five-year horizon, something to which our own research, incorporated in this book, has aspired. With our survey, we also established a benchmark for how organizations were positioned with cloud services as at 2013. A major focus of this book is to indicate how organizations can move forward up the learning curve toward becoming what we call cloud corporations. We will also provide context and time horizons for the playing out of the factors that bear on how organizations and their stakeholders can make reliable progress.

Having set the context for the emergence of cloud computing and pinpointed where corporations are in their adoption patterns, we now, in chapters 2 and 3, move to considering in detail cloud as both a technical innovation – based fundamentally on virtualization, shared computing provision, and the Internet and also a product of a distinctive service-based perspective on the provision of advanced information and communication technologies.

CHAPTER 2

The Technology Trajectory

INTRODUCTION

In this chapter we focus on the technology developments leading to
cloud computing and the challenges and opportunities this turbulent
technology landscape presents for business. We discuss how organizations need to deal with technological shifts and paths of innovation
and how technical innovations have been and can be diffused into
business and management practices to become the 'new normal.'

While the subject of cloud is being discussed everywhere, there is
a lack of substantive, objective evidence not just about technological
trajectories but also about the potentially more far-reaching business
implications of cloud. It is important not to buy too heavily into the
language of 'all change' and radical transformation and crucial to
avoid the related response to business hype and fashions that one
book title dubbed rather acerbically 'fad surfing in the boardroom.'

Cloud must be seen in the context of previous so-called 'revolutions' – particularly in technology and in services outsourcing. Indeed,
from one perspective cloud can be portrayed as a 'back to the future'
phenomenon – for example, there are resonances of application
services provision, shared data centers and even systems network
architecture (SNA), with its data and application 'bunkers' feeding
multiple devices. Is cloud really just a more open SNA on steroids?[1]
We pursue this idea further in chapter 8. Meanwhile, in this chapter we
focus on the fundamental technologies represented by cloud and point
out some significant differences from what has gone before – not least
more powerful computing/processing capabilities, fatter transport
pipes, broadband wireless access, and more open and flexible protocols. As we pointed out in the Introduction, organizations are more

prepared to build and use these capabilities due to dynamic changes in internal and external factors – competition/innovation, globalization, user demographics, management readiness, and supplier ecosystems. Moreover, cloud has real consequences, not all of which are fully or well understood, and we are finding that expectations are running very high, particularly amongst business users. So organizations and CIOs need to be anticipating and planning the journey now for the major changes that will begin over the next three to five years and which may fully realize their potential only sometime after 2020.

CLOUD COMPUTING AS TECHNOLOGICAL INNOVATION

Far from the ephemeral image it suggests, 'cloud computing' is in reality founded upon innovation in two solid technologies: networks and data centers. These technologies have changed considerably in the last 20 years as the Internet has exploded from a research tool for universities to a central infrastructure for most peoples' lives and commerce.

The idea of providing computing as a service through networks dates back to the 1960s,[2] when the provision of 'computing utilities' became a driving force behind the early development of the Internet,[3] Renting mainframe computing time from 'service bureaus' for payroll calculation was a frequent occurrence as the cost of mainframes was greater than could be justified by most enterprises. In the 1980s, IT infrastructure became more distributed through mini and micro-computing and the 'network' began to be a central component of corporate IT[4] through client/server computing and, in the 1990s, 'application service provision' (ASP).

As the 1990s progressed, various high-profile ASP services emerged, capitalizing on the World Wide Web (e.g. Hotmail), as a means of outsourcing applications as a service. Relatively short-lived perspectives like NetSourcing[5] also emphasized this process of outsourcing applications over the Internet. It was, however, the 'dot-com boom' in the late 1990s and early 2000s that began an explosion of interest in outsourcing applications as both networks and Internet software matured. Early ASPs failed partly due to insufficient bandwidth and computing power.[6] However, the dot-com boom resulted in a large increase in global fiber-optic networking, dramatically reducing latency and costs.

The profusion of high-bandwidth fiber-optic networking laid during this boom has provided near limitless bandwidth and low latency across many parts of the globe (swathes of Africa, for example, are yet to benefit significantly, though this has been changing in the last few years). It is these connections that have seen transatlantic telephone calls change from slow crackly satellite links into the high-quality, low-latency and near free calls we enjoy today. As Andrew Blum[7] recounts in his book *Tubes*, in the Western world these fibers are being laid at a phenomenal rate, connecting the major global Internet exchanges in places like London, Frankfurt, Tokyo, and New York with smaller exchanges across the world. However, physical location still matters and the typology of the Internet can still dictate the quality of the connection provided. It is for this reason that the second key component of the cloud – the data center – must be located close to high-quality fiber-optic connections. This mandates that the network connections of provider and user *both* matter.

Similarly important is the data center housing the computers and storage needed for cloud services. A data center is nothing more than a room designed to house computers and associated hard drives that are accessed remotely. They require three key connections – power, cooling, and networking. The first two of these account for over 53 percent of the running cost of a data center[8] (with land itself accounting for around 7 percent) and are the reason many large data centers are located close to cheap power in cool climates. The economics of managing data centers is, however, a complex science. Recent innovations in processors allow them to run much hotter and therefore change the economics of data center location and cooling. Such innovations continue and assumptions regarding the cost benefits of large data centers must be continually re-evaluated.

Coupled with innovations in networking and applications, the last ten years have seen a huge range of innovations in the management of data centers. These have included the emergence of a means of coordinating the 'on-demand' provision of large-scale computing resources, achieved by drawing on innovations around scientific supercomputing at places like CERN and by virtualizing commodity hardware.[9] These innovations allowed companies such as Google,

Facebook, and Amazon to develop the dull gray warehouses in which 'cloud computing' resides. Line after line of racks contain tray after tray of computing 'blades' (circuit board-like servers designed to be packed closely together), each housing large numbers of processors or terabytes of disk storage. The size of these data centers allows them to capitalize on economies of scale in terms of physical resource (cooling, power) and human resource (one engineer can tend to thousands of processors).

Cloud computing, then, is about harnessing this technology to provide computing applications run from data centers around the globe that appear as responsive and interactive as they would if they were running locally in the small server rooms most companies had until recently.

This industrialization of IT infrastructures and the transfer of computing activity from individual PCs and private data centers to large, external, public data centers accessible over the Internet became known as cloud computing. This shift 'to the cloud' is perhaps more accurately described as a move to computing being provided by large pools of automated, scalable computing resources and associated applications.[10] The move to scalable data centers allowed computing resources to be purchased (or, perhaps more accurately, rented) on demand and in a scalable manner via the Internet. Around 2008, the term cloud computing began to be used to reflect the use of the Internet (usually represented figuratively as a 'cloud' in diagrams) to connect to such services.

This focus on the Internet and scalable external data centers is reflected in the most widely adopted technical definition of cloud computing from the U.S. National Institute for Standards and Technology (NIST):[11]

> Cloud computing is a model for enabling ubiquitous, convenient, on-demand network access to a shared pool of configurable computing resources (e.g. networks, servers, storage, applications, and services) that can be rapidly provisioned and released with minimal management effort or service provider interaction.

In figure 2.1 we give the conventional depiction of cloud computing, based on the work of NIST.

FIGURE 2.1 | Cloud Computing Characteristics and Service and Deployment Models

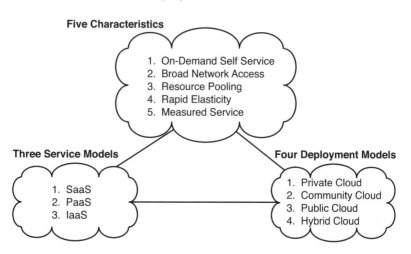

Five Characteristics

1. On-Demand Self Service
2. Broad Network Access
3. Resource Pooling
4. Rapid Elasticity
5. Measured Service

Three Service Models

1. SaaS
2. PaaS
3. IaaS

Four Deployment Models

1. Private Cloud
2. Community Cloud
3. Public Cloud
4. Hybrid Cloud

Source: Based on NIST.

Note that the NIST definition focuses on the cloud as a platform for running applications. But whilst this is an important element, it downplays the role of applications that run on these platforms. Alternative definitions, such as those provided by Boss et al.,[12] emphasize both the platforms and the types of application that run on them. For them, the platform 'dynamically provisions, configures, reconfigures and de-provisions servers as needed,' allowing applications to scale through their hosting in large data centers. Applications are 'extended' to be accessible through the Internet, thus using the large data centers and powerful servers to host them. In Boss et al.'s definition anyone can access such applications via an Internet connection – highlighting the significance of the access device such as PCs and laptops, tablets, smartphones and other forms of mobile computing.[13]

Within this book we offer a slightly different definition from these technologically focused ones. *We define cloud computing as the evolution of a service-based perspective on computing based on innovations in shared computing provision that improve simplicity, scalability, and efficiency.*[14]

CLOUD FOR COST REDUCTION AND GREEN IT

One claim frequently made about cloud is that it enables very big reductions in the cost of computing. To some extent, these claims are made to appeal to the primary reason businesses have sought out cloud adoption. Recall our 2013 survey finding (see chapter 1) that the top-rated business objective for clients, suppliers, and analysts alike was cost efficiency, followed by scalability, rapid deployment, avoiding the complexity of managing IT, and ensuring high security. It is worth pursuing this issue a little at this early stage, linking it with the 'green' issue to demonstrate the complexity in what we mean when we speak of 'cost.'

Network connectivity improvements allow cloud companies to locate data centers where power and cooling are cheaper and, potentially, more environmentally friendly. Due to their large size, such data centers can also benefit from economies of scale in electricity, bandwidth, operations and staff, and software and hardware, leading to reductions in the costs of these resources by a factor of five to seven.[15] However, for large companies that have already undertaken extensive consolidation of their existing infrastructures, the cost savings associated with moving to the cloud may be significantly lower.

It has been argued[16] that these cost benefits and decisions to use environmentally friendly power sources allow cloud to improve the 'green credentials' of its users by reducing the environmental impact of their IT. A Greenpeace report, however, criticizes cloud computing for hiding energy consumption costs within service charges and thus actually making it harder for companies to evaluate their environmental impact.[17] For example, an Apple iCloud data center is estimated to require the equivalent power to 80,000 U.S. homes,[18] yet its users are unable to identify their personal contribution to this power usage. Further, cloud computing has allowed the innovation of many consumer services which rely on power usage in the data center (such as Google's Voice-Search and Apple's Siri). Such innovation and new cloud computing services are hardly likely to cease and so the demand for computing, and the subsequent environmental damage, will, we believe, likely increase rather than decrease as cloud computing develops.

Beyond the cost savings detailed above, which arise from data center consolidation and location, particular types of computing demand can gain specific cost savings. These include situations where demand for IT services varies considerably over time, where demand is unknown, and where the short-term rental of extensive computing facilities offers cost savings over long-term utilization of a small number of servers.[19] As Gray[20] analyzes in detail, cloud costs are based on the characteristics of use in relation to networking, computation, data access, and data storage.

In summary, there are specific reasons why cloud computing can offer cost savings, though what is meant by cost is not simple. Our research also uncovered cost advantages coming from the pay-as-you-go/pay-per-use rental model of cloudsourcing, the reduced cost of technology investment, and 'speed-to-use,' i.e. rapid deployment and the lower cost of innovating. But, as we will discuss below, for enterprises, the decision on cloud is, and will increasingly become, more complex than purely cost advantage.

THE DESIRES FRAMEWORK – EVALUATING THE TECHNOLOGY OF CLOUD

One of the key challenges in considering a move to cloud computing is evaluating effectively the technology opportunities and risks. To assist in this process, in this section we outline a framework that should be used to develop comparisons between cloud computing and existing forms of IT.[21] The framework is based on four key dimensions, against which cloud computing should be compared. These are presented as 'desires' – reflecting the coveted, aspirational nature of cloud computing in comparison with existing computing. We use the word 'desires' here also to signal the importance for business users of the service component in cloud computing. Ultimately, business users do not buy technology but a capability, a service that deals with a business problem, issue, or need. Therefore, business users have 'desires.' The dimensions of these desires are not mutually exclusive, but rather aim to cover the key technical innovations and changes associated with cloud. The dimensions are: equivalence, variety, abstraction, and scalability.

The framework is shown in Table 2.1. Let us now introduce each of its dimensions.

Table 2.1 ▌ **The Desires Framework**

Technological Desire	Definition
Security **Equivalence**	The desire to receive a technical service that is at least equivalent in security to that experienced when using a locally running server.
Availability **Equivalence**	The desire to receive a technical service that is at least equivalent in availability to that experienced when using a locally running server.
Latency **Equivalence**	The desire to receive a technical service that is at least equivalent in latency to that experienced when using a locally running server.
Variety	The desire to receive services that provide a level of complexity (variety) commensurate with the operating environment.
Abstraction	The desire that non-pertinent complexity be hidden, in particular that the complexity of managing the underlying IT infrastructure and software be abstracted and hidden.
Scalability	The desire to receive a service that is scalable to meet demand.

Equivalence

Cloud computing is often intended to replace existing, locally hosted technology infrastructure. As a result, the first technological desire is the desire for equivalence. This is the desire that the cloud provider must endeavor to guarantee security, availability, and response time that are at least equivalent in quality to those experienced with a locally running client/server service on a local area network.[22] The provision of such equivalence is central to the technological realities of cloud computing and this can be understood in terms of three aspects: security, availability, and latency. If this desire remains unfulfilled, cloud adoption is unlikely to proceed. It should be noted that security, availability, and latency are the technical subset of equivalences that should be identified for a cloud computing adoption decision. In addition to these technical elements, managerial and organizational equivalences such as contracts, service level agreements, and risk should be considered.

Security Equivalence

A significant challenge in providing the desired technological equivalence concerns security.[23] This topic dominates much of the existing cloud computing literature and we will deal with the issues in detail in chapters 4 and 5. There is a perception of insecurity in housing data within the cloud, as one of our interviewees stated: 'there's a great confidence and comfort that you get if you walk around your server racks, as you hug the hardware. ... there's a sense that you can actually physically go there and deal with [problems].' In practice, it is a detailed technical question as to whether a cloud data center wholly connected to the Internet is inherently less secure than a data center on a private network when access to the network itself is possibly via the Internet.[24] Indeed, as networks themselves become virtualized, such questions become increasingly complex.[25]

A key challenge for cloud computing security relates to the context in which the computing occurs. Cloud providers who operate globally distributed networks of data centers may face specific security risks (for example in terms of terrorism or cyber-attack) that may also present unique legal issues regarding liability for security infringement. For example, large, shared services may increase the risk of having data accidentally searched or seized by authorities who may be seeking another user's data.

Similarly, certain user contexts have specific security demands (for example government or financial services). Government security requirements may result in enhanced levels of security assurance in the marketplace from cloud providers who wish to be eligible for government contracts. This supports Nelson's[26] belief that governments can encourage new cloud services. Indeed, outsourced hosting services are already employed in many industries for highly sensitive data, including many general practitioners in the U.K., who host health records in a secure cloud.

Owens suggests that the large scale of many cloud providers presents particular problems for security, both technologically and organizationally.[27] The security challenges associated with any off-site hosting of data and services (i.e. outsourcing or cloud) include determining who can access customer data, denial of service attack prevention, perimeter security policy, resource starvation, data back-up and compliance. In addition, there is a need to trust systems administrators, whether in the cloud or within the private data center.

The co-hosting of many companies' data in a cloud data center can introduce distinctive risks. As the CTO of a multi-channel marketing company stated, 'People hack brands,' and the risk of a competitive brand 'sharing' a cloud provider cannot be easily calculated. For example, one unintended consequence of Amazon and DynDNS hosting WikiLeaks was that these services were targeted by hackers with consequent effects on other users or their services.

Although cloud services may change the security risk profile, it was also suggested in our own interviews that the cloud providers may be better able to manage security, respond to distributed attacks, and invest in sophisticated security hardware and software – facilities that are unavailable to all but the largest enterprises. Cloud providers may be able to spot unusual activity that the individual companies would be unable to see by using security analytics to identify unusual behavior patterns among pools of similar enterprises.

Moreover, given the relative novelty of cloud, providers are sensitive to the reputational dangers of security breaches, as the CEO of a cloud company told us:

> If the data center blows up, I'm going to be in the newspaper more often. I don't want to be in the newspaper more often, I need a [business continuity] solution and a [disaster recovery] solution … I'm not saying I'm doing it to avoid the newspapers. I don't want my customers not to have access to their [records].

Another interviewee argued that:

> Cloud is as secure as traditional, really … From a high-level security point of view I'm not particularly concerned at all because [they will be using] the latest operating systems patch, all those sort of things. The basics are always going to be there. (CTO marketing company)

Indeed, cloud can simplify security issues for organizations by outsourcing them to companies with specialist security measures and skills.[28] Durkee, however, is critical of this outsourcing of responsibility, suggesting that it creates the risk of skills attrition – as companies that outsource to the cloud lose the skills to evaluate and manage their cloud providers.[29] A number of guides now exist to provide support for auditing cloud computing risks.[30]

In our view, the challenge of security equivalence has less to do with security issues *per se* than with the ability of companies to evaluate the benefits and risks of cloud-based systems. In undertaking such evaluation, organizations need to look past the idea of 'security issues' and take more meaningful evaluations of risk.

Security equivalence therefore concerns the 'operational security of the business and the integrity of the party with which you choose to work' (senior executive from data center and infrastructure consultancy); and evaluating operational security and risk is standard practice today. As Steve Ballmer of Microsoft usefully summarized:

> as soon as you start pooling computing and data in new and interesting ways, really defining and really being careful about weighing up who owns what data and how it is controlled and used is a fundamental responsibility of every participant in that chain.[31]

Significant emphasis is therefore placed on cloud providers demonstrating their security credentials transparently. For example, Amazon has moved to acquire existing security standards (e.g. ISO 27001) for its cloud service. One cloud provider interviewed agreed that transparency was important:

> We allow any of our customers to come in and do their own ... testing, for example. They can try to hack the system as part of their due diligence. They could come in and tour our data centers and talk to our security experts. (Director of Platforms at SaaS company)

Given the steps taken by cloud providers to increase the transparency of their security provisions, it is important to question the extent to which concerns about security equivalence are genuine or whether they are based on an unrealistic assessment of current security risks or are simply a defense mechanism proffered by beleaguered IT departments who fear that their entire *raison d'être* will be lost to the cloud. We pursue these issues further in chapters 4 and 5.

Availability Equivalence

Although locally hosted infrastructures are themselves fallible, with occasional downtimes for system upgrades and in response to component failure, successful cloud services must be able to match, if not exceed, the availability of local data centers and their disaster prevention and recovery systems. While a key benefit of cloud is dispensing with these redundant (and thus often unused) internal disaster prevention systems, users must be assured that availability is a key concern for their cloud provider. As a result, cloud providers expend considerable effort in monitoring, managing, and predicting the performance of their cloud services, particularly as outages receive considerable press attention.[32]

An important driver of availability equivalence is the extent of capacity planning and capacity management by cloud providers. In order to anticipate and plan for changes in demand, cloud providers and researchers are developing sophisticated business analytics techniques that are believed to provide better insights into likely demand peaks so that they can continue to operate within the service levels (including availability equivalence) offered to their customers. Metrics are increasingly generated, monitored, and shared in real time with customers (e.g. http://trust.salesforce.com and http://status.aws.amazon.com), with some external parties producing similar metrics (e.g. http://www.awsdowntime.com). Cloud providers believe that allowing customers to view availability statistics, incidence statistics, and solution statistics builds trust. Financial transparency is also necessary for cloud companies, as the risk of cloud provider bankruptcy (and resulting unavailability) remains a significant concern among many users.[33]

An important lesson from studies of outsourcing relates to the notion of the 'winner's curse.'[34] The winner's curse occurs when a supplier wins a competitive bid but discovers that it is unable to make a profit from, or even deliver on, the contract. For example, an outsourcing provider wins more outsourcing contracts than it was expecting. As a result, it finds itself unable to adequately support all its contracts, with the unintended consequence that either all customers receive substandard service or some customers (typically pre-existing ones) end up with poorer service than they had initially. Similar problems could arise if a cloud provider suddenly finds itself stretched to provide quality services (including availability) to all its customers.

Latency Equivalence

A third aspect of equivalence that is desired for successful cloud implementation is latency. This means ensuring that the end user perceives no additional performance lags when they are interacting with a cloud-based service. To a large extent, the investment in fiber-optic cabling has helped ensure this and, for global companies that face internal network latency issues when offices that are a long distance from their central data center, the use of cloud computing providers with multiple data centers may offer significant performance improvements.[35]

However, while much cloud computing literature suggests that latency is no longer an issue, our interviewees were more cautious. One service provider noted that:

> lots of people who work in networking say the cloud is fundamentally flawed because the network is the biggest constraint. You can put compute at the end of the network but if the network is limited, then no matter how powerful it is, you've still got that constraining factor.' (Data center consultant)

Indeed, companies such as Akamai.com and BT have specialized in responding to the challenges of latency for cloud companies and their users.

The extent to which this is a problem is relative to the application. For database usage where large records must be locked from other users during updates, latency can be a significant problem, whereas small database look-ups can be unproblematic:

> [For] customers in Australia doing address look-ups from our U.K. hosting providers ... [i]n spite of the fact that some of the databases being queried

are really significant … (20 million [records]) … the actual query response time is really quick. (CEO of SaaS company)

Another cloud user highlighted the importance of the cloud providers' internal network in issues of latency,[36] noting: 'I need to make sure that I'm dealing with providers that can provide the capacity and reduced latency that I need' (consultant at company providing cloud software). Similarly, latency remains an issue in developing countries and this may jeopardize their desire to capitalize on the benefits of cloud.[37]

Hybrid Clouds as a Response to the Failure of Equivalence

For companies that desire security, availability, and latency equivalence but are unable to satisfy these desires with pure-play cloud offerings, there is growing evidence that a hybrid model, in which a service is divided into components according to the differing equivalence demands, is likely to be used. Here those components for which appropriate equivalence is achievable use the cloud, whilst other components, perhaps with higher security or latency demands, remain local. For example, whilst cloud services may be suitable for government systems with higher security levels, for example those related to terrorism, they may remain within local data centers because cloud providers cannot guarantee security equivalence (additionally, such systems are more likely to provide bespoke functionality). Such hybrid models are found in other domains as well, including media companies:

> whenever there was something that had huge security issues, or data needed to be stored somewhere we knew for various laws, [we] would … probably build a slightly hybrid system, that maybe had a box that we were in control of, to store core data, and everything else was in the cloud. (MD for global media company)

This hybrid model was also employed by a cloud provider of health records that hosted 25 million patient records. Because of intermittent networks (i.e. problems with latency equivalence) and the need to update records centrally without problems, the company relied on local cloud-access devices (PCs, iPads, etc.) running local software 'apps' to ensure that the medical records would be available even if the network failed or became slow, and to ensure that updates to records ran fully and safely. In the CEO's words, 'pure cloud is too dangerous in clinical terms.'

One provider suggested that the only viable option for enterprise class systems where legacy systems exist is to employ a hybrid model: 'I think it's hybrids, it's absolutely 100 percent hybrids at the moment. Nobody's doing a 100 percent pure cloud play as we speak, to my knowledge' (consultant to cloud providers).

Variety

As we saw in figure 2.1, the most widely adopted categorization of cloud computing services focuses on the provision of computing itself 'as a service' (aaS), considering differences between software (SaaS), platform (PaaS) and infrastructure (IaaS).[38]

SaaS is defined as a software application accessible through the Internet. It is currently the most mature and largest part of cloud use. **PaaS** provides a cloud-based platform that can be harnessed to develop applications using the PaaS-specific programming approach. Companies can use PaaS to develop custom applications or write software that integrates with existing applications. A PaaS environment comes equipped with software development technologies like Java, Python. and .Net. These allow customers to start writing code quickly and, once written, the code is hosted by the service provider, thus making it widely available. **IaaS** is the most basic and generic category. It consists of servers or storage capacity or bandwidth available over the cloud. IaaS thus provides a virtualized computer via the Internet – a virtual computer upon which the user can install their own operating system in order to run applications they write in any programming approach. IaaS gives access to computing power to clients not wanting responsibility for installation or maintenance.

These distinctions are intuitively appealing. However, they are logically problematic. IaaS, PaaS, and SaaS all involve Internet-based access to software – the virtualization software that provides simulated computing instances for IaaS, a platform operating system for PaaS, and an application for SaaS. As they all provide software systems, the only significant differences between them relate to the extent to which they are general purpose (what we define as 'variety') – and thus the capacity of the user to adapt the service in order to match the variety required for their business environment. Further, these distinctions are founded in existing forms of computing (i.e. the virtual computer or software). Here, therefore, we do not follow the traditional use of SaaS, Paas, and IaaS and instead focus on the underlying *variety* of cloud computing services.

Variety, as used here, is a measure of complexity and relates to the number of possible states in a situation. The term is used to denote the desire that the cloud service must provide requisite variety, that is, variety greater than or equal to the variety required by the user of the cloud service to face the complexity of their business environment. Put simply, a cloud service must provide sufficient variety – in terms of its functionality or its ability to be programmed and altered for users – to meet users' needs. Thus the variety of a service is related to the *'number of distinguishable states that it could take on'* in use.[39]

Variety for cloud services is more helpfully understood as a spectrum. This spectrum starts from the most specific transactional cloud service with extremely limited variety. An example is Bit.ly, which takes a URL string and returns a much shorter URL string – it is very simple and gives no opportunity for tailoring or programming the service and thus exhibits low variety. The spectrum then moves through to cloud computing services that exhibit extremely large variety – approaching a universal Turing machine,[40] with infinite storage and processing – and happen to be accessible through the Web. The huge numbers of computers deployed in the grid computing model, or Amazon's Elastic Computing cloud (http://aws.amazon.com/ec2), are examples of cloud services with extremely large variety. Such a service can be adapted in a multiplicity of ways to respond to the complexity of users' business environments.

This spectrum thus encompasses SaaS (with various levels of variety depending on functionality and tailorability) through PaaS (an arbitrary point on the spectrum dependent upon the level of variety offered by the PaaS platform) toward IaaS (with large-scale virtual computing instances and thus very large variety).

One problem is that users must attempt to contract for services without necessarily knowing the variety they will need in the future.

As one interview highlighted, this is a difficult challenge: 'Every single vendor in the world will tell you ... their product is more ... flexible than everyone else's ... You can't possibly prove that in a request for [a] proposal to provide a cloud service' (architect at SaaS company).

We believe that using the concept of variety will improve the ability of companies to evaluate the decision to move to the cloud. In particular, when evaluating any cloud service, this concept demands that the variety of that service be evaluated alongside the variety required by the organization for that service. For example, in evaluating an e-mail SaaS service, this concept leads to questions about whether the service can be extended or configured and the features it provides, that is, evaluated against an assessment of the necessary variety demanded from e-mail within that organization. Similarly, when selecting a PaaS service, variety helps the evaluation of whether the platform is sufficiently various to match the requisite variety of the service for which the platform is intended.

Abstraction

Abstraction is the process of hiding non-pertinent detail and only dealing with generalizations; in this case we use the term to relate to the desire to abstract away the complexities of managing and operating the underlying IT infrastructure and software of the IT service.

Cloud concerns computing services provided by layers of technology that are abstracted. For Weinhardt et al., such computing services are built on three layers – infrastructure, platforms, and applications, with differing business models at each level.[41] Iyer and Henderson add collaboration to this list – reflecting the collaborative nature of many such services.[42] Youseff et al.[43] define cloud in terms of abstraction as 'a new computing paradigm that allows users to temporarily utilize computing infrastructure over the network, supplied as a service by the cloud-provider at possibly one or more levels of abstraction.' These authors see five layers of abstraction including hardware and operating system kernel, cloud software infrastructure (i.e. computational resources, storage, and communications), then cloud software environment (also called the platform layer) and finally applications.[44]

For users of cloud services to exploit variety in order to respond to the complexity of their problems, there is a necessary degree of unintended complexity created by the cloud service itself, to which the users must themselves respond. Such complexity is created by the underlying computing infrastructure of the cloud service (the need to manage computers, power and cooling, storage, input–output, scale, backups, redundancy, and so on) and how successfully such infrastructure is abstracted. Thus, there is an inverse relationship between variety (that is the complexity of a cloud service that users require to match their needs) and abstraction (the complexity of a cloud service that users usually wish to reduce and have abstracted).

The desire for abstraction is, therefore, also a spectrum from the least abstracted computing hardware (a physical machine hosted in a provider's data center and requiring the user to manage the whole application stack and the physical machine) to the most abstracted service. Our interviews suggested that abstraction from the underlying hardware was a significant desire due to the difficulty of managing the whole application stack in on-premises IT: 'the value proposition of going to the cloud is that they realize that they cannot do IT as well as a cloud vendor like [our company]' (supplier senior executive).

Abstraction of Computing is the Key to Cost Reduction

One of the highest-variety and least abstracted cloud computing services is IaaS through its provision of large numbers of abstracted computing instances (for example, Amazon EC2), using the technologies of virtualization and workload management.[45] Virtualization is the most discussed form of abstraction within the cloud computing literature and amongst practitioners but has existed for decades on mainframes, providing multiple isolated duplicate simulations of a physical computer on one actual physical computer.[46] In this way, a single computer can host many simulated computers (virtual machines) using so-called hypervisor software. The emergence of cloud coincided with the availability of virtualization on commodity hardware using hypervisor software from VMware, Microsoft, Oracle, Red Hat, and Sun.[47]

Such abstraction of computing within cloud providers' data centers allows the use of cheap commodity hardware and enables the elasticity, load balancing and economies of scale that are fundamentally driving cloud computing's adoption and underpinning its economic model. Crucially for cost reduction purposes, by automatically allocating these virtual machines to physical machines (and moving them amongst physical machines, or even archiving them to disk) it is possible to manage the demand for computing effectively across an entire data center or even the world.

Such 'statistical multiplexing' can, for example, allow a European holiday company's website (used extensively at the start of the year when people book their summer holidays) to reside alongside a consumer retail company (used heavily toward the end of the year) thus increasing utilization rates for the shared hardware. Renting virtual machines from a cloud provider (rather than running a data center) removes the challenges of cooling, power, upgrades, failed disks, and so on.

Abstraction Makes it Harder to Manage IT

There is also evidence, however, that abstraction within cloud computing makes it harder for companies to evaluate the quality of the underlying IT and can lead to poor understanding of the nature of the service provided (and poor ability to evaluate its value). As one interviewee highlighted, the provision of a virtual machine through the cloud creates significant complexity for the user: 'Amazon … don't provide any managed service; it's all up to you. They provide the infrastructure; you've still got to manage the back-up, potentially, and what goes on within Windows and Linux and at that level.' Indeed, many organizations fail to effectively risk-assess the use of cloud.

At the other end of our spectrum are highly abstracted services such as software applications. One such example is e-mail service provision. These services are very specific in their purpose and are thus standardized for large numbers of users. They are very useful, as the problems faced by many organizations are (or can be) standard and exhibit low variety: 'When you look at the complete coding that you need in your company, maybe less than 10 percent is really strategic coding or coding for strategic function. Ninety or even more is standard' (consultant).

Scalability

Scalability describes the ability to quickly add or remove resources in varied granularity to allow the better matching of resources to workload. In this context, elasticity is a measure of the rapidity of such scalability. Traditionally, these granular elements were servers, which were slow and expensive to install or remove. By providing a platform that 'dynamically provisions, configures, reconfigures and de-provisions servers as needed,'[48] cloud computing offers the ability to scale elastically. For some, such elastic scalability is 'the true golden nugget of cloud computing and what makes the entire concept extraordinarily evolutionary, if not revolutionary.'[49]

Scalability is central to cloud computing, and among cloud computing proponents the narrative of elastic scalability has been highly influential. Many dot-com business failures were caused because the start-ups had limited Web-server capacity. When their sites gained media attention, these servers were quickly overwhelmed, slowing the sites or making them unreachable, leading customers to drift away. This famously happened, for example, to Friendster.com – in this case to the benefit of Facebook.

More recently, the ability to scale computing elastically through the use of cloud servers has enabled dot-com start-ups like Animoto. com to match their growing demand.[50] Upon launch, Animoto faced a doubling of its server loads every 12 hours for nearly three days. Using an Amazon cloud infrastructure it grew from 50 to 3500 servers during this time – a scaling no company could possibly match if procuring and installing traditional servers.

Such elasticity allows cloud providers to align their offerings with customers' demands and provide the illusion of unlimited computing that can be purchased 'on demand' on a pay-as-you-go basis quickly and easily. As one interviewee stated:

> if you request provisioning on a server, you should get that within a matter of hours. And you should also be able to turn off the use of the server or storage within … a matter of hours. And that should be reflected at least within monthly billing. (services director)

Despite the professional and academic literature being vocal in support of scalability, many interviewees were more circumspect. The time to provision additional resources may be a key differentiator among cloud providers; however, one specialist interviewee suggested that the industry was reluctant to support self-service provisioning for enterprises on demand:

> In my experience both from the service provider side and the enterprise customer side, I think they have to go through a cultural shift and a mindset shift to accept allowing their end users to do on-demand, self-service provisioning. What I'm seeing is that, on the service provider side, they're still wanting to … work within the context of their managed services. Likewise on the enterprise customer side, I've seen resistance from IT at the management level [to] … the concept of allowing their end users within the enterprise to do self-service, on-demand provision[ing]. (computer consultant)

Scalability and the Impact of Variability in Demand

Within certain industries, spikes in demand are standard, retail being an obvious example, and this makes scalable cloud-based resources an attractive option. For example, within the television industry:

> demand was very spiky. If something was promoted on the telly, then people would, for the next three minutes, go on-line and then never again … we were forever having servers going down. It was too expensive to manage that peak … We spotted the capability of managing spikes very easily through cloud computing.

Contemporary computer science research has also highlighted the challenges of modeling peak demand and demonstrated the complexity of efficiently managing the scaling of cloud resources.[51] Even within businesses without such spikes, the management of scale is difficult and it is usual to over-provision IT hardware. As one interviewee told us:

> Typically … they look at a project [and] implement enough IT infrastructure to support that project for up to three years. And typically you might find that only 50 percent of that capacity is used up until the third year of

the project ... It's spent two years sitting around doing nothing. [An elastic cloud] model means that people could ... literally turn on the tap faster when they need more power, turn it down when they need less, and pay directly for that.

In this way, scalability can lead to a decline in the average amount of computing commissioned by giving users confidence that they do not need to over-provision, or hold onto unused resources, as they can acquire them when needed in minutes. The net effect of these patterns of behavior is to reduce headline demand for cloud services, although cloud providers need to be able to respond to the demand levels hidden behind these behaviors.

Elasticity is not without its problems, as certain applications cannot be scaled elastically (relational databases in particular). Cost calculations for elastic demand are complex and can be unpredictable. Moreover, as cloud computing expands, it is likely to face the challenges of scaling cloud data centers. Indeed, an IBM paper suggests that as applications and users of cloud computing grow in number, scalability problems are likely to increase.[52]

The Challenge of Managing Scale for Cloud Providers

Given the previous discussion about abstraction and variety, it is reasonable to expect that cloud providers offering abstracted computing instances (at the level of IaaS or PaaS) will find fewer challenges in managing scalability than companies offering highly abstracted applications (e.g. SaaS). In addition, experience of managing these processes will inevitably prove significant, giving companies that have operated large abstracted data centers (e.g. Microsoft, Google, and Amazon) an advantage over new entrants – a point Microsoft's Steve Ballmer made: 'We learnt from Bing [its search engine] about huge scalability of data centers and this feeds into cloud applications, where scale is important.'[53]

For software companies used to delivering software as a packaged, shrink-wrapped product but forced to move to cloud, the ability to manage large data centers and elegantly scale their software for large numbers of users is very new and challenging, a point made by one interviewee:

In a traditional software world you might not need to worry about the performance of the service … You don't know the target hardware. It might be someone else's problem. When you're the provider, you're the one throat to choke. (SaaS marketing VP).

For many interviewees an important consequence of adopting cloud was to provide a strategy 'for when they are going to sunset some of the existing on-premises technology' (Global software development manager), which can lead to cost savings and a reduced environmental impact. The cloud is simply a means of achieving this.

CONCLUSION

This chapter has outlined the technological dimensions of cloud computing as they exist today, describing these through a Desires Framework. This framework both catalogues the key technological dimension of cloud computing and provides a useful benchmark against which specific cloud computing services can be evaluated. In particular, if you are considering cloud computing, an analysis of the equivalences necessary, the variety required, the levels of abstraction, and the need for scalability is a very good place to start.

This technology landscape changes rapidly, however. In 1965, Geoffrey Moore published the paper that set out his 'law' for the inextricable rise in computer capacity for a given price.[54] Less law than manifesto for the fledgling integrated circuit company Intel, Moore's law has been remarkably successful in describing decades of decline in the cost of computing. Similar predictions for the capacity of hard disks and networks appear to hold up. Moore's law as a past indicator suggests also how the economics of cloud computing could change rapidly. There is some evidence for this. For example, recent advances in chips that allow data centers to run at higher temperatures erode the perceived advantages of large data centers (with their huge cooling systems). Similarly, software improves and begins to allow the simpler management of small data centers and appliances.

In 2008 Larry Ellison, CEO of Oracle, was highly skeptical of cloud computing and famously said:

The interesting thing about cloud computing is that we've redefined cloud computing to include everything that we already do … The computer industry is the only industry that is more fashion driven than women's fashion. Maybe I'm an idiot, but I have no idea what anyone is talking about. What is it? It's complete gibberish. It's insane. When is this idiocy going to stop?[55]

Ellison has changed his opinion a little in the intervening few years, but in some ways he was right. While, as we describe above, there are some fundamental technological innovations at the core of cloud, these are not revolutionary. As he goes on to explain in the remainder of this speech, whether in cloud computing or in existing computing models, it is all 'just computers running software connected to networks.' *Where* those computers are is less significant than is sometimes implied. *What* software they run (and therefore the services they provide) is more important, as is *how* they are managed and *by whom*. It is for this reason that the next chapter attempts to distil from the cloud computing debate the fundamental innovation in *service* that cloud computing brings.

CHAPTER 3

The Service Trajectory

INTRODUCTION

Cloud computing is the consequence of the evolution of two distinct strands: technological innovation – based around virtualization and shared computing provision – and a distinctive service-based perspective on computing. Following from this dual-strand perspective on cloud computing, we argue in this chapter that the drivers of the near-term development of cloud computing will have their origins in both strands. We have already seen in the previous chapter, with the Desires Framework, how important it is to see and focus on the business service dimension inherent in cloud developments. In this chapter we develop the notion of the service trajectory with cloud. On a larger canvas, based on our interviews and analyses of the IT industry, we identify three big impacts that relate to the service trajectory in cloud computing. These are: a radical **shift toward service performance**, a **move from products to business services** and a radical **reconfiguration of the supply industry**. In practice, as will emerge, these three shifts present major challenges to the IT supply industry and also to its user organizations.

In this chapter we also identify that these developments emphasize *the service-dominant logic* inherent in cloud computing. Here, we add to the technological picture of cloud emerging from chapter 2, by describing and assessing the role of this service-dominant logic, showing that it makes sense to speak not just of SaaS, IaaS, and PaaS, for example, as we did in chapter 2, but also of efficiency, creativity, and simplicity as services. But first we turn to the near-term developments and cloud trajectory.

NEAR-TERM DEVELOPMENTS

In our first survey, of the 21 percent of survey respondents who were in an IT role in client organizations, 90 percent had an influence on IT investment decisions in their department (48 percent with significant influence, 42 percent with some influence/input). A further 40 percent of respondents were in business and operations functions (i.e. not IT-related roles) and of these, 85 percent had influence on IT investment decisions in their function (35 percent significant influence, 50 percent some influence/input). This suggests that our survey respondents' decisions represent the likely direction of cloud services in the coming years.

FIGURE 3.1 ▎ **The Status of Deliberations about Cloud 2011–2013**

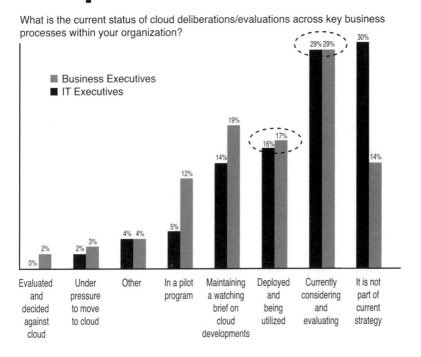

What is the current status of cloud deliberations/evaluations across key business processes within your organization?

Sample: 628 enterprises
Source: HfS Research and the Outsourcing Unit at the London School of Economics.

Although it is common to think about technology innovations over the next five to ten years, our survey suggested that developments in cloud were likely to be found in many organizations between 2011 and 2013. Thus, while around 16 percent of these respondents were 'maintaining a watching brief on cloud computing' and 17 percent had already deployed some cloud services, a further 29 percent of respondents were 'currently considering and evaluating' cloud services.

In terms of existing cloud services, corporate e-mail, websites, storage, and customer relationship management were already cloud based for 20 percent of respondents, with similar numbers planning to make the transition, representing a doubling of cloud usage in the 2011–2013 period.

When asked what proportion of their IT budget would be allocated to cloud services, 44 percent of respondents suggested that at least 10 percent would be allocated to cloud in 2012/13 (23 percent suggesting that it would be 10–20 percent of their budget, a further 21 percent suggesting over 20 percent). (A lower proportion of respondents were uncertain (11 percent) or didn't know (16 percent) about their future cloud budgets.) These trends were more marked for business executives with significant influence on cloud investment decisions in the near term and less marked for IT managers. Whilst these IT managers did not foresee as much investment in the 2011–2013 period, over the next five years they expected similar levels of investment as business managers.

As recorded in our 2013 survey (see chapter 1), it would seem that these predictions of near-term growth in cloud usage have largely been borne out. A slowdown in growth in 2012 was followed by an acceleration in moves to cloud across 2013. However, these near-term developments give a very incomplete picture of the larger, longer-term, radical shifts in service implied by cloud, and it is to these that we now turn.

THE LONGER-TERM SHIFTS

In our first survey, nearly two-thirds of business and IT executives saw cloud as an enabling business service and IT delivery model that would *drive innovation* in organizations, while half saw it as a new technology platform that could *transform organizational forms*. If cost advantages from moving to the cloud figured highly on the executive radar, around half of business executives saw cloud as innovatory in getting access to and implementing best-in-class business applications more quickly, in supporting moves to a distributed virtual organization, and in enabling a refocus away from IT and onto transforming the business.

We shall address further these two themes – innovation and changes in organizational forms – in chapters 6 and 8, but taking into account the technology developments we described in chapter 2 and our more comprehensive research findings, we suggest that there will be a more fundamental shift to cloud, though over a ten-year rather than a five-year horizon, from a cost agenda to a growing innovation agenda. This agenda at the organizational level will, in our view, move cumulatively over time from IT operational innovations, through an increasing number of business process innovations to product/service and market positioning innovations.[1] These will be discussed in more detail in chapter 6. But this is only looking at the implications of cloud and the innovative opportunities it presents at an organizational/competitive level. Looking across our present study, we identified three much larger impacts that the technological developments cloud embodies make both more likely and more necessary. These developments are thus both opportunities and challenges. And all three relate to changes in the service dimension that cloud brings. Let us consider these in more detail.

CLOUD AND SERVICE PERFORMANCE

Our first finding is that *cloud escalates greatly the importance of service performance in the external IT and business services industry*. The role of service has been key to the IT and business services industry.[2] But at the same time, in a series of studies across industries and countries, we have shown through survey and case study work that the BPO industry's record on providing service (as opposed to services) has been very mixed indeed.[3] We have found that this situation has been slowly improving over the last five years, but has this been fast enough to meet rapidly rising expectations emerging on two major fronts?

On the first front, the indications are that customers are becoming both more knowledgeable of the services they are buying and also more demanding of them. A 2010 Competitive Enterprise Initiative (CEI) survey is typical in confirming that customers are challenging companies to sit up and take notice of their needs and if they are not willing to care for their customers, the customers will go elsewhere. The survey found that 86 percent of customers quit doing business with a company after a bad customer experience – up 27 percent from four years earlier. Even in a 'down' economy, customer experience remained the top priority: 60 percent of customers will always or often pay more for a better experience. The survey also confirms the importance of speaking live with a service agent and having interaction with the company and the growing importance for the customer experience of web information, Twitter, and social networks.[4]

On the second front, the emergence of cloud makes the role of service much more differentiating of suppliers than before. Wolfgang Faisst of SAP illustrates this well for us:

> [With cloud] you do not have all the buffers between you and the customer that correct problems, like consultants or internal IT people. You have the direct link with the customer and that means that you have to change yourself to make a software service really ready. In the past we have thrown 170 software DVDs over the fence and said, 'Okay, it's yours now. Try it and good luck.' But now we deliver a service that needs to run from the first time on. That means day by day, every hour we are faced with customer needs and that also educates the software vendor to become really a true service player in terms of high customer service, higher than ever before in terms of easy-to-use and flexible software.[5]

Cloud developments and the high customer expectations emerging from our survey mean that IT and business service companies have to massively 'up their game' on service. Cloud business models make service a much more differentiating and competitive component in any customer offering. A way of understanding and dealing with this step-change is to think in terms of what needs to be measured. A CEO we interviewed put it succinctly: 'I am moving to only two sets of metrics – customer satisfaction and key business performance indicators.'

In the cloud world, the customer experience of service is going to be key, yet few current cloud companies are focused on this metric. One way forward is to import service knowledge from other, more service-focused, industries in terms of people and practices. A way of directing this is to move more ambitiously toward applying more service-based metrics. In figure 3.2 we show a way of directing attention to the fact that in cloud what matters is not just what the service organization does, nor what it provides, but what the customer actually experiences.

FIGURE 3.2 | The Four Big Metrics for Cloud

- **Quantity** – how many we did in how much time
- **Performance** – quantity versus target
- **Value** – did it make business sense?
- **Quality** – did our customers like what we did?

SERVQUAL dimensions:

'Tangibles'	=	Physical evidence – the physical facilities and equipment available, the appearance of staff, how easy it is to understand communication materials
'Reliability'	=	Accuracy and dependability – performing the promised service dependably and accurately
'Responsiveness'	=	Timing and speed – helping customers and providing a prompt service
'Assurance'	=	Relevance and trust – inspiring confidence and trust
'Empathy'	=	Attention to user – providing a caring and individual service to customers

In figure 3.2 we show that the traditional measures of quantity and performance remain important, though even more important is the value metric – gauging performance against key business performance indicators. In addition a heavily charged emphasis needs to be placed on *what the customer experiences* through utilizing service quality metrics (see SERVQUAL dimensions, figure 3.2).[6] Research regularly finds *reliability* to be the single most important quality dimension, but the others accumulate an impact and several are quite subjective, needing care, experience, and insight into how they can be delivered to specific customers. In cloud environments we would expect both clients and suppliers to be assessing performance on these types of dimensions, thus raising the standards for cloud service across the board.

CLOUD AND BUSINESS SERVICES

Our research also points to a second long-term shift. *Cloud accelerates the existing shift from IT-based products to business services.* Just as there has been a rising aspiration to move from IT inputs and service level agreements to business outcomes, so there is a continuing shift in the IT and business services market from IT products toward business services. Moves to the cloud accelerate this shift. Some of this can be glimpsed with, for example, Microsoft's Office 365, providing a 'pay-by-the-drink' service for constantly updated office software instead of a customer having to buy a copy of the software for every PC. Why should a customer be expected to download an iTunes update every two weeks and maintain huge libraries of files, when services such as Spotify offer music in the cloud without regular software updates? SAP has been separating its classical ERP business from its SAP OnDemand, while Oracle has been making the same move, with the same language, with Oracle On Demand. The concept here is to collapse the distance and implementation time between the IT product and the business services it supports.

As one (early) example amongst many of this trend, consider Qantas, which has moved its massive Frequent Flyer program onto a cloud-based computing platform in order to keep up with growing demand. Its 22-year-old Fortran-based system was replaced by an On Demand service provided by Oracle, incorporating a scalable architecture designed to cope with changes in demand. Using Oracle's Siebel Loyalty and On Demand offerings, the system is able to provide consistent service to some 7 million members, whilst also dealing with rapidly growing activity. Qantas also sees the new platform as providing the opportunity to target loyalty promotions and extend its loyalty program by introducing new partners – something that would have been difficult with the old system.

As a series of innovations, the speed of this trend from IT products to business services is dependent on two functions. The first – illustrated by the Qantas case – is the degree to which client and suppliers work together to identify and deliver upon the business service possibilities created by the imaginative deployment of cloud-based technologies. The second – to which we alluded earlier – is the role of service integrators in configuring hardware, software, cloud capabilities, and cloud suppliers into new value propositions, commoditizing technology and supplier complexity into offerings experienced as relatively straightforward business services.

CLOUD AND THE SUPPLY INDUSTRY

The third shift we identify, which in some ways is a product of the first two, is that *cloud leads to reconfiguration of the supply industry.* Our research strongly supports the view that cloud technologies will combine as a major disruptive innovation for the IT industry, with widespread anticipated knock-on impacts for businesses across sectors and economies. Marketed as platform independent, scalable, and cost effective, cloud computing promises to deliver IT resources as a utility similar to water, electricity, gas, and telephony. It is seen as a new paradigm for provisioning hardware and software resources over the Internet, where the management and location of physical computing resources are shifted from local to external providers. As we have seen, cloud computing is increasingly being offered by established IT service providers such as Amazon (Elastic Computing Cloud), Google (App Engine), Microsoft (Azure), and Yahoo (Y!OS) as well as by emerging providers such as Zoho. Cloud-based service revenues have been projected to grow globally from $17 billion in 2009 to anything between $44 billion and $60 billion in 2013.[7]

What will be the substance of this rupture and what changes can we expect? A useful way of thinking about the cloud future is in terms of two scenarios. The one advanced by the media and the industry is an 'all change' scenario. This is not surprising given that the industry has clearly reached a trigger point and has, in Geoffrey Moore's phrase, 'crossed the chasm,' rapidly making large-scale cloud investments that are both offensive and defensive. These are seen as strategic bets on the future but are also part of an effort to mitigate risks and not get left behind. Invariably, as we saw in the

1995–2001 e-business era, such a rhetoric of transformation tends to underplay the complexities of adoption and diffusion of innovation. The empirical studies demonstrate that there need to be antecedents for innovation in terms of right structure, absorptive capacity for new knowledge, and a receptive context. The innovations themselves need to demonstrate attributes such as relative advantage, compatibility, low complexity, trialability, observable results, and potential for reinvention (see chapter 6). Client organizations and the industry need to be ready for innovation. Diffusion of innovation requires complex communication, influence, and implementation processes.[8]

Given these realities, it is more likely that a 'hybrid' scenario will play out. The full evolution by businesses to the major set of technologies cloud represents will take at least ten years. In the first five years suppliers will continue to develop and sell their capabilities, while innovation and change will occur within the industry as clients also learn to exploit cloud opportunities more extensively, beyond a cost, scalability, and speed remit. Such a picture is much more consistent with our study findings and the views of the experienced clients, suppliers, consultants, and analysts whose views we have sought.

Let us look at this hybrid future, as shown in figure 3.3, in more detail. For the business, we can define the shift in computing we are observing in our research in terms of the business need for cost/rationalization, agility, innovation, and consumerization. For IT suppliers, cloud enables both consumerization and elasticity. The challenge for the supply side is to reconfigure the industry to meet the business services made possible by cloud. The effect of the shift is already evident. Few enterprise products are being created that are not cloud-enabled. Industry is focusing on providing services, not software. Computing is increasingly commoditized (standard processing or storage units) or consumerized – purchased off the shelf and competing on functionality rather than performance statistics.

That something is up in the supply industry was graphically illustrated in June 2013, when Oracle and Microsoft announced plans to work closely together in the cloud.[9] Subsequently, Oracle unveiled other partnerships, with Salesforce.com and NetSuite, together with a new, cloud-compatible version of its database software. The partnership between Oracle and Microsoft is especially striking because the two firms – and their high-profile co-founders, Oracle's Larry Ellison

FIGURE 3.3 | **The Cloud Rationale: Toward Cloud Business Services**

and Microsoft's Bill Gates – have a long history of business conflict, not least in the 1990s, when Oracle tried to promote an alternative to personal computers to limit the influence of Microsoft's Windows operating system and Microsoft began competing with Oracle's core database business. Why the new partnering? Because both were being wrong-footed by the speed at which business customers were shunning their costly packaged software and maintenance contracts in favour of cloud-delivered services. Microsoft and Oracle both have their own web-based offerings, but they face strong competition from, for example, IBM and Amazon, the latter having built a dominant position in cloud infrastructure. To avoid being left behind in the drift to the cloud, Oracle and Microsoft wanted to show that their services work well together to win customers who fear being locked into a single firm's products. Over the years both have ensured that Oracle's database software runs smoothly on servers using Microsoft operating software. But, in the new commitment, Oracle will also ensure that various parts of its software run well on Azure, Microsoft's cloud platform, while Microsoft will promote Oracle's database software and other products to Azure customers.

So, clearly, IT service suppliers are already moving to reconfigure the industry to meet the business services made possible by cloud. We envisage that this shift will lead to a stratification of the industry, as shown in figure 3.4. At the bottom of the industry stack shown in figure 3.4 we will continue to see production and commodity processing, storage, and communications infrastructure. This infrastructure will mostly be targeted at supporting what we term the 'cloud power stations.' In the long term, we believe that PaaS will be the main choice for enterprise businesses because of its abstraction. These PaaS power stations (the first examples are being created by Google and Microsoft) will supply the raw computing potential for most enterprise applications – and will provide the elasticity required. We see PaaS as successful because of its ability not only to hide unnecessary complexity but also to provide value-added services such as authentication, databases, and integrated development environments (IDEs).[10] The impending 'data deluge' – referred to by Hey and

Figure 3.4 | **Cloud and the New Stratification of the Supply Industry**

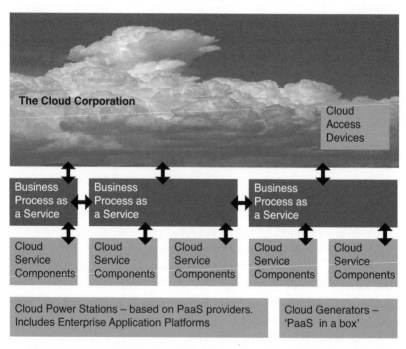

Trefethen and *The Economist*[11] – faced by enterprises exploiting data analytics, business intelligence, and integrated services will demand efficient data-support and database technologies: not just based on SQL but also supercomputing-based data management (Google's MapReduce[12] is a contemporary example).

For niche markets 'PaaS in a box' may emerge, drawing on the container data center model, but with monitoring and maintenance provided by power station providers. IaaS will, however, most likely remain central but increasingly hidden. We anticipate PaaS and SaaS providers exploiting IaaS providers to create value-added services. Further IaaS will remain for niche applications – particularly those founded on open source software.[13] We also envisage the emergence of open source PaaS clones based on commodity IaaS – just as JumpBox.com provides platforms based on open source software using Amazon EC2 IaaS service.

Above these power stations will run business services. We envisage these as the evolution of SaaS. Founded upon PaaS (and sometimes IaaS), such services will be smaller and more easily integrated. We envisage a fragmentation of this SaaS market into interoperable and thus easily integrated 'cloud service components' allowing smaller SaaS players to develop complete suites of services to compete with existing industry behemoths. These services will be integrated to create business-process-as-a-service (BPaaS) using basic glue and interface programming. BPaaS will be created either by cloud service component producers (with expertise in their component offerings – examples might include Oracle, SAP, and SaaS providers) or by systems integrators with specialist understanding of industries and their specific requirements.

These amorphous BPaaS offerings will be the point at which enterprises of all sizes interact with the cloud. Their amorphous nature will allow easier collaboration between enterprises, which can easily share elements of the applications with third parties – just as salesforce.com currently offers salesforce-to-salesforce (S2S) integration – and thus enable the creation of new forms of enterprise based on closely integrated business services.

Access to these services will be through commodity networking and IT. Enterprises will not necessarily have to install their own networking, instead relying on wimax, public wi-fi and 4G. Their IT equipment will be commodity-consumerized Internet access devices including smartphones, tablets, TV screens, and PCs – with minimal configuration to access the enterprise's cloud portals. Designing IT architecture will thus be the design of the digital enterprise – and thus management and IT consultancy will merge in places.

How will this model affect the traditional IT and business process outsourcing industry as cloud takes hold in the market? Far from cloud being the harbinger of the 'death of outsourcing,' we expect a significant increase in the use of external service provision, resulting in a much smaller internal IT function (see chapter 7). This scenario is based on the likelihood of an increasingly diverse and dynamic provider community, but one organized along three principal value trajectories to manage different levels of complexity: a relatively small group of bulk providers of utility and platform services; a much larger group of specialist providers with distinctive industry or functional expertise; and a very small group of service integrators with deep consulting and technology skills who can partner with enterprises to integrate, manage, and continuously optimize a bespoke services ecosystem, helping them become true 'cloud corporations.'

TOWARD A SERVICE-DOMINANT LOGIC

What will be the consequence of these radical shifts on service? The answer is: a move toward a service-dominant logic, which forms a key part of the jigsaw that is cloud and the development of the cloud corporation. Cloud providers invariably already present their offerings using the phrase XX-as-a-service. But what does this imply? In this section we explore the notion of a cloud service in more detail. We do so by drawing on our cloud research streams and reviewing the marketing literature on value creation through a service-dominant logic as well as the business abstraction that the service perspective can provide. We then review different attributes that are typically required of cloud services, such as efficiency, creativity, and simplicity, as well as the constraints on those attributes.

The traditional way of thinking about value is that it is created by the provision of goods and services.[14] Thus, in the context of cloud computing it is the provision of scalable, shared computing resources that enable organizations to generate value. This goods-dominant logic has been challenged by an alternative *service-dominant logic*. This suggests that value is always only created by the user and that, as a result, all exchange is based on service. Indeed, 'when goods are involved, they are tools for the delivery and application of resources.'[15] That is, rather than being an end in themselves, cloud computing resources are best seen as a distribution mechanism for service provision. Cloud providers cannot 'deliver' value but can only offer 'value propositions' that the customer takes advantage of. The service-centered view is also inherently customer oriented and hence relational.[16]

Grönroos gives the example of buying food for a family meal as an illustration of the shift from a goods-dominant logic to a service-dominant logic. According to him, the groceries are bought by customers in order to assist them with a service that should create value for them:

> Groceries are not bought for the sake of having them in store. They are bought in order to provide input resources in the process of cooking dinner for the family, for example in order to have a nice family occasion around the dining table.[17]

Thus, from a business value perspective, cloud computing is not bought for the sake of having access to specific pieces of hardware and software systems. Instead, it is bought in order to achieve particular business aims and objectives. Indeed, for most business managers, cloud computing means that they do not have to know or worry about the technological details of computing products but can, instead, specify their requirements in terms of what they would like to achieve; the business functions that provide value for their organization. Thus, most managers will say that they want a reliable e-mail service to enable them to create business value by allowing staff to exchange messages and share calendars rather than specifying that they want to run Microsoft Exchange 2013 on a computer running a ×64 architecture.

Taking such a service-based perspective means that using cloud computing will increase the ability to transform enterprises by driving down the overall cost of doing business, by reducing the cost and time needed to configure applications and by simplifying the overall process of integrating technology into the business process.

From a more technological perspective, Iyer and Henderson were among the first to present cloud computing as a shift in emphasis to service: 'With cloud computing a product-centric firm-based model for applications and systems can be transformed to a global, distributed, service-centric model (where 'service' means an IT service that the firm can use).'[18] In much the same way, Durkee's analysis incorporated service dimensions, defining cloud computing as the provision of computing 'services' on a demand-driven, pay-as-you-go basis with little or no commitment.[19] In this way, cloud extends existing service concepts of Web services and application service provision (ASP).

The service perspective focuses on the economic exchange associated with consuming cloud services as, in this perspective, cloud computing services are rented in contrast to more traditional assets that are procured. This has immediate consequences for enterprise budgeting as it enables the IT resource to move from capital expenditure to operational expenditure. More generally, however, a service-dominant logic perspective toward cloud desires emphasizes 'the outcomes realised by customers instead of the process or act of provision to customers.'[20] Although service perspectives are relatively well understood in some fields, in the context of computing resources the services perspective is relatively less well understood and potentially much more transformative.

Thus, the service dimension of cloud sees cloud as providing more than just an alternative delivery and pricing mechanism for packaged software. Cloud service becomes the application of competencies (skills and knowledge on data center design and software innovations) through deeds, processes, and performances for the benefit of the business user. Key elements within this service dimension are the extent to which cloud enables creative use of technology for business purposes, the simplicity with which such innovations are enabled, and the efficiency of such enablement. It is helpful at this stage to classify these potential benefits in terms of three service dimensions: efficiency, creativity, and simplicity, which we shall explore in the following sections.

EFFICIENCY AS A SERVICE

Cloud computing has most often been marketed on the basis of the cost savings that can be achieved through the economies of scale that the technological infrastructure underlying cloud computing enables (see chapter 2) as well as the lower environmental impact of equivalent computing. For example, governments often find that the distributed nature of their organizations – arising from their bureaucratic work – results in a proliferation of under-utilized local servers and duplicated support roles. Coupled with a failure to take advantage of the potential purchasing power that a single (government-wide) IT procurement function could obtain, this results in significant costs, which could be reduced substantially simply by consolidating data centers and sharing the overheads among more users. When coupled with innovative procurement arrangements that potentially offer a computing service across the whole of government, these cost savings will provide headline-grabbing efficiency improvements. In the U.K., it has been argued that the government's cloud proposals could save over a billion pounds.[21]

These benefits do not necessarily automatically accrue from the adoption of a particular form of technology and there is an increasing realization that some enterprises, particularly those with well managed, existing large data centers, may find limited efficiency improvements by adopting cloud services. Efficiency is therefore not just a feature 'of the technology' but also of how the technology is used in practice. Therefore, efficiency considerations must be evaluated by customers on the basis of their use of the service and should include consideration of the various 'hidden costs' associated with cloud. These include the cost of back-sourcing services if demands change and thus the risk of 'lock-in' to a service (due to switching costs) as well as the cost of managing the contract with the service provider.

CREATIVITY AS A SERVICE

Once enterprises move beyond the efficiency gains that cloud services can provide, they soon become particularly interested in the extent to which cloud can enable creativity and innovation by lowering the transaction costs associated with innovation and enabling the development of value networks.

Low Friction Creativity from Cloud Services

Experimentation is a key enabler of creativity and yet the traditional ways of managing computing infrastructures introduce delays and inhibit experimentation due to the lead time for provisioning and configuring, which could be weeks or even months. The ability to cut that cycle down by a couple of weeks or even to shrink it down to days has two important benefits. First, it translates into pure cost savings. Second and perhaps more significantly, this speed of response opens up novel business opportunities that could become a significant competitive advantage, allowing enterprises to take advantage of shifts in the marketplace. It has been argued that adopting cloud services can reduce the time taken to innovate and to bring innovations to market, since you can turn on infrastructure very quickly and essentially bring new products to market much more quickly. Missing from this narrative of speedy innovation, however, is the concern as to whether such speed introduces pressure on IT departments to reduce the time for traditional planning, user requirements elicitation, and analysis activity, thus introducing new risks.[22]

However, it is always possible that cloud can reduce the risk of innovation as upfront commitments are lowered and sourcing decisions can be made in a rhythm that is much more closely aligned with the enterprise's business cycle. Such optimistic views support Owens's assertion that 'elasticity could bring to the IT infrastructure what Henry Ford brought to the automotive industry with assembly lines and mass production: affordability and substantial improvements on time to market.'[23]

Another consequence of the service perspective is that cloud computing exhibits the characteristics of what Christensen describes as 'distributive innovation,'[24] whereby there are lower barriers to market entry and therefore previously excluded market participants (including emerging countries and small to medium-sized enterprises) can gain access to markets. Creativity also emerges from the ability to exploit cloud services in a 'low friction' way, allowing innovation because the technological functionality behind the scalability of cloud services allows the trialing of niche services in an agile manner with low risk. For example, a supply chain optimization company within the automotive industry can have its services 'plugged into' existing inventory systems.

What is much less clear, however, is the extent to which enterprises have the skills and motivation to exploit such opportunities, as all too often their existing mind-sets will determine the extent to which they can truly innovate. Ciborra, for example, presents the case of AT&T, which bought the Italian computing manufacturer Olivetti because it wanted to transform itself from a telecommunications company to an information-based company. Over time, however, the telecommunications engineering mind-set at AT&T reasserted itself, Olivetti was sold off, and the company reverted to being an enterprise that provided telecommunications solutions.[25]

As Porter and Hammer and Champy showed some time ago, this question of willingness to transform in the light of new technological opportunities has existed throughout the history of strategic information systems, with technology either driving or following organizational changes.[26]

'Business agility' can be defined as an organization's ability to appreciate and respond to change[27] and, together with speed to market, is proving to be essential for business survival. As a result, there is a significant desire for agility characterized by speed, nimbleness, and lightness, and this is closely related to, and sometimes replaces, creativity.

The time to provision that has hampered creativity has also been seen as a constraint on agility[28] and results in a phenomenal increase in the weight of expectation falling on the IT function. The business pressure on a Chief Information Officer is today shifting from whether or not something can be done to how quickly it can be achieved (see also the Allergan case in chapter 4 for an illustrative example).

Emerging Cloud Value Networks for Innovation

Brynjolfsson and colleagues note that those enterprises that 'simply replace corporate resources with cloud computing, while changing nothing else, are doomed to miss the full benefits of the new technology.'[29] For them, cloud provides services which must be exploited by companies in their innovation processes through the reinvention of services. Central to this is the need to understand how portfolios of information services are brought together to support service provision to customers. Thus, while cloud provides services in an abstracted, scalable form with varying levels of variety, such services typically need to be integrated, configured, and reconfigured to enable the creative provision of service to customers. This might be achieved by combining elements with low levels of abstraction (such as hardware platforms offered as a service PaaS) with elements at higher levels of abstraction (and less flexibility), including forms of SaaS.

Such an arrangement mimics the more traditional supply chains, where intermediary service providers depend on other service providers to enable them to support their customers. Such cloud supply chains raise important challenges in terms of how the intermediary service providers can ensure that their suppliers provide levels of service that will allow them to honor their own service level agreements with the end customer. Whilst for many this might involve careful consideration (and monitoring) of the service levels offered by the lower-level cloud providers, some cloud intermediaries have chosen to manage this risk directly, for example, by using the flexibility offered by cloud provisioning to use a range of lower-level providers. If one fails to provide the required level of service, they simply switch to a different provider, in much the same way that the end customer can choose to switch to a different intermediary provider.

This process of 'reconfiguration' of the IT value chain is proving not to follow a simple linear coordination and reveals high levels of complexity. Leimeister et al. propose a focus on the emergence of 'cloud value networks,' which emerge 'as some kind of marketplace, where various cloud computing resources ... are integrated and offered to the customer.'[30] Within these networks various types of participant are found.

This view reflects a service-oriented architecture perspective, using cloud services in much the same way as globalization has reconfigured product supply chains.[31] Such an approach is likely to lead to cloud ecosystems involving 'the fruitful interplay and co-opetition between all players that realize different business models in the cloud computing context.'[32] Here, it will be down to the ingenuity and the inventiveness of the client and the client's integrator to configure capabilities that will enable the client to do things differently and innovatively. In particular, such an approach will depend on a process of collaboration that is defined here as a cooperative, commercial arrangement in which two or more parties work jointly in a common enterprise toward shared goals. The early days of outsourcing focused primarily on cost minimization and latent antagonistic relationships between customer and service provider. Unsurprisingly, this severely limited the amount of innovation that would arise and outsourcing organizations slowly realized that there is a very strong correlation between levels of collaboration and innovation within and across organizations.

In the context of outsourcing, our study carried out in 2011 of 26 organizations that had moved to 'collaborative innovation' in their outsourcing relationships revealed that all of them experienced IT operational innovation while 21 were getting business process and 7 business product/service innovations.[33] Innovation through cloud will also come from an acceleration of such collaborative tendencies, but, as has been found in more traditional outsourcing arrangements, this will be a challenge to many client and provider organizations alike. Simply put, superior performance will require a step-change in client–provider and provider–provider relationships in terms of objectives and behaviors. This step-change needs to be toward new forms of collaboration involving mutual flexibility, trust, reciprocity, risk sharing, and investment in resources and time, and it needs to be executive led.[34]

A specific and important example of such creativity is the emergence of business intelligence through cloud computing.[35] This allows all sizes of businesses to exploit business intelligence across their processes and in collaboration with other businesses within their value networks. For example, a clinical systems cloud supplier could pool the clinical data in its servers and undertake real-time data analysis using the data from thousands of individual doctors' businesses held in the cloud. We turn again to the theme of cloud and innovation in chapter 6.

SIMPLICITY AS A SERVICE

Cloud computing in several of its forms involves the outsourcing of the skills and knowledge traditionally held by IT departments (such as configuring and managing servers), and organizations need to gain knowledge of how their chosen cloud provider (outsourcer) operates and how they will ensure that the service is provided as contracted. There are costs for enterprises in gaining such knowledge including the costs associated with the contractual arrangements that underpin the use of cloud services. As a consequence, effective cloud services will require this knowledge exchange to be as simple as is practicable.

On the one hand, contracts for cloud services are becoming simpler by 'disentangling' the complexity of the underlying hardware, for example by abstracting and by limiting the variety of a cloud service. The resulting simplicity can be reflected in simpler and more standardized contractual arrangements for the purchase of services by a larger number of customers. For example, through Amazon Web services it has become possible to procure 750 hours of a Microsoft Windows Server Micro Instance with 613 MB of memory and 32-bit and 64-bit platform support. Given this standardization of hardware, it is increasingly possible to condense the contract into an easily digestible form. When serving volume markets, the contracts have to be fairly simple and certainly would not contain the tens of thousands of pages found in long-term outsourcing contracts.

Such standardized and simpler contracts for well-defined cloud services allow the use of simpler high-volume purchase channels such as credit cards with automated 'zero touch' interactions between user and provider. Abstracted computing services are rented for a specific period in non-uniform patterns (supported by scalability). As the full cost of the service is included within this price, the purchaser can avoid complex cost calculations (for software licenses, hardware costs, support, power and cooling, ground rental, etc).

This also reflects a consumerization of IT services (see above). Customer-focused IT (such as Gmail, Dropbox, and iCloud) are beginning to be employed within businesses. Similarly, enterprise IT providers are packaging their services in a simpler structure – a consumerized 'retail model' was pioneered by Amazon – that welcomes all-comers and accepts anyone with a credit card.

The Value of Simplicity

Traditionally, IT costs have been both hidden and complex. For example, whereas servers and IT support staff are explicitly included in the IT budget, power consumption/cooling costs are less frequently explicitly budgeted as IT expenditure. Whilst power consumption is negligible for an individual server, it becomes significant for a large data center. Cloud providers are able to monitor usage patterns and demand through pay-as-you-go purchases and can gain knowledge of market demand.

The Limits of Simplicity: Service Level Agreements

One area where simplification can make things harder for both contracting parties is service equivalence. Traditionally, for outsourced infrastructure the service level agreement (SLA) contract provided knowledge of the quality of service expected in comparison with internal service provision. Such contracts were mechanisms for negotiating the relationship between IT vendor and client, establishing trust and anticipated risk. At present, however, cloud SLAs are often weak and ineffectual for this purpose (see also chapter 4). Meaningful SLAs are few and far between and even when a vendor does have one, most of the time it is toothless. In part this is because many companies provide the same SLAs for all users and, unless the cloud provider has segmented the marketplace by price, it is not possible to 'purchase' a higher level of service availability or quality. Part of this weakness in SLAs might be a consequence of service providers worrying about the unintended consequences of hosting large numbers of users on a single platform or server, as this multiplies their risk of a breach of the SLA. As a consequence, current SLAs are usually poor signals of total cloud performance.

CONCLUSION

How to position the cloud's likely impacts? Long wave researchers posit a regular cyclical pattern for each Kondratieff long wave – a long climb out of depression through recovery and prosperity phases, leading to a maturity phase, whose shallow decline leads to a steep fall in a depression phase. In our view, cloud represents a further progression of technical innovation within the fifth Kondratieff long wave. In 2011, growing cloud investment and technical innovation had not yet been matched by a large market. But by 2013 this was changing and we expect over the next five years increasing technical innovation starting to diffuse to a wider range of applications and to find a broader market. It may well be that within the long wave, cloud moves through both the prosperity and maturity phases over the 2010–2025 period. Long wave theorists would see such a period marked by considerable technical innovation and the transformation, in the context of Internet developments, changing major areas including working lives, business models, leisure patterns, and the structure and shape of business organizations themselves. One would expect an acceleration also of business institutional changes typical of the fifth long wave, namely in network structures for organizations, alliances, joint ventures, and outsourcing.[36]

In all this we have pointed to some major near-term developments, in particular a relatively fast take-up of the new cloud services being made available from 2014 and over the next five years, together with technical and contractual advances that would render those services robust and more attractive to clients. Client appetite is likely to move from a *cost reduction* agenda to a *cost plus* innovation agenda, with clients becoming more ambitious about wanting not just IT operational benefits but also business process and market innovations from cloud adoption. We return to this theme in chapter 6.

At the same time, we point to cloud implying and, indeed, making necessary, three longer-term, major game-changers – radical shifts toward service performance and from products to business services and a radical reconfiguration of the supply industry. These long-term shifts represent major challenges for the IT services industry, in particular requiring the adoption of a service-dominant logic, offering efficiency, creativity, and simplicity as a service, as detailed in this chapter. If in this chapter we have examined the challenges for the IT/cloud supply industry, in the next two chapters we examine the major challenges faced by cloud user organizations in their shifts toward cloud corporations.

CHAPTER 4

The Challenges

INTRODUCTION

In the near term, cloud computing faces a number of challenges clearly identified by our research. These include legal and regulatory compliance considerations, security and privacy issues, managing the contractual relationship between client and cloud provider, including lock-in and dependency, as well as managing the very flexibility that cloud provides. Nevertheless, many of these types of challenge have been faced previously and effective solutions have evolved. For example, safe harbour provisions address legal and regulatory issues about transferring data abroad and over 25 years of IT outsourcing have resulted in a skill base that is capable of managing contractual relationships with key partners. End-user computing, whether in the form of desktop computers or, increasingly, smartphones, has become effectively integrated within the IT infrastructure of most organizations. Cloud computing can, and should, learn from these experiences if it is to achieve its full potential. In this chapter and the next, we report on the five major challenges identified by our research and discuss ways forward.

CLOUDY BUSINESS: PERCEPTION GAPS ON RISK AND EXPECTATION

One major finding from our research is that not every party sees the challenges presented by cloud computing in the same light.[1] This in itself adds to the challenges associated with cloud and the future of business as it implies a need to recognize and act on the different assessments of what the key cloud challenges are. When we asked client companies whether cloud business services brought new business risks into play, senior business executives registered their top five concerns as data security and privacy, followed by data being housed offshore, compliance/regulatory issues, exit strategy and lock-in risks, and the credibility of suppliers. On the other hand, some 30 percent suggested that there was a real risk of their businesses suffering if they did not adopt cloud services. Such executives could see cloud being some 20–30 percent of their IT budget within the next 18 months.

Senior IT executives weighed risks differently. They agreed that security and offshoring of data were significant new risks introduced by moving to cloud. However, they also saw some issues as much greater risks than did the business executives. This was particularly true of the risks inherent in cloud exit strategy and lock-in. In practice, senior IT executives have greater concerns over all contractual issues with cloud. But they also rated the risks much higher than business executives for compliance and regulatory issues, disaster/recovery of data, and availability of quality external support. They also saw the business detriment of not adopting cloud business services as a much lower risk than did their senior business counterparts. *This points to a major challenge in organizations as they move to cloud, namely: how to bridge the cloud 'risk perception gap' that exists between business and IT executives.*

At the same time, we found business executives having high expectations of their internal IT departments, 40 percent of them saying that they would rely upon their internal IT staff 'extensively' to deliver cloud and another 40 percent relying 'moderately' on them. Business executives' expectations about what cloud could deliver to the business are also running high, with 50 percent or more citing the gains as cost reduction for business applications and their configuration, much quicker provision of business applications, new ability to access best-in-class applications, and the facilitation of a virtual distributed organization. Our interview research found IT executives positive but much more circumspect about what cloud could deliver, especially in the short time horizons mentioned by their business executive colleagues. They were much more aware of the difficulties of transition and the multiple, detailed relationships and actions that had to be handled, in order to move to cloud. They invariably suggested longer time horizons for implementation and for fulfilling the business potential of cloud. *This suggests that a major challenge also needs to be managed going forward, namely the cloud 'expectations gap' manifestly existing between senior business and IT executives.*

These two gaps – on perceptions of risk and on expectations – frame the substantive cloud challenges our research has identified and which are the subject of this chapter.

CLOUD – THE EMERGING REAL CHALLENGES

Cloud computing is far from mature and it remains unclear to what extent fears on cloud computing are reasonable in the long term, or represent another example of 'FUD'[2] – the fear, uncertainty, and doubt instilled by those with a stake in an old computing model against the new, innovative entrant. This uncertainty was reflected in our interview evidence, with many technical specialists believing that the concerns are over-played but remain, in the words of one, a 'stigma' on cloud computing. Security, offshore data housing, lock-in and compliance are key concerns emerging from our survey results, especially from an IT executive perspective (see figure 4.1). However, in assessing the challenges of cloud computing over the medium term, there is a need to avoid focusing wholly on these concerns. The technology is changing, legislation is uncertain and decisions cannot be made in absolute terms but must be made in relation to, for example, current data-center options and risks.

There are numerous challenges facing organizations when considering cloud computing. In chapter 2[3] we presented four desires that might drive the move to cloud: equivalence, variety, abstraction, and scaling. The particular desires that drive the move to cloud affect the timing of when a business goes to cloud, what 'cloud' it should go into, whether to focus on IaaS, PaaS, or SaaS, how to develop the necessary skills, and how to maximize existing data-center investment while moving to the cloud. All these decisions are about desired results, but also concern risk.

FIGURE 4.1 | Comparative Risks of Business Cloud Services

How much of a concern are the following business risks posed by cloud business services to your business function, compared to your existing risks for non-cloud services?

■ Business risks are greater   ■ Business risks are similar/no change   ■ Business risks are lessened

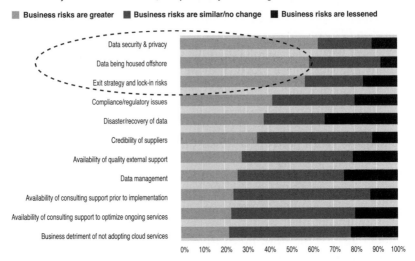

In the analysis here, however, we focus on the five challenges which seem particularly critical at this stage in the development of cloud use within organizations. For each challenge we discuss its relative importance, the likelihood of its impact changing over time, and the potential responses business can make to the challenge.

Challenge 1: Weighing up the Security and Legal Risks

As shown in figure 4.1, our survey suggests that data security and privacy, together with offshore data housing and security, are perceived to be the most significant risks for cloud – a result supported by our interview evidence.

Offshore data concerns revolve around the problems of legislative compliance when data crosses borders. In the short term, most companies can avoid these by using domestic cloud facilities, although those in smaller jurisdictions may struggle to access the two cloud data centers necessary for disaster recovery – something container data centers may help address. In the longer term, we anticipate that market developments and new legislation will improve this situation. Therefore, legal challenges are unlikely to be an intractable barrier to adopting the cloud.

Security concerns are more complex. Potential adopters are concerned about the security of data outside the corporate firewall, though many companies regularly rely on hosting services.[4] As just one example we researched, many general practitioners (GPs) in the U.K. use hosted services for health records. Within the U.K., GPs are small businesses that typically maintain their own computer infrastructure. This is costly and time-consuming, and ensuring adequate data protection and data recovery is difficult. EMIS, a leading provider in this area, offers GPs a secure, fully hosted solution as an alternative. EMIS hosts the patient data at two data centers that have been accredited by the National Health Service (NHS) as having no single point of failure, thus providing the required disaster recovery facility and business continuity for such important data.[5]

The cloud does bring some new risks. For example, people hack brands. Thus, hosting in a multi-tenancy environment alongside other brands may increase risk (e.g. hosting WikiLeak led DynDNS and Amazon to be targeted by a DDoS[6] attack that endangered others using their services) – a risk which is hard to calculate. This risk also needs to be understood in the context of risks inherent in existing systems, which are multiple, such as poorly implemented policies, employee breaches, and systems failures. Furthermore, the risks of cloud computing are mitigated to some degree by the new security benefits it offers. Virtualization and multi-tenancy have been around for 30 years[7] and are rapidly maturing. Also, various new security applications (such as encrypted file systems and data-loss prevention systems) exist. Cloud providers are often better managed and can invest in more sophisticated security hardware and software – for example, analytics of unusual behavior across the vast numbers of virtual servers. Beyond this, their scale enables effective responses to large DDoS attacks through high levels of redundancy.

Concerned enterprises can employ hybrid clouds – where most servers are in the cloud, but key data is hosted internally and linked to the cloud. Alternatively, they can employ data-governance solutions (such as PerspecSys.com for the SalesForce platform) that automatically replace corporate data with anonymous identifiers as the data leave the firewall, though both involve cost and processing overheads.

The real challenge, therefore, is not so much the legal or security issues but *the ability of companies to weigh up the benefits and risks* of such disparate systems and manage them effectively, in particular when they are new and immature. Cloud security concerns the 'operational security of the business and the integrity of the party with which you choose to work' and evaluating these would seem to be standard practice today.[8] As Steve Ballmer, CEO of Microsoft, usefully summarizes:

> As soon as you start pooling computing and data in new and interesting ways, really defining and really being careful about weighing up who owns what data and how it is controlled and used is a fundamental responsibility of every participant in that chain.[9]

However, until cloud providers better understand enterprise security demands and reflect these in their contracts, evaluating their security provision remains difficult. In such circumstances enterprises may well need to seek expert advice to assess the risks pertaining. Amazon's 2010/11 focus on acquiring security standards (e.g. ISO 270001) was a welcome development. However, the indications are that security and privacy issues concerning the Internet and cloud have not gone away, but may well be multiplying. Moreover, different regulatory agencies across many economies are endeavoring to keep pace with the security and privacy implications of cloud developments. Therefore, we will spend more time in the next chapter dealing with the issues and regulatory responses.

Challenge 2: Defining the Relationship through Contracting

Cloud computing contracts are hybrids of outsourcing, software, and leasing and are becoming major contractual agreements.[10] Such contracts are focused typically upon the service level agreement (SLA) regarding security and service quality.

In chapter 3 we pointed out how service was a key component of cloud and a key expectation amongst cloud users. Despite this, we found many cloud providers struggling to provide the robust SLAs enterprises expect for their data centers. This is due in part to technical problems but also to the cloud business models we have seen. Multi-tenancy multiplies the risk for the cloud provider (and hence the cloud user). Moreover, statistical multiplexing – hosting virtual machines with different demands for different times to enable high resource utilization – can lead to service delivery failures if demand patterns change. Network latency between cloud provider and enterprise is beyond the provider's control,[11] though services such as Akamai[12] can enable some level of management. SaaS providers often share a single platform for all users and thus cannot provide differentiated SLAs.[13]

As a note of caution, we found that many cloud supplier business models are not that focused on providing enterprise contracting requirements. As one respondent told us:

> The problem with cloud services today is that many of the service providers have not evolved to the point that they are comfortable being custodians of data because, frankly, many of the service providers used to provide product and they never had to sign up for it and they don't understand what it means to have that liability.[14]

At present, their businesses continue to expand despite the often relatively low compensation offered for breaches of SLAs.[15] Competition should improve this situation, as should the development of cloud standards. As another respondent told us:

> I'm sort of hoping for an ITIL.v.4[16] that's more cloud ready. You still need change management, you still need to keep track for compliance of where data is, but a lot of those constructs don't quite fit in the cloud world.[17]

It has been argued that contracting for cloud is simpler, as only one contract is required – not the usual three: software, hardware, and systems integration.[18] In reality, however, few SaaS or PaaS meet all functional requirements and thus contracting for cloud services involves 'ecosystems' of SaaS, PaaS, and IaaS providers that must be integrated to provide complete solutions. Similarly, IaaS and PaaS involve traditional software licenses, which can prove problematic for the cloud.[19] It is this network of interactions within an ecosystem that increases complexity for SLAs. As one supplier executive put it:

> If you were eventually to go to a completely 100 percent utility model, the complexity would come between the numbers of players that you'd need to engage to offer the rounded solution. And that's where the complexity would lie, in the interactions between the players.[20]

In response, companies should evaluate cloud SLAs in relation to their business's risk-management profile as well as the ecosystem of cloud providers and their SLAs. Where the offered SLAs are inappropriate, companies can seek to exploit multiple IaaS and PaaS cloud providers for the same service. In this way, they can fashion their own guaranteed up-time by creating virtual points of presence at extremely low cost. Alternatively, they could engage a service integrator to perform this function. The Media Agency RAPP takes the first approach to critical infrastructure:

> If we're doing anything that has to be 100 percent up-time … we would make sure that we've got enough points of presence globally and enough redundancy in each of those points of presence to get round any issues. So we don't particularly worry about the SLA. You will never guarantee a 100 percent up-time regardless of whether it's infrastructure, hardware, or virtual. So if you want 100 percent, you need to pay for this extra deployment, you know, in another place.[21]

Creating such value-added SLAs on top of cloud environments is likely to be a key role for service integrators – which is a step beyond systems integration. Here, they can manage the entire ecosystem for their client and provide a simple SLA in return:

> An example of that might be if a customer has industry regulatory compliance process that none of the cloud vendors would offer out of the box. But we provide the plumbing to enable that application to be in compliance with industry regulations. So, for example, in the pharmaceutical industry,

they have to comply with the 21-CFR PAR-11 regulation. Microsoft don't provide that out of the box but this is where SI and the consultant can provide a turnkey solution sitting on top of that platform as a service. And we sell that back to the customer.[22]

We therefore believe that in-time SLAs for cloud will better represent the needs of companies – and that SLAs will be created for ecosystems of cloud services by systems integrators.

SLAs: Bigger Challenges than You Think

When it comes to SLAs, the client using the cloud is faced with a real challenge. Small new cloud SaaS providers that are increasing their business and attracting more clients to their multi-tenanted data center are unlikely to provide more usefully defined SLAs for their services than that which a data-center provider can offer where it controls all elements of the supplied infrastructure. Why would they? Their business is growing and an SLA is a huge risk. One part of this is that with a multi-tenanted structure the breach of one SLA is probably a breach of a lot of SLAs – the pay-out might seem meager to a single client but will be large for a SaaS provider. Furthermore, with each new customer the demands on the data center, and hence the risk, increase. Therefore, the argument is that, as SaaS providers become successful, the risk of SLAs being breached might increase.

There is, however, a counterpoint to this growth risk. As each new customer begins to use the SaaS, they will undertake their own due-diligence checks. Many will attempt to stress-test the SaaS service. Some will want to try to hack the application. As the customer base grows (and moves, probably, toward blue-chip clients) the seriousness of this testing will increase. Security demands in particular will be tested as bigger and bigger companies consider their services. This presents a considerable opportunity for the individual customer/user. For with each new customer comes the benefit of increased stress-testing of the SaaS platform – and increasing development of skills within the SaaS provider. While the SLA may continue to be poor, *the risk of failure of the data center may well diminish as the SaaS grows*.

One experienced consultant usefully described SLAs in this way:

A lot of businesses are used to the SLA concept. They've got a legal team or a commercial team who can do that reasonably well. But the devil is in the detail … In really defining … it's your typical technology-meets-business mind-set. Defining the level of SLAs required, what to ask for from a vendor when it comes to cloud, when it comes to software as a service. It's more important now to get it right because it's outsourced, and how do you manage that? Thus the devil is in the detail – in knowing, when it comes to cloud, exactly what you've got to be granular with. Without the granularity, it's ineffective.[23]

A Different Approach to SLAs

To invoke a contract is, in effect, a failure in a relationship – a break-down in trust. Seldom does the invocation of a contract benefit either party. The aim of an SLA is thus not just to provide a contractual agreement, but rather to set out the level of service on which the partnership between customer and supplier is based. In this way, an SLA is about the expected quality demanded of the supplier and, with the development suggested in the last section, the expected quality may well increase with more customers – not decrease, as is usually envisaged for cloud. SLAs for cloud providers may well be trivial and poor, but the systemic risk of using cloud is not as simplistic as is often portrayed. While it is unsurprising that cloud suppliers may offer poor SLAs (it may not be in their interest to do otherwise), this does not mean that the quality of service is, or will remain, poor.

So what should the client consider in looking at the SLA offering in terms of service quality? We would suggest three assessments:

1. How does the cloud SaaS supplier manage its growth? The growth of a SaaS service means greater demand on the provider's data center and, hence, greater risk that the SLAs will be breached for their multi-tenanted data center.

2. How open is the cloud SaaS provider in allowing testing of its services by customers?

3. How well does the cloud SaaS provider's strategic ambition for service quality align with its customers' desires for service quality?

Challenge 3: The Lock-in Dilemma

Exit strategies and lock-in risks are key concerns for cloud contracts. For any technology provision there is always a switching cost, but for cloud providers there is significant incentive to attempt to exploit lock-in. If computing were to become a fungible commodity in a liquid cloud marketplace, then costs would fall to marginal cost – and profits would thus be slim. *Like Telcos before them, cloud providers will tend to focus on maximizing switching costs while remaining competitive.*

We identify two forms of lock-in for cloud services, which we term technology and institutional lock-in. **Technology lock-in** concerns the cost of mobility of business service between cloud platforms. In general, IaaS has the lowest switching costs, with SaaS and PaaS switching costs higher but related to the nature of the business services. For IaaS, however, there is also lock-in to the virtual machine's operating system and application stack, which should be compared with PaaS. Further, SaaS and PaaS create network effects (it is more economic to purchase further services compatible with existing services), thus increasing lock-in. Network effects are highly significant for the envisaged ecosystems of cloud services.

Institutional lock-in is seldom considered. Here we are referring to the lock-in encountered when technologies become embedded within organizational routines and users' work practices. For SaaS (and to a lesser extent PaaS) such institutionalism can have a serious impact on the ability to switch and thus represents lock-in. In contracting for a cloud service, both types of lock-in should be considered. An example of institutional lock-in is the institutional investment made when adopting a particular e-mail system – such as specialist configuration and training activities.

The risks of technological lock-in should be considered in the cost of contracting for services. Contracts are likely to focus on increasing lock-in as competition reduces margins. Competitors, however, will focus on reducing switching costs for dominant players. Specialist services (e.g. http://www.cloudswitch.com) and systems integrators will help, but such services can themselves become locked in.

Challenge 4: Managing the Cloud

Perhaps the most significant challenge for organizations and CIOs is the predicted extinction of the corporate IT department in the face of cloud computing. Nicholas Carr has polarized the cloud debate, arguing that:

> In the long run the IT department is unlikely to survive, at least not in its familiar form. It will have little left to do once the bulk of business computing shifts out of private data-centres and into 'the cloud'. Business units and even individual employees will be able to control the processing of information directly, without the legions of technical specialists.[24]

Such prognostications of the 'end of corporate computing' lead IT executives' policies to appear tinged with self-interest and out-dated, so reducing those executives' capacity for action. In response, we see such statements as founded upon the belief that computing will be 'solved' in an 'always near future.'[25] One is reminded of Ken Olson's pronouncement as president of DEC in 1977, which also pushed computing in the direction of suppliers: 'there is no reason anyone would want a computer in their home.' Such a view then saw corporate exploitation of computing as static. Nicholas Carr's view on cloud tends to underplay technical issues, transition, legacy systems, and the economics of different technical arrangements. But it is not a new view, either. It should be noted that similar predictions were made in the early 1980s in response to the introduction of the microcomputer and yet, ultimately, IT departments were needed to achieve control over and gain value out of disparate and uncoordinated PC purchases.[26]

As we have noted in other chapters and elsewhere,[27] cloud change is likely to be slower and less linear than suggested by the more dramatic predictions (see especially chapter 6). Cloud technologies are being applied and tested in highly complex markets, with many different interests in play based on multiple kinds of relationship. In the long term, cloud computing is likely to be the impetus for a fundamental change in underlying technological capability. However, our research suggests that this technology environment will be a hybrid of the new and the old, rather than a radical departure. Cloud computing in the short term is still likely to be disruptive. We therefore see two key challenges in managing the immediate transition period before longer-term, deeper changes can be achieved: maintaining strategic control and managing cloud services.

Maintaining strategic control. The strategic relationship between IT and business is challenged by cloud – as it was with the introduction of the microcomputer.[28] SaaS companies, such as SalesForce. com, are directly marketed at the end user rather than at corporate IT[29] and many end users already exploit cloud services in response to perceived deficiencies in corporate IT provision without consultation with the IT department.

Once introduced into the enterprise, cloud services can be updated, morphed, and changed easily by technology providers without the control or direction of the IT department. New functionality is immediately available – and it is in providers' interests to develop functionality that leads product use to expand, become more institutionalized, and spread across the organization. For example, SalesForce.com (traditionally focused on sales) now incorporates corporate social networking through its Chatter product. As Robin Daniels told us:

> Chatter is really about picking the best that we've wanted from the consumer Web from Facebook … and Twitter and putting that inside of the enterprise so there is virtually no training involved, there's nothing to do really from an administrative perspective, 'cause you just turn it on and suddenly it's there[30]

If such cloud services align with a specific business function's power, such adoption could alter the organization in favor of that business function. The simplicity and low cost of such technology adoption means that IT strategy must move up to CxO level and continue to be seen as vital or IT will have difficulty controlling its proliferation.

Managing cloud services. Organizations are still slow in developing management capability and principles for operating with cloud services. Such strategies should focus on the multiple contracts needed for a cloud ecosystem. Monitoring usage, SLAs, performance, robustness, and business dependency are vital. Most cloud providers demonstrate the robustness of their infrastructure through real-time monitoring services.[31] Such services should be monitored, but internal cloud monitoring should also be introduced. Support from cloud providers can be variable, and organizations should develop their own support services either internally or with third parties.

Cloud computing offers significant opportunities for new competitors. Initial economic analysis of cloud suggests that its removal of capital expenditure will lead to an increasing number of agile SMEs entering marketplaces.[32] Monitoring such cloud-based competition, and the opportunities for competition through cloud services, should become part of corporate strategy.

Finally, as the 'Internet generation' continues to enter businesses, their demands for consumerized services, and their often limited understanding of Internet boundaries, will put pressure on IT strategy. IT will need to develop strategies for rapidly improving end-user applications to reflect the demands of this generation as they enter managerial roles, or it will risk losing the argument for strategic IT.

Challenge 5: Dealing with the Integration Challenge

While the integration challenge does not emerge strongly from surveys on cloud, the problems with integration emerged very powerfully from interviews with corporate, and especially IT, executives. Many suggested that integration was actually the *key* challenge with cloud and that those who solved this challenge would be in the vanguard of cloud use and exploitation. A superficial look at cloud computing indicates, of course, that there should not be an integration issue. Cloud is all too often presented as taking problems away. The IT/cloud service company and its partners will run the technology (the 'pipes') and look after service; the business executives can get on with focusing on business objectives, while the IT function can act as knowledgeable broker, helping to leverage IT/cloud services supply for business advantage. A similar, somewhat simplistic, view was taken of IT outsourcing in its early days in the 1990s.[33] But with cloud, as then with IT, corporations, especially large corporations, are rarely finding it so easy. Why is this?

Well, consider figure 4.2, which maps the major components that need to be integrated. Getting the business on side and behaving in disciplined ways is historically hard and this is unlikely to cease with cloud. We know that building the retained organization to take advantage of cloud technologies is vital but also difficult and an evolutionary process. In fact this emerged so powerfully from our research that we devote the whole of chapter 7 to this part of the integration story. If technology governance was a challenge in the past, then, our respondents tell us, cloud introduces new and more immediate risks. On IT strategy, there is the potential to let the new technologies overwhelm the achievement of alignment with business goals and needs. There is the question of fit with the more conventional external IT services and also with the legacy environment. Also with cloud, not just systems integration, but, as we saw in chapter 3, also *service integration* between end users and multiple internal and external cloud services becomes more critical for achieving the potential business benefits. Finally, governance and interoperability in the larger cloud ecosystem also become key.

FIGURE 4.2 | **The Cloud Integration Challenge**

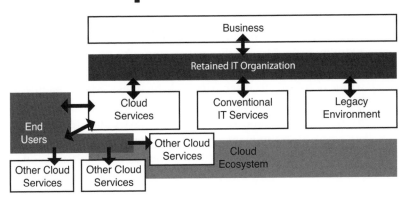

Source: Ricky Santos, Chief Architect, Accenture, 2010.

The likelihood is that the integration challenge will be a long-run one, but also a matter of choice for the more mature users of cloud. Thus, a senior IT executive at a global pharmaceutical and health care company told us:

We're not so romanced by cloud – that it is 'just plug and play' or, 'Oh, we have cloud, we don't need an IT shared service team'. Our projections show cloud becoming part of the environment but not replacing the entire environment. We think cloud will replace a fair amount but we always think there will be other, [let's] call [them], 'conventional IT shared service requirements' still out there. We'll still build the servers and still have capacity for applications and solutions that we keep in house.[34]

How do corporations begin to address such a set of challenges? It turns out that they are not insurmountable, even though such issues may lead to more delays in cloud adoption than many would like to think. Allergan, a $5 billion U.S.-based multi-specialty health care company operating in over one hundred countries, provides one illustrative example.[35] Given the five-year strategic business plan to accelerate growth through product innovation, market expansion, and depth of customer relationships, the CIO established that IT's central role was to facilitate business agility. Between 1997 and 2006, to achieve business efficiencies, the company had already built a single global ERP. Its business units began adopting cloud-based capabilities from 2005, but it was only in late 2010, to enhance business agility, that Allergan adopted a 'cloud first' policy. Henceforth, before buying or building additional systems, it reviewed whether a viable public cloud option existed. The company moved from cloud supporting non-core low security risk business competencies to using public cloud services for non-core processes with high data-security requirements and some core business competencies with low data-security requirements. Allergan's cloud-vendor assessments found suppliers with data-security processes as thorough as its own. Allergan planned to have more than half of its application portfolio within the cloud by 2014. In IT management terms, it had made the big jump – enabled by cloud – of moving from delivering IT solutions to brokering business capabilities.

One can see in this example all the integration challenges we raised above being worked through. For the IT executives at Allergan three challenges emerged as the significant ones. The first was the need for a carefully designed and executed data architecture. Different countries had different rules about transferring data (see chapter 5); moreover, data integrity depended on clarifying data ownership.

The second challenge was re-skilling IT professionals – an issue we deal with in detail in chapter 7. The third challenge was governance, in particular addressing the continuous trade-offs needed between having stable enterprise-wide platforms and responsive local plug-and-play services. Business relationship managers helped here, as did a company-wide Technology Steering Committee, where business executives had the major voice in prioritizing and approving new platforms and IT/cloud-based business capabilities. The result? Cloud gave the company long-term financial predictability and flexibility, reduced capital investment significantly, and offered a faster way to deliver new capabilities. The greatest cloud impact, though, has been how plug-and-play allowed Allergan to respond rapidly to unique business needs.

Mooney et al. suggest from this case and others six imperatives for preparing for the cloud: rethink the IT value proposition; re-architect the existing digitized platforms by reducing their scope; redesign IT governance; re-allocate IT budgets; refocus on user needs and preferences; and redevelop the IT organization.[36] In practice, this is quite a familiar list and has applied whenever new technologies have emerged across the four eras outlined in chapter 1 and been incorporated into business operations. The lesson here is that integration challenges do not go away with cloud; they are still present, though sometimes different, and always need significant senior executive, operational manager, and specialist attention.

Our most recent research into large companies extends these findings.[37] The pioneering corporations included a major global retailer, a health company, and a service provider. In all three, cloud had, in the period between 2010 and 2013, moved to a more mainstream role. Enabling this, these organizations had very clear cloud policies; they avoided building silos in the cloud; their internal applications were being developed to be 'cloud ready'; and internal IT skills were being re-oriented from '*plan, build and run*' to '*broker, integrate and exploit.*' As one example of clear policies, the retailer had three cloud fitness criteria: data sensitivity had to be medium or low; the load had to be low, unpredictable, or highly variable; and (technical) integration issues had to be simple or few. The position was that if these three criteria were favorable, cloud was an option, but a commercial comparison still had to be made between an in-house and a cloud solution. The retailer had a number of other strong policies. These included:

1. Data separation (multi-tenancy) – appropriate (logical) data isolation controls

2. Encryption and data access, involving requirements for data storage and clearance of storage after use

3. Rules for privileged access

4. Logging and breach disclosure requirements

5. Authentication requirements

6. A written and approved exit strategy for each and every cloud solution to get data back in a usable form that allows us to transfer it to a different cloud provider or in-house system.

To enable internal applications to be cloud ready, the policies included:

- Be prepared to run distributed – applications components may be distributed.

- Manage own performance and resources – meter own resources, e.g. call an API to add another virtual machine or another gigabyte of storage; you cannot rely on data center staff to add processors or disks.

- Build in tolerance for failure.

- Adopt services-oriented architecture (SOA) – 'the SOA model of a few years ago is now a necessity in the cloud.'

- Enable third-party services (e.g. authentication) – 'applications have to be written in a way that enables a third-party authentication service and can live with multiple identity sources'[38]

In these illustrative examples one can observe corporations ahead of the game in making themselves 'cloud ready' for the long term while already having a track record of adopting cloud in public and private versions and also as SaaS, PaaS, and IaaS, and even as BPaaS. The message? If integration challenges have been inhibiting all too many corporations, then, nevertheless, there are already exemplars for how these challenges can be dealt with.

CONCLUSION

Having identified five major challenges that need to be addressed, we will conclude by noting some subsidiary issues and by making explicit some challenges latent in the above that may well become more apparent over time and come to haunt moves to cloud. One recent detailed listing of technical barriers[39] is consistent with our own findings, some of which are mentioned above. These are: availability/business continuity; data lock-in; data confidentiality and auditability; data transfer bottlenecks; performance unpredictability; scalable storage; bugs in large distributed systems; rapid scaling; reputation fate sharing; and software licensing.

On latent challenges, we have been picking up potential tensions between clients' need for command and control and the fact that cloud may well require a relearning for the internal IT department, in effect enabling them to move back to a bureau-sharing style of management (see chapter 8 and also chapter 7 for the possible implications for the IT function). There are also tensions between this and supplier strategies for becoming systems integrators and/or primary contractors for cloud. What degree of service commoditization is optimal for a specific supplier, taking into account not just price to client and cost to supplier but also long-term competitive positioning in the marketplace? Moreover, if suppliers are going to offer increased commoditization of service, how does this fit with client organizations desiring customized services to support business agility and differentiation? These tensions are not insoluble but they are latent challenges to clients and suppliers alike given the present state of evolution to cloud. Maybe the biggest latent challenge lies in the belief that cloud will take the pain and the problems away. We might call this the '*false security*' offered by cloud.[40]

In reality, cloud is unlikely to solve all the technology problems of corporations and government agencies. Indeed, as we discussed above, cloud may well create new ones of integration, when to make

'go' (let's do it) or 'drop' (let's stop doing it) decisions, which infrastructures to rely on, what to keep control of internally, and which
part of the business – back-office, operations or strategic positioning – cloud can really help in. We are sure that cloud represents a
considerable opportunity, but the challenges to realize its potential,
especially for business advantage, remain formidable. In the next
chapter we continue this focus on challenges by revisiting in more
detail the high-profile issues of security and privacy. And here we
deal with a complex set of issues concerning both perceptions and
realities of the ever-changing risks.

CHAPTER 5

Security and Privacy Concerns Revisited

INTRODUCTION

The most frequently raised concerns about cloud computing relate to the security and privacy of data held in the cloud. In some cases, we found that these concerns were actually preventing the adoption of cloud services, a point confirmed by Everest Group research in 2013 (see chapter 1). In other cases, security and privacy increased the costs of adopting cloud by requiring increased diligence in assessing cloud suppliers. Finally, there is also the perspective, uncovered in our interviews, that these concerns can be exaggerated by IT departments who are reluctant to cede further control over, or out of, the IT function – departments, perhaps, that have learned their own lessons from the outsourcing revolution.

The purpose of this chapter is to contextualize these concerns and assess them in terms of legal and business requirements. This will be undertaken by looking at specialist guidance offered by various privacy and security specialists. More generally, it is important to develop a risk-based assessment of the privacy and security concerns that arise when moving to the cloud, so as to better appreciate which risks can be mitigated by an effective cloudsourcing strategy, which can be addressed by cloud providers, and which are the unavoidable risks of doing business.

THE BUSINESS BASIS OF SECURITY CONCERNS

Many of the privacy and security concerns raised in this context are a direct consequence of the nature of the cloud proposition, particularly in these early years of cloud adoption, when the benefits have been invariably presented in terms of cost reduction. According to this view, cloud computing transforms the nature of IT provision from specific, internally hosted and managed IT resources to commodity hardware and software platforms hosted outside the organizational boundary. In order to provide the lowest-cost offering, cloud providers may switch the customer's data and processes from one hardware instantiation to another and it is precisely this switching that raises the privacy and security issues. From a security perspective, if critical data and processes are hosted on various 'random' hardware instantiations, significant risks are introduced for the customer:

- How can the customer be sure that their data and processes are not accessible to staff working for the cloud service provider, to other customers running their services on the same hardware environment, etc.?

- How can the customer be sure that, when the use of the hardware comes to an end (either when demand patterns change and cloud hardware is decommissioned or when the cloud provider relocates the customer's services to other, cheaper computing resources) any data stored on that hardware is irreversibly removed? Alternatively, if there are legal obligations on a company to retain data, what guarantees are there that the data will remain available for the retention period (often measured in years)?

- If the cloud provider is hosting mission-critical services, how can the customer be sure that its disaster recovery plans are effective?

- Is there a risk that, despite claims that the choice of cloud provider is open and based on commodity hardware, there will be attempts to lock in the customer (see chapter 4) – either by using slightly non-standard hardware configurations or because of the sheer impracticality of transferring data and processes to another provider at contract renewal time?

- What are the risks of using a cloud data center that is co-hosting many companies' data? 'Sharing' a cloud provider with other brands can have unintended consequences that cannot be easily calculated. For example, as previously noted, one unintended consequence of Amazon and DynDNS hosting WikiLeaks was that these services were targeted by hackers, with consequent adverse effects on other users of their services.

Cloud providers similarly face their own version of these challenges:

- What levels of staff accreditation need to be implemented to demonstrate to customers that our staff will not misuse the data held on our cloud hardware? Would offering on-site security inspections reassure customers about security concerns or would the costs of doing so be prohibitive?

- What forms of data-wiping need to be offered to customers? How computationally expensive are these processes and how would this affect the cost of the cloud service? Would it be appropriate to offer these services at a premium or is it better to develop an architecture that offers this functionality to all users?

- What disaster recovery mechanisms should we have in place or should we limit the service we offer to simple hardware platforms and put the responsibility for disaster recovery on the customer? How will our reputation be affected by a major outage?

- How do we find a balance between offering commodity products sold on the basis of price and service quality and offering distinctive capabilities that might raise customer concerns about lock-in?

THE LEGAL BASIS OF PRIVACY CONCERNS

Whilst many of the security concerns outlined above are driven by business needs (of the customer and of the cloud provider), concerns over the privacy of personal data are directly linked to specific legal requirements regarding the processing of personal data. For example, the EU Data Protection Directive (translated into specific national legislation, such as the U.K.'s Data Protection Act) places specific obligations on companies handling personal data.

What do we mean by personal data? In the U.K., personal data is defined as data which relate to a living individual who can be identified from those data, or from those data and other information that is in the possession of, or is likely to come into the possession of, the company, which includes any expression of opinion about the individual and any indication of the intentions of the individual.[1]

Let us take the U.K. as a sample jurisdiction. The U.K. Data Protection Act defines the *data controller* as the entity who decides how and why data is processed. The actual processing of the data may be handled by another party. The *data processor* processes the data on behalf of the data controller. In many situations the data controller and the data processor are in the same organization but, with the growth of cloud and outsourced services, the data processor is increasingly not part of the same organization as the data controller. Regardless of the relationship between the data controller and data processor, it is the data controller who remains responsible for ensuring that 'their' processing complies with the Act, whether they do it in house or engage an external data processor. Outsourced data processors are therefore not directly subject to the Act. Where roles and responsibilities are unclear, the Information Commissioner's Office states that they will need to be clarified to ensure that personal data is processed in accordance with data protection principles, adding that for these reasons organizations should choose data processors carefully and have in place effective means of monitoring, reviewing, and auditing their processing.[2]

Although the Data Protection Act applies to all personal data, extra requirements apply when handling 'sensitive personal data,' which is defined as data relating to the racial or ethnic origin of the individual, their political opinions, their religious beliefs or other beliefs of a similar nature, whether they are a member of a trade union, their physical or mental health or condition, their sexual life, the commission or alleged commission by them of any offense, or any proceedings for any offense committed or alleged to have been committed by them. In addition, certain regulated industries impose their own best-practice requirements in relation to the handling of data related to their industry.

The seventh data protection principle of the U.K. Data Protection Act provides that: 'Appropriate technical and organizational measures shall be taken against unauthorized or unlawful processing of personal data and against accidental loss or destruction of, or damage to, personal data.'[3]

The eighth data protection principle provides that:

> Personal data shall not be transferred to a country or territory outside the European Economic Area unless that country or territory ensures an adequate level of protection for the rights and freedoms of data subjects in relation to the processing of personal data.[4]

It is this requirement that becomes important in the context of cloud computing. To simplify the presentation, this chapter adopts the terminology whereby the cloud customer is a data controller as defined by the Data Protection Act and the cloud provider is the data processor. In the case where the cloud provider is offering software-as-a-service (SaaS), rather than infrastructure or platforms as a service (IaaS or PaaS), it is possible that it might actually be considered as a joint data controller rather than a data processor.[5]

Thus, there is an obligation on a cloud customer who uses a cloud provider as a data processor to ensure that personal data is not transferred outside the European Economic Area unless that country or territory ensures an adequate level of data protection rights. Only a few countries are judged by the EU to offer an 'adequate level of protection' outside the EEC. These include Switzerland, Argentina, and Canada. Alternatively, the cloud customer could ask the permission of every person whose data was being processed. More practically, cloud customers might be able to use a cloud provider with a data center in the EU and ensure that the data is only held there. For example, Amazon EC2 offers a choice of location for some of its cloud services: U.S. East Coast, U.S. West Coast, Asia, or Ireland.

In many cases, however, the cloud provider will be unable to provide a guarantee that the personal data is held on cloud hardware that is located within the EEA or in a suitably accredited location. Further complications arise if the cloud provider further outsources some of its processing to additional parties (perhaps to address load balancing issues). In these circumstances the cloud customer is even further removed from the actual processing and the existing contractual relationship with the cloud provider may not explicitly consider this situation.

Failure to address privacy and data protection concerns adequately can result in the cancellation of cloud services. For example, in June 2013, the Swedish Data Inspection Board issued a decision that prohibits the nation's public sector bodies from using Google's cloud-based apps including calendar, e-mail, and data processing functions.[6] The ruling was based on a risk assessment by the board and on perceived problems with the contracts offered by Google. According to the Swedes, the contracts give Google too much covert discretion over how data can be used and leave public sector customers unable to ensure that data protection principles are adhered to. Several examples of the kinds of deficiency in the contract were noted, including uncertainty over how data may be mined or processed by Google and a lack of knowledge about which subcontractors may be involved in the processing. The assessment also concluded that there was no certainty that, or when, data would be deleted after expiration of the contract.[7] In 2012, the Norwegian data protection authority insisted on contractual adjustments for similar reasons before they would permit Norwegian local authorities to use Google apps.[8]

GUIDANCE AND ADVICE ON PRIVACY AND SECURITY ISSUES

At first sight, these privacy and security concerns threaten to leave cloud computing dead in the water. However, numerous bodies had issued advice and guidance on these issues by mid-2013. For example, the European Commission has a new strategy for unleashing the potential of cloud computing in Europe, which it claims will result in a net gain of 2.5 million European jobs and an annual boost of €160 billion to EU GDP by 2020.[9] According to the EU, the strategy is designed to speed up and increase the use of cloud computing; key actions of the strategy include developing standards on issues including data portability and reversibility, EU-wide certification schemes for trustworthy cloud providers, and the development of model 'safe and fair' terms for cloud contracts.

The first outputs from this work will be the 'safe and fair' contract terms.[10] These are needed, according to Neelie Kroes, Vice-President of the European Commission, because 'people don't always understand the terms in their contract: what they're paying for and what they can expect.' She particularly highlighted the concerns of small and medium-sized enterprises

> who might hesitate to use the cloud because of fears that they will not meet their legal obligations, or who might be worried that they get locked in or stranded by changes of technology or service by cloud providers. They don't want the risk of getting mired in foreign court cases in foreign languages; nor of exposing the data which may be their business's life blood to security risks or breaches. And they cannot afford costly legal fees to figure all this out case by case.[11]

More specific guidance comes from detailed reports such as the 'Sopot memorandum' produced by data protection commissioners from different countries to improve privacy and data protection in telecommunications and media.[12] The guidance notes that, at present, with the increased globalization of data processing (perhaps, more accurately, the use of 'multiple locales (data centres) distributed across different jurisdictions and different private operators'[13]) there is a lack of transparency about cloud service provider processes, procedures, and practices, including whether or not cloud service providers sub-contract any of the processing and, if so, what their sub-contractors' processes, procedures, and practices are. The commissioners note that this lack of transparency makes it difficult to conduct a proper risk assessment, as well as increasing the difficulty of enforcing rules regarding data protection.[14] Important consequences of this lack of transparency include data being transferred to jurisdictions that do not provide adequate data protection, acts in violation of laws and principles for privacy and data protection and the data controller accepting standard terms and conditions that give the cloud service provider too much leeway, including the possibility that the cloud service provider will process data in a way that contradicts the controller's instructions.[15]

The International Working Group on Data Protection in Telecommunications suggested that the adoption of cloud computing should not lead to a lowering of data protection standards as compared with conventional data processing; that data controllers should carry out the necessary privacy impact and risk assessments (if necessary, by using trusted third parties) prior to embarking on cloud projects. They also recommended that cloud service providers further develop their practices in order to offer greater transparency, security, account-ability, and trust in cloud solutions, in particular regarding information on potential data breaches, and more balanced contractual clauses to promote data portability and data control by cloud users.[16]

The U.K.'s Information Commissioner's Office issued similar guidance on cloud computing.[17] This noted that by processing data in the cloud 'an organization may encounter risks to data protection that they were previously unaware of' and suggested that data controllers take time to understand the data protection risks that cloud computing presents. In addition to the points noted above, the ICO's guidance points out that it may not be necessary to move all data and process-ing to the cloud and that many data protection risks may be mitigated by separating out the processing of personal data from that of non-personal data. The personal data could be processed internally and all other data processed in the cloud. This avoids the legal uncertainties associated with cloud-based data. Processing data in the cloud also often results in the creation of audit records and other metadata. If these data are associated with particular customers, then these meta-data are themselves personal data (as they can be associated with an identifiable individual) and are subject to the provisions of the Data Protection Act.

Whilst much of this guidance is written from the perspective of allowing/encouraging businesses to keep using cloud services, there is some guidance that is presented firmly from the perspective of the citizen whose personal data might be held and processed in the cloud. For example, in 2012, the European Parliament issued a report that explicitly sought to protect privacy in the cloud[18] (rather than just ensuring compliance with existing data protection legislation). The report suggested that the challenge of privacy in the cloud has been underestimated if not ignored completely and that the main concern for private citizens was not so much the possible increase in 'cyber' fraud or crime but rather 'the loss of control over one's data.'[19] The report argued that from this perspective the most disruptive feature of cloud computing had nothing to do with technical or business innovation but was instead where 'it breaks away from the forty-year-old legal model for international data transfers.'[20] As a result, they argued, consumers' fundamental rights, as embodied in data protection, were lost in a complex mesh of contracts and service level agreements (SLAs) with private sector companies that are cloud providers. Further effects on the legal rights of citizens regarding their data arise in the context of 'exceptional measures' taken in the name of security and counter terrorism. As the report noted, this is particularly significant in the U.S. context, where both the Patriot Act and the U.S. Foreign Intelligence Surveillance Amendment Act (FISAA) 2008 have been enacted.

That is, jurisdiction matters. The legal environment that applies to cloud providers (and particularly the regulations that apply to the location where they host their infrastructure) can limit any protections that citizens may expect with regard to the processing of their data. For example, a number of companies claim that U.S. 'safe harbor' certification legalizes transfers of EU data into the U.S. cloud.[21] According to the European Parliament report, §1881a of FISAA created mass surveillance specifically targeted at the data of non-U.S. citizens located outside the U.S. (as would apply to cloud computing). The law was passed in the aftermath of allegations of 'warrantless wiretapping' of U.S. citizens after accounts emerged in 2005 that, in violation of strict constitutional protections, surveillance of Internet and telephone communications of U.S. citizens (and legal residents) had been conducted. After various legal measures and cases reviewing the relationship between U.S. citizens and others, Congress enacted FISAA in 2008.

The use of these types of power re-entered the public imagination in May 2013, when whistle-blower Edward Snowden revealed that the U.S. PRISM program had been surreptitiously surveying the communications data of U.S. and non-U.S. citizens, with allegations that the U.K. government was also monitoring this kind of data.[22] Technology companies and cloud providers like Google and Yahoo noted that they were not even allowed to disclose the information they were forced to disclose to the U.S. government. This highlights the risk that cloud providers may be forced to disclose their clients' data and may not even be allowed to inform the clients that this has taken place.

RESPONDING TO PRIVACY AND SECURITY CONCERNS

Given the range of concerns that the corporations moving to the cloud face, it is unsurprising that a range of responses are available. In addition to the guidance outlined above, there are further options that organizations can use. The specific configuration of options will be determined, to a large extent, by the maturity of the marketplace and the internal capabilities of cloud customers and providers. Some options are technologically driven whilst others are business choices that will reflect the risk profile of the enterprise.

Technological Responses

There are a range of technological responses to privacy and security concerns. One important development highlighted in the recent EU Data Protection Regulation[23] is the concept of privacy-by-design and, similarly, security-by-design. It is widely recognized that bolting privacy (and security) functionality on top of an existing system is frequently ineffective and always more costly than designing systems where these capabilities are built in from the start.[24] Thus, enterprises seeking to use cloud services and cloud providers in the hope of increasing their market share at a time of low trust in cloud computing services might adopt privacy-by-design-style thinking when developing their applications and services.

One example of such an approach, which seeks to address the problem of concerns about third parties gaining unlawful access to data held on cloud servers, is to build cryptographic techniques into the cloud infrastructure. These techniques encrypt data (both personal data and enterprise data) as they move to and from the cloud in much the same way as it is now possible to encrypt personal data held on smartphones and tablets. These encryption services might be administered by the cloud customer, or might be offered as a value-added service by the cloud provider. In each case, nevertheless, there can be significant computational costs associated with the encryption/decryption process. In addition, there may be liability issues associated with encryption services offered by the cloud provider: if they have provided this customer with the decryption keys, what assurance do you have that they haven't shared the same keys with other parties?

The complexities and costs of managing the various encryption keys, issuing replacement keys, and authorizing and de-authorizing key users, are well understood in mainstream computing environments and are increasingly being appreciated in the cloud context. As with many of these responses, their successful implementation will depend to a large extent on the internal capabilities and organizational learning of all parties in the cloud supply chain (see chapters 3 and 7).

A related technological response is to have strictly enforced access controls associated with cloud data and processing. These access control mechanisms help ensure that only suitably authorized role holders are able to gain access to or modify data and processes in the cloud. When successfully implemented, these techniques open up the possibility of innovative cooperation along an entire production supply chain. For example, rather than having production and distribution data held by one of the hubs in the supply chain, all this data could be held in the cloud, each part of the supply chain having (suitably controlled) access to the part of the data that they need for their own part of the production process. Again, there is growing evidence of the complexity of managing this task within modern enterprises, where role definitions are increasingly fluid.[25]

Another technological mitigation involves the choice of cloud model that the enterprise adopts. For example, in some circumstances an enterprise might benefit from using a 'private cloud' rather than a 'public cloud.' That is, it creates its own data center within the organization's boundaries. This data center can still offer the benefits of scalability and rapid provisioning of computing resources, as well as the cost reductions associated with consolidated data centers, but without running the risk of external organizations having access to the data.

Another alternative, suggested above, is a hybrid cloud model, whereby some data (typically the data that need to be protected in terms of data protection legislation) are kept 'in house' whilst less sensitive (or mission critical) data are held in a public cloud. In practice, however, the boundaries between what should be kept in house and what could be held in the public cloud are not clear cut. For example, office productivity tools like e-mail and document processing can frequently be provided at lower cost in the public cloud (e.g. Google Apps) but may, in fact, contain personal data or commercially sensitive information that the enterprise deems should be kept in house.

Cloud providers are also seeking to signal their security credentials transparently. For example, as noted elsewhere, Amazon has moved to acquire existing security standards (e.g. ISO 27001) for its cloud services.

Business Responses

In addition to technological responses to cloud privacy and security concerns, there are a range of business responses that can be adopted. Assuming that the enterprise has actually read and understood the terms of the contract offered by the cloud provider, the enterprise could use the provider's risk profile to determine whether it is prepared to accept those terms or demand counter-terms. In some cases of a 'one size fits all' type of contract (such as those offered by Google Apps to local authorities in Scandinavia) the opportunity for negotiation may be limited. In other cases, on seeing a pattern of specific requests for certain services or warranties, the innovative cloud provider may offer a range of pricing options for customers to choose amongst, thus segmenting the market place on the basis of price and (additional) services offered.

For example, a cloud provider might offer potential customers the opportunity to do their own penetration testing of the cloud provider or allow them to inspect the physical security of the data center or the vetting process for staff hire. In other cases, third-party certification agencies might be prepared to assure the enhanced security and privacy claims made by the cloud provider. In each of these cases, however, a cloud customer needs to be aware of the 'winner's curse' phenomenon we met in chapter 2. Recall that the 'winner's curse'[26] kicks in when, for example, an initially successful cloud provider who gains customers by offering higher levels of service loses that capability as it becomes 'too' successful and is unable to hire or retain key staff or expand its hardware capabilities reliably.

Another response involves the close monitoring of SLAs to ensure that the cloud provider is actually providing the level of service that they had initially promised (discussed also in chapter 4). Achieving this requires the development of in-house contract monitoring capabilities (described in more detail in chapter 7). It also, of course, involves ensuring that the original SLA was read and understood. In the case of commodified cloud resources, if the SLA is standard for that market segment but doesn't quite match the customer's needs, the cloud customer must make a risk-based assessment about whether to accept a contract with an SLA that is an imperfect match for its requirements.

Another consideration, particularly at the commodity end of cloud SLAs, is: what happens if the promised service levels are not met? This is where the enterprise's real understanding of its cloud computing becomes paramount. The failure for 24 hours of a cloud service that allows a retailer's customers to locate their nearest store is likely to cause fewer problems than the failure of the retailer's order processing system for 24 minutes. In the case of a failure to meet agreed service levels (and this might only be spotted by active contract monitoring by the customer), the terms of the contract need to specify the compensation. In many cases, this will be limited to refunding the usage fee for the period of interruption, which may only be a few dollars. Close reading of the contract/SLA will reveal what actions the cloud provider agrees to undertake and what actions it does not. For example, following a failure of Amazon's cloud services in 2011, many of Amazon's customers 'discovered' that they cannot depend on having multiple 'availability zones' within a specific region as insurance against system downtime.[27]

Given uncertainty about the effectiveness of SLAs and the potential costs of monitoring performance, some businesses take a very different approach to managing their cloud risk profiles. That is, rather than closely monitoring the SLAs they have with their cloud providers, they mitigate their risks by drawing on a broad pool of potential cloud providers. If one cloud provider appears to be performing at a substandard level, they simply reduce their usage of that service and switch on alternative cloud providers (see also chapter 4).

Finally, it should be recognized that although cloud services may change the security risk profile,[28] cloud providers may also be better able to manage security, respond to distributed attacks, and invest in sophisticated security hardware and software – facilities that are normally unavailable to all but the largest enterprises (see chapter 2). Indeed, cloud providers may be able to spot unusual activity that the individual companies would be unable to identify, by using security analytics to identify unusual behavior patterns among pools of similar enterprises.

CONCLUSION

Because of the high profile they receive in the context of cloud and use of the Internet generally, we have devoted an entire chapter to security and privacy concerns. The chapter builds on the previous chapter in raising nine key questions on those issues that businesses and their service providers face and that they invariably struggle to answer. We also highlighted that there is increasing legislation in the security and privacy areas, both generally and specifically with regard to cloud. While businesses would frequently like to ignore such legislation, not only will the legislation not go away but legislatures are increasingly trying to catch up with the implications of Internet-based technologies and putting in place controls and penalties for non-compliance wherever possible. This impacts on cloud clients and service suppliers alike.

We noted that, at first sight, using the European Union and U.K. examples as our benchmark, developments in legislation, guidelines, and codes of practice on these privacy and security concerns threaten to leave cloud computing dead in the water. Clearly, there is an increasing burden of regulation to comply with. However, we also noted the range of initiatives by regulatory bodies offering guidance and advice. In the EU, the first outputs from this work are the 'safe and fair' contract terms. More specific guidance comes from detailed reports such as the 'Sopot memorandum' produced by data protection commissioners from different countries with a view to improving privacy and data protection in telecommunications and the media. Similarly, the U.K.'s Information Commissioner's Office issued guidance on cloud computing to help businesses. But other initiatives are not so much on the side of business as in support of the citizen, so that, in all this, we emphasize that *jurisdiction matters*. As one example we cited shows, the legal environment that applies to cloud providers (and particularly the regulations that apply to the location where they host their infrastructure) can limit any protections that citizens may expect with regard to the processing of their data. Faced with these complexities, the chapter spelled out a number of practical technological and business responses to security and privacy concerns arising when moving to the cloud.

This chapter has highlighted not just security and privacy concerns but also the race different jurisdictions are having to try to place some control and assurance around the issues raised by moves to the cloud. Such efforts emerge as invariably lagging behind what the technologies are making possible and where businesses want to take the innovation potential seemingly inherent in further cloud adoption. One cumulative effect may be an actual drag on the diffusion of cloud-enabled innovations. But this is only one factor amongst many others that make the cloud diffusion process much less straightforward than many pundits have chosen to present it. The next chapter addresses this topic – the speed of diffusion and likely types of innovation enabled by cloud.

CHAPTER 6

Cloud and the Diffusion of Innovation

INTRODUCTION

The First Law of Technology applies to cloud. The law says: *We invariably overestimate the short-term impact of new technologies, while underestimating their long-term effects.*[1] In his work on the future of the Internet John Naughton makes a strong case for this law. Certainly, it is clear that if the much hyped take-off period from 1995 ended in the bursting of the 'e-business bubble' in 2000/01, all predictions of its impact now have to go way beyond the technology and hi-tech sectors, into widespread social, economic, indeed global impacts.[2]

Many researchers who take a big picture perspective see us as on a fifth Kondratieff long wave cycle of innovation and technological change, this time based on a raft of transforming technologies in the form of computers, telecommunications, and biotechnology.[3] The past 30 years have seen the rise of a digital age based on massive computing power, the Internet, high-speed data transmission, mobile communication, and, most recently, the cloud, which represents a potentially highly disruptive convergence of these developments. However, it is important to locate cloud in the long wave and as part of Internet development, rather than as a relatively autonomous group of technologies with immediate, radical impacts.

This is all to dampen down anticipation of radical innovation when it comes to cloud. There are three major reasons for seeing the impacts of cloud as emerging more slowly and over a much longer time horizon than many commentators are suggesting. The three reasons are related to the process of diffusion of innovation. One is that *a technical innovation, or set of technical innovations like cloud, typically goes through three phases – invention, commercialization, and diffusion.* By 2013, cloud was still predominantly in the commercialization phase, though diffusion of parts of cloud business services, as with many Internet-related services such as eBay and Facebook, could be very rapid. A second reason is that *diffusion of an innovation is rarely steady and linear.* Rather, research shows that it tends to follow an S-curve, starting quite slowly, needing to demonstrate many attributes, and passing through several phases before being fully adopted. Clearly, cloud will be on a far from frictionless journey toward having substantive impacts on individuals, organizations, sectors, and economies.

Finally, *cloud and its developers and users are on a learning curve that will take considerable time to climb before the sizeable impacts anticipated actually materialize.* In our view, looking across the evidence already accumulated in this book, there are near-term developments involving a relatively fast take-up of new services, together with supportive technical and contractual advances. Here, the cost imperative has been strong and will dominate, but organizations and providers will mature in their ability to manage services. This will enable them to move to more innovative uses of cloud computing at the organizational level. We see this learning strand as accelerating over the next ten years.

CLOUD AND INNOVATION

As pointed out in chapter 3, cloud computing is the product of two developmental strands. The first strand emerges from technological innovations such as virtualization, high-performance networks, and data-center automation. The second strand emerges from a more distinct emphasis on service-based perspectives, which shifts attention from the management of technology assets to consideration of customer value deriving from the use of technology services. But while the benefits of cloud computing are often presented in financial terms as cloud offers a subscription-based/pay-as-you-drink model that moves IT expenditure from capital expenditure to operational expenditure budgets, the long-term benefits of cloud computing are unlikely to be restricted to (or be driven by) simple cost savings. Instead, this combination of computing trends offers the potential for innovative business practices to enterprises adopting cloud computing.

Achieving innovation through cloud resources is a two-stage process that involves an enterprise first *adopting* cloud computing and then *innovating*, using those cloud resources. Enterprises will seek to achieve benefits simply from adopting cloud computing but are likely to benefit further from innovations enabled by cloud. Hence, any limitations or delays in either activity will influence the long-term benefits of cloud and so it is important to understand the limitations on the adoption of cloud as well as those factors that inhibit innovation through cloud.

There is growing evidence that developments in information technology often move in packs. This seems to be the case with cloud. It was the interactions between base technology developments, technology service improvements, and technology process advances that allowed Internet computing, and will allow cloud, to make radical IT-based innovations. These characteristics, however, do not ensure that cloud technology will be widely adopted.

In chapter 3 we saw three major disruptive impacts associated with the increasingly rapid development and deployment of cloud technologies. These are: service performance, cloud as a business service, and radical changes in the supply industry. Related research sees the cloud disruptive sequence being

- new delivery models

- technology disruption

- restructuring of the IT industry

- disruption of other industries.[4]

Although cloud computing involves technological disruption, the effects of this are likely to be cumulative and ongoing. Cloud introduces new delivery models that will mature over time. Our own most recent work has been particularly interested in what factors will shape these delivery models and how these delivery models will drive innovation through the need to grow the service dimension and produce business services.

Once adopted, the kinds of innovation that cloud computing affords exist at a variety of different levels. These include:

- **IT operational innovations** – technology and IT operational and personnel changes that do not impact firm-specific business processes

- **business process innovations** – that change the way the business operates in some important ways

- **market (business product/service) innovations** – that significantly enhance the firm's product/service offerings for existing customers or enable entry into new markets.[5]

In common with many other cases, the innovation trajectory for enterprises using cloud is likely to be cumulative, starting mainly with IT-operational innovations then gathering pace over time in business process and market innovations as enterprise capabilities adapt to the new technological environment. For example, Retana et al. show how the self-service nature of the cloud makes firms both consumers and producers, or co-producers, of cloud services.[6] They suggest that in order to understand the drivers of cloud adoption and usage it is important to pay attention to firms' knowledge, skills, and abilities in co-producing the service, which are known to be key determinants of the adoption and usage of other self-service technologies.[7]

Antecedents to Cloud Adoption and Innovation

Although the potential for innovation through the use of cloud is considerable, the speed of such innovation is likely to be shaped by four key antecedent factors that affect the adoption of cloud. The first of these is *the attributes of the technology itself*. Greenhalgh et al. identify a series of important attributes of a novel technology that will affect its diffusion. Does it give relative advantage? Is it compatible with existing ways of operating? What is the risk level? Is it too complex or is it administratively feasible? Is it easily trialable, with tangible outcomes? Is technical support given? Is there potential for reinvention?[8] It would seem that the technological basis of cloud computing has many attributes that should support the rapid diffusion and adoption of cloud.[9]

The second antecedent factor is that in pursuing the adoption of such novel technologies, *organizations, providers, and providers' partners will need to become much more collaborative than ever before*. Collaboration is here defined as a cooperative commercial arrangement in which two or more parties work jointly in a common enterprise toward shared goals. Ongoing research in outsourcing has identified a very strong correlation between levels of collaboration and innovation within and across organizations. Simply put, superior performance through innovation is made feasible by cloud adoption, but this will require a step-change in client–provider and provider–provider relationships in terms of objectives and behaviors. This step-change needs to be toward new forms of collaboration involving mutual flexibility, trust, reciprocity, risk-sharing, and investment in resources and time, and needs to be executive led.[10]

In the context of outsourcing, our study carried out in 2011 of 26 organizations that had moved to 'collaborative innovation' in their outsourcing relationships revealed that all of them had experienced IT operational innovation while 21 were generating business process and 7 business product/service innovations.[11] Innovation through cloud will also come from an acceleration of such collaborative tendencies, but, as has been found in more traditional outsourcing arrangements, this will be a challenge to many client and provider organizations. We therefore employ the concept of *cloudsourcing* as the situation where an organization using cloud computing adopts many of the best practices and lessons learned from outsourcing in order to achieve collaborative innovation in the enterprise context.

The third antecedent factor is *the speed with which diffusion through informal, unplanned communication and influence moves to formal, planned dissemination*. There are already clear signs that with cloud there is a real uptake across the supply industry and all other major economic sectors on this antecedent factor. This continued to accelerate across 2013.

The fourth antecedent factor is *the innovation implementation process*. This includes the range of practical factors that support or slow an innovation's progress from design to adoption, diffusion, and usage, through to exploitation. Key issues here are:

- the sectoral structure, absorptive capacity for new knowledge, and sectoral receptiveness to change

- adopter attributes

- organizational readiness for innovation

- how easy the innovation is to assimilate – is it a complex, non-linear process, with many 'soft' elements?

- the quality of the organization's implementation processes.[12]

Our research suggests that the implementation challenge is very real in the context of cloud, particularly for large organizations with a big legacy of IT investments, infrastructure, and outsourcing contracts. There are also cultural, structural, and political legacies that will shape and determine the speed of implementation, exploitation, and reinvention. Our cloud research suggests that these challenges are very real and pervasive, cannot be assumed away, and may well be particularly significant for large organizations with a large legacy of IT investments, infrastructure, and outsourcing contracts. There are also cultural, structural, and political legacies that will shape and determine the speed of implementation, exploitation, and reinvention.

Of these antecedent factors, by mid-2013 only the third was unequivocally supporting cloud adoption and exploitation. However, the pace was beginning to increase in the other three areas. There could be a rapid acceleration in innovation if the supply side is ready with manifestly advantageous new services and if both sectors and client organizations see those advantages and apply them quickly and in a wholesale manner.

Our own research at the organizational level reviews the status of the four antecedent factors listed above and suggests that the claimed benefits of cloud are somewhat overstated. The challenges are larger and there is more friction associated with the adoption of cloud. Cost savings will come through, but the business benefits will need an eight- to ten-year rather than a five-year horizon to come to fruition. We also anticipate initially more process innovation – associated with net job losses – as a result of cloud, before job-creating product innovations come through, and would therefore predict much smaller net job creation from the cloud, especially for the 2011–2016 period.

These remarks frame our study findings on what innovations clients will be anticipating and seeking from their moves to cloud. Based on our earlier research, chapter 3 pointed to three major disruptive impacts associated with the increasingly rapid development and deployment of cloud technologies.[13] We are confident in saying that the changing technological base, as detailed in chapter 2,[14] together with these three big disrupters, will channel many innovating practices toward service, the development of business services, and reconfiguration of the supply industry.[15] But these trends will also free up creative space for further innovations in client businesses and other sectors with which they connect. The next sections present empirical evidence on further innovation from our research base (see Introduction). In this chapter we consider the critical issue of the level of executive readiness and expectation on innovation, what these further innovations might be, and the likely trajectory they will take. We distill these findings into four main areas: executive support for the cloud innovation agenda; innovation through infrastructure and service; changes in the IT function; and long-term moves to what we call the 'cloud corporation.'

EXECUTIVES AND CLOUD: SUPPORT FOR AN INNOVATION AGENDA

Cloud computing appeals to business and IT executives. In our survey (see figure 6.1), around 65 percent of business executives believed that cloud drives down the overall cost of business applications, 50 percent believed that it facilitates a virtual/distributed organization and 60 percent of these executives believed that business applications can be provisioned far more quickly when they are in the cloud. Whilst the business appeal of cloud might appear to be driven solely by cost and efficiency savings, our survey also provides strong support from business executives for the claim that 'cloud enables us to focus on transforming our business and not our IT.' Fifty percent of respondents agreed with this statement. In the same

FIGURE 6.1 | Executive Support for Cloud Computing

To what extent do the following aspects of the 'cloud' value proposition appeal, as it pertains to your job? Answer selected: 'Appeals to a great extent'

■ Business Executives   ■ IT Executives

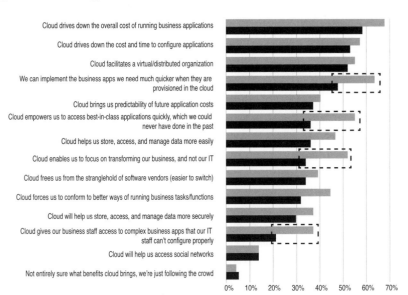

Sample: 628 enterprises.
Source: HfS Research and the Outsourcing Unit at the London School of Economics, November 2010.

survey over 50 percent of business executives put as the first and second features of cloud that: 'it is enabling business services/IT delivery model that drives innovation in organizations' and that: 'it is a new technological platform that can transform organizational forms.' Clearly, there is a widespread perception and expectation amongst business audiences that cloud will be transformational. As one of our respondents noted: 'these technologies are enabling companies to do things they never could have imagined before. It changes the financial model of the company. It changes the talent model. It changes just about everything.'[16] Cloud computing allows the business to focus on the tasks it needs and wants to perform, not how they are going to be performed: 'they're going to get a form to fill out that says, "I want to run this workload, I want to run it at this cost, I need this level of performance, this level of availability.'"[17] Cloud offers the opportunity for the focus to be put back on the business function, and not the technology constraints. The business user, as has always really been the case, does not care and does not want to know how the computing is provided. Some of our interviewees made a comparison to the 'net generation's' use of the Internet[18] and smart (phone) mobile devices:

> Now, increasingly, [devices like] my iPad are becoming oxygen for how I need to operate. And I've got an expectation that I can access my business information in real time wherever I am. So I think when IT organizations look to the next ten years, they need to look at the consumer trends that are hitting us right now and start to think … , from an IT strategy [viewpoint], 'How am I going to adapt my business to this trend in consumerization?'[19]

> End users are now expecting, I think we all expect, that we can use multiple devices during the course of a day to access the information we need to do our jobs, right? I've an iPhone and an iPad, I have got a computer, in fact three or four computers. I can go log into my friend's computer, get online, get my stuff that I need. I can access my information from everywhere. And so older applications and older systems that were very locked into only being accessible through terminals and stuff, [are] quickly fading away.[20]

These users want the high level of service that they have come to expect, but tell us they do not know (and do not care) how it is provided. Another common thread from a business perspective is frustration with the limitations of the existing, in-house IT function. For most organizations IT is just a means to an end rather than an end in itself. Some estimates suggest that 70 percent of the IT function is being devoted to 'keeping the lights on.' It is therefore unsurprising that the IT function is frequently seen as unresponsive to changing business needs, that it is perceived as performing indifferently and, typically, has large backlogs of unimplemented applications.[21]

If technology deployment (and the day-to-day management of the IT infrastructure) is moved to the cloud, then arguably some of this unresponsiveness and backlog can be addressed. Whilst this shift might cause short-term disruption for the IT function, long term it offers the opportunity for the (remaining) IT function to become increasingly aligned with the business needs of the organization and to provide innovative, sustainable advantage to the enterprise.

Indeed, some of our respondents argued that the shorter cycle times offered by cloud enable, indeed require, the IT function to be more closely aligned with business needs. Even cloud providers recognize that with a pay-per-drink service model of computing they earn their business 'every quarter or every month, you know, when subscriptions or renewals are due,' as one service manager put it. This forces them 'to align their entire business to the success of that project and the success of the customer.'[22]

From a cloud provider perspective, there is also the question of how flexibly services can be provided, as Jim Spooner notes: 'whether the billing is down to a day, a week, or a month, it ultimately kind of defines how mature you are in cloud.'[23] From a technology perspective, cloud computing offers distinct advantages that are recognized by IT professionals. Although moving to the cloud may be disruptive to the existing IT function, it does allow the forward-thinking, business-focused CIO to have meaningful answers to board-level questions about the current organizational IT environment, including how much it costs and how quickly new services can be provisioned:

> I guess the wise CIOs of today have started to think about how much their services cost and how they can leverage these models within their business or how they can actually terminate existing models to be able to deliver these kinds of levels of services internally. And I think we're seeing that in the … commercial sector people are approaching this as a financial thing, wondering about how they can drive costs out of their business and use these services.[24]

A technological benefit of cloud computing is the more detailed provisioning and planning that managed services can provide. For example, cloud providers can build in detailed performance metrics that can be utilized by clients to optimize their performance. Alternatively, the cloud model allows the IT function to manage its own service level requirements by building redundancy into its cloud provisioning. Therefore, rather than having the IT function worry about providing 100 percent up-time capability from its in-house equipment, it can provide this capability by sourcing the same functionality from a variety of independent cloud providers. In so doing, cloud also offers novel disaster recovery solutions that address many of the pressing concerns of the modern CIO.

Although most IT functions are currently not charged for their consumption of electricity (to power their computers and provide necessary air conditioning), as costs continue to be trimmed across the organization, it is likely that this will begin to happen. Consolidation of IT through cloud computing therefore has the potential to offer significant environmental savings, for example, by locating the cloud service in a zero-carbon facility in Iceland. This also increases the green credentials of the organization.

CLOUD INNOVATION THROUGH INFRASTRUCTURE AND SERVICE

Despite a common myth suggesting that cloud computing is mostly about an alternative payment/subscription model, two critical cloud streams – flexible infrastructure and service – do offer novel opportunities for innovation. The service-based, infrastructural flexibility of cloud promotes the possibility of 'seed and grow' activities, where the capabilities of the cloud are demonstrated through the rapid development of prototype systems. Some of our respondents talked about this capability in terms of 'low friction' activities, echoing the language of transaction cost economics. Whereas previously a decision to prototype a new system might involve the procurement and installation of new hardware (with the associated checks and delays that conventional purchasing requires), cloud provisioning can be implemented rapidly and at low cost.[25]

Such low friction approaches allow a business to experiment and innovate, according to Accenture's Jimmy Harris, 'because you'll be able to acquire these services, use them where it makes sense, and then decommission and get rid of the services when you no longer need them.'[26] The service flexibility of cloud services changes the risk profile associated with innovation. Projects and processes that would have been too risky to attempt if they required a capital investment (say, hiring two servers on two-year contracts) become worth attempting if unsuccessful experiments can be decommissioned easily. The speed of a project in terms of time to market is also affected if it is implemented in the cloud.

Whilst there are numerous examples of rapid prototypes being used to capture the imagination of a corporate board in relation to cloud services, what is less clear is how the organization makes the transition from experimenting with using the cloud as a demonstrator to using the cloud for 'production' systems that, in many cases, have much more stable demand patterns than the systems presently being placed in the cloud.

As is the case with IT outsourcing, there will be distinctive skills required from the in-house IT function, existing system integrators, and outsourcing partners to make the most effective use of cloud computing. For example, when specifying their computing requirements, they will be making their requests in terms of 'power at this rate, computing at this rate, at this level of security, with this compliance requirement, this level SLA.'[27] The skills required to specify and procure cloud in this way will be discussed in more detail in the next chapter.

Perhaps the most distinctive feature of cloud computing from the *service* perspective detailed in chapter 3 is the possibility for innovation that it offers by, in one way, confirming Nicholas Carr's argument that 'IT doesn't matter.' In cloud computing, IT does, of course, matter, but a service perspective allows businesses to think much more about what they need (or would like to have) without having to worry about whether their IT function (or outsourcing partners) have the requisite skills, hardware, or resources to deliver them. As Jimmy Harris notes:

> If you take it to its logical conclusion, most people would want the acquisition and deployment of IT to be secondary. What you would acquire and deploy would be a business process or it would have a business services orientation.[28]

To illustrate this, consider an organization's desire to acquire sales support. That is, the organization recognizes that it needs 'the ability to track contacts, the ability to manage the pipeline, the ability to convert our pipeline into sales, the ability for sales to be recognized as revenue.'[29] This does not (or perhaps should not) mean that the organization knows it wants to go out and buy a particular package. Instead:

> what you would provision in effect is probably a combination of a SalesForce.com, some of the functions from an ERP system or financial management system, etc., and for any given employee they have a certain usage profile, he or she has access to certain functions and you would provision that employee with sales support.[30]

Steve Furminger of RAPP, another of our respondents, made a similar suggestion when discussing how his organization used cloud services to provide solutions for its own (media) customers:

> It's providing us with the ability to create much more, produce many more solutions without having to worry how are we going to do that. Where four or five years ago, or even two or three years ago, that was a massive concern, now we can almost forget the technology and just think, "This is what we're going to do."[31]

The management of cloud services from a cloud provider's perspective also offers opportunities for innovation because there are current shortfalls, as Kevin Lees notes, in terms of 'orchestration, monitoring, performance monitoring, capacity management monitoring and capacity management modeling, and capacity planning'[32] while others, including Jim Rivera and Russell Marsh, see scope for business process automation and integration[33] and automated marketplaces[34] for provisioning.

THE CHANGING ROLE OF THE IT FUNCTION

As noted above, a recurring frustration expressed by many of the executives we interviewed relates to the limitations of the existing, in-house IT function. For most organizations IT is just a means to an end rather than an end in itself. Some estimates suggest that 70 percent of the IT function is being devoted to 'keeping the lights on.' It is therefore unsurprising that the IT function is frequently seen as unresponsive to changing business needs, that it is perceived as performing poorly and, typically, has large backlogs of unimplemented applications.

Cloud computing potentially changes all this. Whilst there will still be key technical roles in enterprises that adopt cloud computing, there needs to be a much greater emphasis on business skills and business orientation in nearly all roles. Even the more technical roles need an increasing amount of business understanding and relationship building. More generally, there is a significantly increased requirement for 'soft' skills across all roles. The major shift is toward fewer personnel, but of very high quality. The recruitment and retention of such a small, high-quality group has always been a major human resource challenge. Skills shortages in the corporation could be a major barrier to cloud adoption and subsequent business innovation. Therefore, we discuss this key issue, and ways forward, in more detail in the next chapter.

Other providers talked of needing to be much sharper on service metrics and transparency, and taking faster corrective action through automation. Much greater operational readiness is needed with cloud on the part of provider staff, but this passes over to client staff, not least because of the internal pressure from client business units to perform faster. For example:

> When it comes to cloud we are discovering that all the internal roles have to be faster acting than before. And while organizations have speeded up, they have not necessarily come up to the speed of cloud, which is instant – well, almost. You have to automate the bureaucracy. Change management, for example: we used to have weekly meetings. With cloud, fast-tracking is almost your everyday. And that means you need to have a robust system that makes assessments and changes really quickly. It means changes in how knowledge and processes are set up, teaming and shared knowledge enabled by automation. On the big picture, this is IT coming up to speed on service with other areas and sectors, as it should do.[35]

Certainly, our research shows cloud implying big changes, refreshed and new skills, and a new innovation role for IT functions if the potential of cloud developments is to be optimized. But as we will now see, the innovation potential of cloud extends a long way past those internal changes in the IT function.

CLOUD AS INNOVATION – SLOW TRAINS COMING?

Let us take stock. Although the perceived benefits of cloud computing are apparent, the analysis of our evidence base suggests that widespread adoption of cloud and, more importantly, the use of cloud for innovation beyond IT operational benefits could be more problematic than would at first appear. By focusing on three aspects (executives and cloud, cloud innovation through infrastructure and service, and the role of the retained IT function), this chapter has so far identified a range of factors that affect cloud adoption and innovation. Some of these factors, such as attributes of cloud computing that can support low-friction innovation and the potential for experimentation that the resulting changed risk profile affords, clearly support the ability to use cloud for innovation and are likely to drive the adoption of cloud by suitably prepared organizations.

Other factors, however, are likely to be more problematic. These might cause enterprises to delay their adoption of cloud computing or limit it to IT operational activities. Others might require the enterprise to develop and retain specialist in-house skills and capabilities. For example, the greater 'operational readiness' that cloud requires, whereby the enterprise might need to be responsive on a daily or even hourly basis, might not be achievable with existing internal capabilities. Similarly, the changing skill sets required of the internal IT department might take some time to achieve; moreover, retaining this capability is likely to prove a challenge for many traditional IT functions (see chapter 7).

What is particularly interesting from this analysis is the realization that whilst cloud has obvious technological benefits, there are also a number of important negative technological consequences. Both are illustrated in table 6.1.

For example, integrating existing legacy systems with the use of 'bring-your-own-devices' (BYOD) by employees may be problematic and there are significant management and operational challenges in moving from projects and demonstrator systems to full production systems (where personal credit cards cannot be used to provision and maintain mission-critical computing resources). According to one of our respondents: 'how the organization absorbs the technology or solution is the gating factor to speed as opposed to the ability to implement the technology itself.'[36]

TABLE 6.1 | **Evidence Relating to Cloud Innovation**

	Executive perspectives on the cloud innovation agenda	The changing role of the IT department	Innovation through infrastructure and service
Attributes of innovation	+ Focus back on business requirements	– Greater 'operational readiness' required	+ 'Low-friction' innovation
Collaborative innovation	+ Increased focus on customer needs along supply chain	– Too much emphasis on headcount/cost reduction	+ Changing risk profile supports experimentation
Innovation implementation process	– Requirement for high levels of service	– IT staff need greater business orientation	– Challenge of moving from demonstrators to production systems
	– Challenge of managing BYOD	– Skills shortage/retention problems	+ Automated marketplace for provisioning

As we saw in chapter 1, our survey in 2013 provided further evidence to support the concerns raised about the assumption that frictionless innovation would arise from cloud adoption. The client, advisor, and supplier communities were asked to rank the top five business objectives clients seek from cloud services from among nine choices. The top-rated business objective by all three communities was cost efficiency, followed by scalability, rapid deployment, avoiding the complexity of managing IT, and ensuring high security. In 2013, innovation through cloud was low on the corporate agenda.

Our analysis would be that business innovation through cloud could be facilitated where there were significant changes in the IT supply market and in the internal IT function, fostering a medium-term situation in which organizations (and consumers) collaborate and interact through configured business services provided from the cloud. CIOs would then consider cloud-based business processes as real services to the business – assessed not as SLAs but against key business performance indicators and profit. Once in place, these cloud business services would allow third parties to be directly integrated within them – accountants, suppliers, and regulators, for example. The traditional role of the systems integrator might thus become, in effect, that of a business integrator: connecting real business services together rather than worrying about technology. For most organizations, such a change would improve their processes, free IT staff time for a business and strategy focus, and allow a much easier relationship with suppliers of services. Such a change would be an example of an incremental innovation, rather than a radical one. In the next section we will finish the chapter by suggesting the three types of innovation cloud can support and how these can move an organization toward becoming a cloud corporation.

INNOVATING THE BUSINESS: TOWARD THE CLOUD CORPORATION

A summary of the possibilities for innovating the business through cloud is shown in figure 6.2.

Most organizations must be, to some extent, ambidextrous.[37] Organizational ambidexterity is the difficult act of balancing two diametrically opposed organizational qualities – adaptability and alignment. **Adaptability** implies nimble, agile change and innovation. **Alignment** means leveraging, exploiting, and maximizing capabilities and resources. Organizations will seek alignment through incremental innovations but they must also continually seek to explore new ground through radical innovations. Architectural innovations establish the platform for achieving both alignment and adaptability. As figure 6.2 shows, cloud offers all three types of innovation. But as a radical innovation in technology, cloud computing offers organizational units a chance to alter radically their business services – most probably through the innovation and collaboration beyond the enterprise we identified earlier. For, as John Seely Brown reminds us,[38] Nicholas Carr's pronouncement that 'IT doesn't matter' ignored the fact that each new computing facility creates new possibilities and options – which can be exploited for market advantage. We believe, therefore, that, for innovative organizational units, cloud computing may provide a platform for radical innovation in business process.

FIGURE 6.2 | **Cloud Computing as the Infrastructure for Business Services within an 'Ambidextrous' and Agile Organizational Form**

Innovation Focus	Proposition	Cloud Services
Incremental Innovation	Cost control through consolidation and virtualization Direct replacement of apps with SaaS	Virtualization Hybrid clouds IaaS SaaS
Architectural Innovation	Improvement in business processes Increased mobility Increased usability and elasticity	Mobilization Consumerization PaaS IaaS SaaS
Radical Innovation	Skunk-work IaaS Collaboration (intra & inter organizational)	Elasticity Consumerization Market-based PaaS SaaS

We see glimpses of this today: Avon exploits a Facebook application to allow its Sales Leaders to socially network. Jim Rivera of SalesForce.com describes the strategy:

> It's these young girls that are on Facebook all day. And they have huge networks of friends ... they're not going door-to-door like they used to and selling a product. It's all about just going out through their network. Well, Avon did a fascinating thing where they built a Facebook application on [the SalesForce] platform and on the Facebook platform, you know, and largely ... plug[ged] in external applications quite easily ... They built this custom application to help manage their network of Avon ladies within Facebook. So now, as an employee of Avon, as an Avon Lady, all I do is ... sign into Facebook. You get all the promotions coming to you. You're understanding what the new products are, what things you should be pushing

and then, within the same application, you turn around and you start to push that out into your network. And it's amazing. So they've actually used that as ... their portal for their sales people in Facebook.[39]

Here, Avon's sales and marketing business processes have moved outside the organizational boundary, creating amorphous collaborations, through sales leaders, with customers and their social networks. We look at this example in more detail in chapter 8, but such collaborative, innovative relationships, supported by BPaaS, hint at a new organizational form – amorphous, agile, ambidextrous (in focusing on delivery but also on radical innovation) – a form we term the *cloud corporation*. Knowing what such an organization might look like is difficult – few commercial enterprises are yet in a position to collaborate and integrate business services sufficiently. We therefore need to look beyond the commercial enterprise. One example exists among the particle physicists working at CERN on the Large Hadron Collider (LHC).

In order to analyze the staggering 15 million gigabytes of data that are being produced every year by the LHC's experiments, they needed to create a global organization of over 140 computer centers (each part of a university or research facility) working together to pool their computing into a Grid Computing Infrastructure.[40] This infrastructure – a kind of globally distributed PaaS service and the bedrock of many cloud technologies – was developed, and is run collectively by this loosely organized group of physicists and their data centers.

Interestingly, though, this new organization connects the computer centers through loose memoranda of understanding and business processes (particularly around support, data analysis, and technology upgrades). Its bureaucratic hierarchies are very limited in scope and power and most work is achieved through collaboration among equals.[41] Crucially, technology (in the form of monitoring, support, and control dashboards) allows collaborators to implicitly understand the state of the grid, of their collaboration, and of their part within it. The technology and the social networking around the technology is taken for granted and institutionalized and is part of their agility – woven within their management practices. For example, when Steve (a collaborator in the U.K.) wished to steer other U.K. collaborators' actions, he did so by 'mashing up' a new BPaaS, which showed, hour by hour, elements of the grid infrastructure that he felt were deficient. Called 'Steve's Jobs,' these new BPaaS provided an incentive and direction to other collaborators to change their work and innovate around them.[42] Particle physicists at CERN are unusual – they have highly collaborative tendencies[43] (which they helped to invent the Web to support); however, we believe that they provide a first glimpse of how an agile, innovative global organization can be created when built upon collaboration and shared cloud-based technology.

The CERN example hints at the genuine possibilities for cloud-enabled businesses. Let us revisit a diagram we saw first in the context of the reconfiguration of the IT supply industry (see chapter 3). Before, we saw it from the supply perspective, but now look at figure 6.3 from a client corporate viewpoint.

FIGURE 6.3 | **The Foundations of the Cloud Corporation**

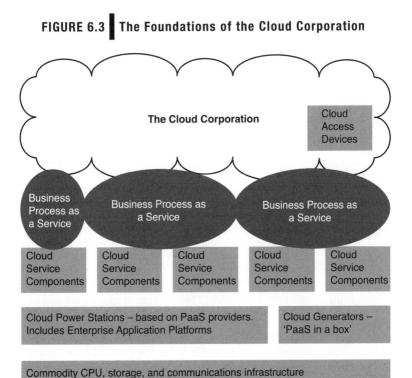

The corporation is going to have to work as hard as the supply side, but in different ways, to put in place the technologies and capabilities needed to harness and exploit the power of cloud technologies. Senior executives are going to have to be on side and influential in driving through the requisite technological, organizational, and capability changes. There will be radical shifts in the role and capabilities of IT functions. Business users will need to develop the maturity to support cloud-based innovation and learn how to exploit the business possibilities created. New contracting forms and relationships with existing and emerging suppliers will need to be thought through and implemented. Business processes will need to be constantly reconfigured. The corporation is going to need to keep fully abreast with advances in technology given the ever improving cost/performance curves of advanced ICTs. And this is just to mention some of the more obvious challenges.

To take on such an agenda, senior executives are going to have to work out an evolution. One path is to plot a trajectory starting with incremental and moving through architectural to radical innovations. We have researched major Fortune 500 companies that were by 2013 already considerably along the path of architectural innovation. Most recently, we have found SMEs already achieving radical innovations, with several examples of 'born-in-the-cloud' start-up companies.[44] As William Gibson acutely observed, the future is already here but unevenly distributed. This is precisely true in the case of the move to the cloud corporation and why in this book we see innovation through cloud being a long-term story.

CONCLUSION

The reality is that cloud computing cannot achieve the plug-and-play simplicity of electricity – at least, not as long as innovation, both within cloud computing itself and in the myriad applications and business models it enables, continues at such a rapid pace. While electric utilities are held up as models of simplicity and stability, even this industry is not immune to the transformative power of IT. Innovations like the 'smart grid' are triggering fundamental changes at a pace not seen since the early days of electrification. The real strength of cloud computing is that it is a catalyst for more innovation. In fact, as cloud computing continues to become cheaper and more widespread, the opportunities for combinatorial innovation will only grow. It is true that this inevitably requires more creativity and skill from IT and business executives. In the end, this is not something to be avoided, but, we suggest, to be welcomed and embraced.

The distinctive features of cloud computing offer many potential opportunities for business innovation, particularly given its service (and service quality) focus, coupled with the flexibility that new technology delivery mechanisms provide. These features serve to change the risk profile of business innovations to the extent that it is now increasingly possible to specify new business processes and their associated required service levels, experiment with them for a short time, and either disband them if they are unsuccessful or rapidly scale them if they have potential.

However, our most recent survey found reasons for qualifying the assumption of frictionless innovation arising from cloud adoption. The challenges are larger and there is more friction associated with the adoption of cloud. Cost savings will come through, but the business benefits will need an eight- to ten-year rather than a five-year horizon to come to fruition. We also anticipate initially more process innovation – associated with net job losses – as a result of cloud, before job-creating product innovations come through, and would therefore predict much smaller net job creation from the cloud than many have been predicting, especially in the short term.

The pattern, therefore, may well follow past diffusions of other potentially powerful technological innovations, including the Internet itself. The technology innovations will move in packs covering base technology and technical service and process innovations. With cloud these innovations in combination are likely to be radical and disruptive, if over a longer period than many are anticipating. From a business perspective, these technology innovations will have a cumulative impact on the possibilities for more business-focused innovations, though these will be through the filter of the four antecedent factors discussed in this chapter. From a business executive perspective, the innovation plan then is relatively easy to state, but much more difficult to make the right choices on: navigate the hype, test out the capability, find the useful application, ensure the capability to leverage, and learn further how to exploit the innovation for strategic, business purposes. And move from cost gains through incremental, architectural, and radical innovation to the cloud-based, agile, ambidextrous organization.

CHAPTER 7

Management: Building the Retained Organization

INTRODUCTION

Earlier chapters have pointed to the promise of cloud. Generically, the promise is: speed, payment based on consumption, lower costs, clearly defined services managed to appropriate services levels, on-demand availability, and scalability. There is simplicity (complexity hidden from view), allowing a focus on business requirements, strategy, and innovation, away from day-to-day maintenance and technology issues.[1] We have also pointed to the challenges presented by cloud computing technologies, their likely impacts and their potential for incremental, architectural, and radical innovations for the business. The opportunity is clear:

> We are virtualizing the enterprise at a business and operating model level. Companies are using technologies converging in cloud, coupling that with greater reliance [on] and utilization of outsourcing and really releasing themselves from a lot of the constraints on what they can do as a business. The way we have run business for the last 80 years is on its last legs. The financial model changes, the talent model, so many things; and these technologies are enabling companies to do things they have never imagined before.[2]

However, most of this is before us in a future still undetermined, despite confident predictions of, for example, very large revenues and business benefits from applying cloud technologies within three to four years. It has been said that 'the mark of a successful technology is that it vanishes.'[3] If this is true, then cloud computing has a long way to go; it has been the most visible technology by far in the last four years and this looks likely to continue for the next three.

We are clear that leaders in industry and governments worldwide found themselves, by 2013, on the cusp of potential major deployment of these technologies but at a key '*stop, think, act moment.*' This was nowhere more true than for the technology (IT) functions so key to cloud deployment. In the context of business demands, technological developments, and the maturing of external services, CIOs need to be thinking about and revisiting what their technology organizations will look like three to five years out. Managing cloud deployment on a project-to-project or six-monthly basis is not going to achieve technological integration, optimize cloud deployment, or deliver on the agenda businesses are setting for cloud. CIOs need to be looking at their strategy, capabilities, operating model, and ability to execute. They need to consider how cloud fits with their existing technologies and organization, and its implications for *this* industry and *this* business. Because there is no single cloud and it is going to be different for every organization. Ultimately it is management that will make the difference. And for management there is a (very large) sting in the tail. The next ten years are going to see a massive scaling of data, which needs to be managed. According to Chuck Hollis of EMC: 'the twin benefits of cloud are saving on IT and agility, but the result at the end of the journey is big data.'[4] This is an issue we deal with in more detail in chapter 9. In the face of the forthcoming data explosion, the problems organizations have always had with optimizing their use of information are just about to get much, much more difficult. This brings to the fore the need for organizations and their technology functions to resist the old compulsion to merely straightjacket the data explosion with superior technology. Instead, they need to rethink themselves as digital businesses and address the importance of business analytics for guiding strategic action and operations.[5]

Therefore this chapter suggests ways forward for management. It is designed to help senior executives think through the role, capabilities, and evolution of the technology function over the next five years in the light of business imperatives and cloud developments.

CLOUD: FROM EXPECTATIONS TO THE ART OF THE POSSIBLE

Business executive expectations on in-house IT staff to deliver on cloud have been high. Our 2011 survey found 80 percent relying on in-house staff. At the same time, business executives expect much more use of external services for supporting the move to cloud, with 40–50 percent surveyed recognizing benefits for governance support, business process transformation, change management, and communications and IT maintenance and support. Interestingly, IT executives also look for external assistance but with mainly technical issues – IT configuration and integration, data security, data management, and governance.[6] The overall message is that the IT function cannot manage the move to cloud by itself. However, there is widespread recognition that it needs to retain key capabilities. Our recent outsourcing survey gives provider insights into what these need to be, though their perceptions underrate the role of cloud skills because many of their customers were not yet making significant moves to cloud (see figure 7.1). At the same time our, and other, research shows many CIOs and IT functions lacking the knowledge to move decisively on cloud computing.[7] In practice, we found this to be a major reason for organizational delays in moving to cloud. One strategist summarized this point:[8]

> I think it's very early days actually. … companies are only starting to realize that your organization needs to change and evolve and update. Many people in IT organizations are still seeing this as quite a threat. They're seeing it as outsourcing … Actually, this is an opportunity for career development, for individuals to grow and really change what they do: from doing things themselves to actually managing the provision of some of these new cloud services. We are going through an interesting time ourselves from a strategy perspective in terms of our capabilities and we are looking at the IT operating model, and figuring out how internally our IT function needs to change.

In fact, to deliver on business expectations and cloud potential, those charged with technology leadership have to prepare themselves for some radical changes, whose path and pace of evolution must be carefully delineated. Cloud signals significant changes in functions

FIGURE 7.1 | Management of Outsourcing Relationships

In your view, how important is it for your clients to have the following in-house skills/capabilities for managing outsourcing relationships? (Outsourcing advisors)

■ Essential   ■ Useful   ■ Not needed

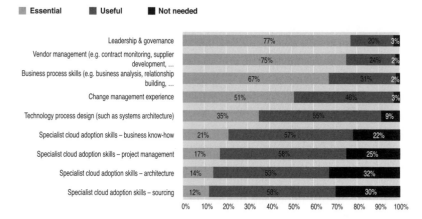

	Essential	Useful	Not needed
Leadership & governance	77%	20%	3%
Vendor management (e.g. contract monitoring, supplier development, ...)	75%	24%	2%
Business process skills (e.g. business analysis, relationship building, ...)	67%	31%	2%
Change management experience	51%	46%	3%
Technology process design (such as systems architecture)	35%	55%	9%
Specialist cloud adoption skills – business know-how	21%	57%	22%
Specialist cloud adoption skills – project management	17%	58%	25%
Specialist cloud adoption skills – architecture	14%	53%	32%
Specialist cloud adoption skills – sourcing	12%	58%	30%

Sample: 318 outsourcing advisors and 544 outsourcing suppliers
Source: HfS Research and the London School of Economics Outsourcing Unit, July 2011.

and roles for internal IT. The IT function has been on a journey for some decades from being a back-office technical function to a service-oriented provider that delivers business value operationally and is managed by business and technology leaders as a strategic business resource. One of the much touted purposes of outsourcing has been to accelerate this process, freeing up internal capability to become more business focused and strategic in contribution.[9] Our research shows that cloud is already accelerating this process and, to fulfill the real business potential of cloud will require significant changes in the way internal IT resources are organized, staffed, and managed. This conclusion is reached through reviewing our ongoing research in four streams. This suggests four converging journeys that technology leaders need to pursue if the potential endpoints, in terms of management capability to deliver and run an integrated technology-with-cloud platform, are to be realized (see figure 7.2).

Our work on the evolution of the IT function (stream 1) establishes that the IT shop needs first to establish itself with the business as a competent technical service. On this foundation it can develop into a strategic partner with the business – a process requiring a reorientation of goals, culture, and skills in both IT and lines of business – in order to leverage IT as a strategic business resource. With this in place IT can become a small, high-performance team organized into retained core capabilities that elicit and deliver on business requirements, design and maintain the blueprint for the technology platform, manage large-scale outsourcing, and provide leadership, coordination, governance, and organization. However, technology cannot be leveraged strategically and for business innovation without a) senior executives and business units being fully engaged in funding and playing pro-active roles in designing, developing, and deploying these technologies and b) IT achieving a step-change in its outsourcing maturity toward collaborative innovation with suppliers (stream 2). Cloud developments (stream 3) fit this context by bringing new technological capabilities and related challenges and opportunities that will, as we detail below, require major shifts in

FIGURE 7.2 | **Cloud Implications for the Retained Technology Function**[10]

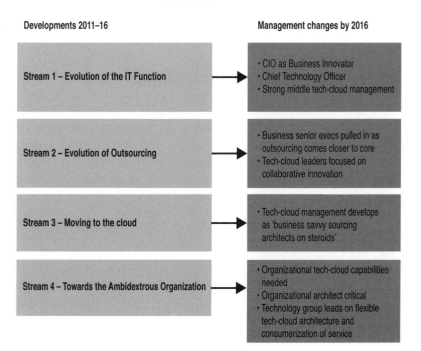

internal management, skills, and capabilities if cloud deployment is going to deliver on the promise and innovations we documented in earlier chapters.[11] But for cloud technologies to be fully exploited for business advantage, the rest of the business will also need to develop new organizational IT and organizational architecture capabilities. These will fit with the technology architecture, strategy, and operations becoming increasingly embedded in business practices, the convergence (stream 4) founding an ambidextrous, more digitally based business (see chapter 6).

If this forward vision seems ambitious, it does actually represent a realistic convergence whose emerging shape we have been tracking through a range of research studies stretching back to the start of the commercial development of the Internet in the mid-1990s.[12] Below, we discuss how this world can be, and is being, managed into existence. We start by detailing the retained capabilities necessary for running the future technology function. We point to specific management capability challenges already emerging with cloud deployment and describe how the technology function can be evolved, along with business readiness, for leveraging for business advantage the ever-developing technology platform and applications.

CLOUD MANAGEMENT: THE FOUNDATIONS

In the face of turbulent technology, we have consistently found that an emphasis on technology and technology-related skills guarantees adoption *but rarely exploitation*. There was still, in 2013, a danger of a lot of cloud offerings being technology solutions in search of business problems. To get cloud onto a more strategic agenda and identify the relatively few applications that produce disproportionate business value, the technology function needs to shift from its traditional skills, roles, and values.[13] In practice, with each technology cycle, cloud being but the latest, and with ever increasing usage of the external services market,[14] our ongoing research demonstrates that high-performing technology functions are managed by a relatively small internal team of highly capable, demand-led, and primarily strategy- and business-focused people. Here we focus on the technology function, whose role is central to cloud deployment. However, the same logic applies to, for example, the human resource, finance and accounting, procurement, and administrative functions.[15] The model provides a strong foundation for managing existing technologies and remains robust in the light of our present findings on cloud services, but throughout we elaborate where it needs new emphases and more granularity.

The internal group responsible for the technology platform and applications, including cloud, needs to deliver on four core tasks:

- **Governance**, including leadership, organization, and coordination. This involves aligning dynamically the technology function's activities internally and with those of the organization as a whole. The goal: governance. Essential capabilities: leading; informed buying

- **Eliciting and delivering on business requirements**. A demand-driven task concerned with defining the systems, information, and processes to be provided and how they can be leveraged for business purposes. A key emerging role here is supporting, even catalyzing, business innovation through technology. The goal: business value creation. Essential capabilities: business innovating; business systems thinking; relationship building

- **Ensuring technical capability**. A supply-focused task concerned with defining the blueprint or architecture of the technical platform used over time to support the target systems and processes and dealing with risks inherent in non-routine technical issues. The goal: IT and business architecture. Essential capabilities: architecture planning and design; making IT and process work

- **Managing external supply**. This concerns arriving at and managing sourcing strategy. It requires understanding of the external services market and the ability to select, engage, and manage internal and external technology/cloud resources and services over time. The goal: service delivery. Essential capabilities: service integration; informed buying; contract facilitation; contract monitoring; vendor development.

Looking at figure 7.3, we can see that these capabilities populate seven spaces. The first is a lynchpin governance position covered by two capabilities. Three spaces are essentially business, technology, or service delivery facing. Finally, there are three spaces that represent various interfaces. Let us look now at the roles that enact these capabilities.

FIGURE 7.3 | **Core Capabilities for Technology and Back-Office Functions**

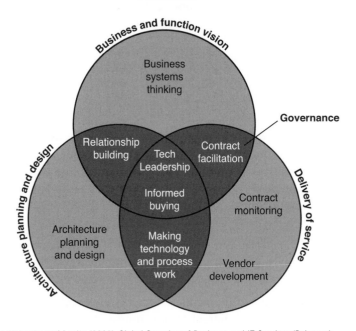

Source: Willcocks and Lacity (2006) *Global Sourcing of Business and IT Services* (Palgrave).

Governance

This task is delivered through leadership and informed buying capabilities. The central **leadership** task is to devise and engage in organizational arrangements – governance, structures, processes, and staffing – that successfully manage internal and business interdependencies, in ways that ensure the technology function delivers business value for money. The key role of the leader is to look for value shifts, listen to the technology, and see where business value in the (cloud) technology is migrating to.[16] The CIO, as leader, will also be responsible for setting up the organization for cloud:

There is a demand management component, which includes the business requirement definition; there is the business case component – does it fit the architecture, is it strategically where we want to go, does it fit our financial model? Then there is delivery – generic program management, methodologies that give you more agility; there is the integration management component – faster, more dynamic procurement, service management; and finally [there are] the skilled people to deliver all this.[17]

In an organization that has decided to outsource most of its technology services, the **informed buyer** role is the most prominent after the CIO. Informed buyers analyze and benchmark regularly the external market for IT and cloud services; select the five- to ten-year sourcing strategy to meet business needs and technology issues; and lead the tendering, contracting, and service management processes. Informed buying also requires an intimate knowledge of suppliers, their strategies and financial strength, and their capabilities and lack of capabilities in different sectors, services, and regions. One informed buyer in an energy company also described the pragmatic aspect to this role:

If you are a senior manager … and you want something done, you come to me and I will … go outside [and] select and draw up the contract with the services supplier, and if anything goes wrong, it's my butt that gets kicked by you.[18]

Cloud requires many changes to traditional procurement. Matthew Coates of Accenture points to one reason: 'My whole way of procuring needs to change because the whole idea of cloud is [that] things are going to be agile.'[19] Cloud also requires the ability to source different technologies and services from a multi-supplier base, on a more dynamic, frequently pay-for-use and pay-as-you-go basis, as well as on more traditional outsourcing contracts and shaping multiple service integration for the business unit customer. In a world that gets increasingly outsourced and cloud-sourced, we are finding that client organizations still under-resource their informed buying capability, when in practice what they need is informed buying on steroids.

Business and Function Vision

In the leading practice organizations we have been studying, **business systems thinkers** from the technology function are important contributors to teams charged with business problem solving, process re-engineering, strategic development, and delivering e-business. Such organizations recognize that business processes should be redesigned in the light of technology, including cloud, potential. Business systems thinkers focus obsessively on aligning strategy, structure, people, process, and technology. One case we researched illustrates the problems faced when this capability is *not* in place. A major insurance company contracted a supplier to deliver a strategic IT system aimed at transforming administrative and customer service systems. However, the business transformation was misconceived as a technology project and the supplier was given primary responsibility and aggressive deadlines. In the event, the supplier failed to deliver detailed business requirements on time and the project was cancelled nine months into the two-year implementation. The CEO learned from this and in later business projects involving technology suppliers insisted that internal 'business systems thinking' capabilities were in place. The danger with cloud is that organizations fail to learn from such experiences embedded in the technology history of almost all large organizations.[20] In cloud research we are finding that business systems thinkers need to be on cloud projects and act as conduits between business demands and the technical architects.

Architecture Planning and Design

The principal challenge to the **architect planner/designer** is, through insight into technology, suppliers, and business directions, to anticipate technology trends so that the organization is consistently able to operate from an effective and efficient technology platform – without major investment in major migration efforts. Planners shape the technology architecture and infrastructure through developing the vision of an appropriate technical platform and through formulating associated policies that ensure necessary integration and flexibility in technology and cloud services. Any outsourcing arrangement provides a strong test of the value of retaining this capability.[21] When it comes to cloud, our respondents suggest that the cloud architect has to be an enterprise architect, SOA architect (most clouds use services architecture), and cloud technologist, the new role emphasis being to increasingly collaborate with business initiatives. David Linthicum of Microsoft describes it well:

> The cloud architect needs to be an expert in the existing cloud computing technology: public, private and hybrid, including IaaS, PaaS and SaaS. You can't build something unless you understand the tools and materials that are available and the same goes for bringing cloud computing technology into the enterprise to form [business] solutions.[22]

According to one senior practitioner:

> I have worked on cloud based systems for years now and the common thread to cloud architecture is that there are no common threads to cloud architecture. The complexities around multi-tenancy resource sharing and management, security and even version control lead cloud computing start-ups and enterprises that build private and public clouds down some rough roads before they start to learn from their mistakes. In the world of cloud computing that means those who are smart, creative and resourceful seem to win out over those who are just smart.[23]

For Frank Modruson, CIO of Accenture:

> The client person who can think about the enterprise data model, how all the technology and data fits together, can conceptualize, plan, and implement; these are the skills going forward – more conceptual, knowledgeable, and architectural. And data modelling [is] a sort of lost art – with cloud, it's back.

Hong Chiong of Microsoft points to in-house capability needed in architecture planning and design on security and compliance:

> When it comes to compliance and security, technology managed by the cloud supplier is only one fourth of the solution. You have to have a standard operating procedure that is well-documented and that people are trained to operate. That has got to come from the customer.[24]

A senior executive in a major IT supplier detailed a further role for the architect:

> The other retained capability that's critical going forward is identity management. So, whether it's a BlackBerry conversation, whether it's the iPad conversation as well, the customers are logging into the systems directly, the organization critically must understand identity management. Because identity management drives the automation of the data center, it drives the automation of the applications, it drives the automation of what happens on a website, it drives the automation of what happens on mobile devices. Most customers we talk to don't have that capability. Why? Because the identity management model was designed for seven, eight, ten years ago and served them well up until then, but now, as we go through this step-change and transformation, understanding that identity drives security, it defines access to information, it defines access to devices, it defines the way that customers log into systems; that becomes a critical capability.[25]

The senior executive cited a case in point of a major insurance company needing to rethink totally how identity systems played within its information technology architecture.

By listening to the technology and understanding the business and its technical configuration, the technical architect ties together cloud strategy and its links with existing technology and develops the coherent blueprint for the migration path.

Delivery of Services

The fourth task, and competency, comprises the capabilities required to manage and ensure external supply. Here, **contract monitoring** involves making inputs into the development and maintenance of a robust contract as the basis for a sound governance framework. The role then leads on to holding suppliers to account against both existing service contracts and the developing performance standards of the services market. Not all potential issues and expectations can be identified at the onset of a relationship, and the contract will be subject to differing interpretations as issues arise. Moreover, there is no standard contract, only standard headings, as each outsourcing and cloud arrangement has its own set of issues and dynamics. While all organizations we have studied recognized the importance of contract monitoring and staffed it at the beginning of their deals, historically, they all too frequently put the wrong people in place, especially in the large deals, underestimating the dynamic nature and extent of the task. Cloud, we are finding, brings a new dynamism to the role – more and more diverse contracts, more instant and transparent information, including information from suppliers, faster response times, new standards of service, and the need to deal with the immaturity of contracting in the cloud eco-system.

Anchored in the supply face of our model, the **vendor developer** is concerned with leveraging the long-term potential for suppliers to add value, creating the 'win-win' situations in which the supplier increases its revenues by providing services that increase business benefits. Given the prohibitive cost of switching, historically, it has been in the client company's interest to maximize the contribution from existing suppliers. It remains so for cloud deals, especially where, as we anticipate, these deals become larger and more complex. In the context of multiple suppliers, not properly managing the vendor set can lead to sub-optimal outcomes, such as loss of technology and process knowledge, lack of innovation, over-spending, and poor quality.[26] It is also important to guard against what we call 'mid-contract sag,' in cloud and other arrangements, where the supplier delivers to the contract, but only to the letter. As one aerospace IT service director puts it:'Yes the supplier can achieve all the things that were proposed – but where is the famous "value-added service"? We are not getting anything over and above what any old outsourcer could provide.'[27]

Compare this with a retail multinational that meets suppliers formally at senior levels to find new ways forward: 'there are certain things we force on our suppliers, like understanding our business and growing the business together' (CIO, retail multinational). While such a concern might not be present in the initial, smaller cloud deals, as these grow in complexity, there is every reason for a client to have this in-house capability, not least to service its existing non-cloud outsourcing contracts.

Interfacing Capabilities

The role holders that operate in the three interfaces in figure 7.3 are crucial for facilitating the **integration** of effort across the four competencies. Operating in the overlap between the challenges of IT architecture design and delivery of IT services is the core capability of **making IT and process work. Technology 'fixers'** are needed to troubleshoot problems and identify how to address business needs that cannot be satisfied properly by standard technical approaches. They understand the idiosyncrasies of the inherited infrastructure and business applications, enabling them to make rapid technical progress – by one means or another. In outsourced environments they also assess and challenge third-party suppliers' claims about technical problems and proposed solutions. Technical staff will need not only a deeper understanding of their traditional core competencies but also a wider skill set to transcend the traditional IT silos and address the fact that cloud encompasses more than one technology. Senior Executives suggested to us, for example, that instead of employing three people to oversee storage, networking, and virtualization environments, companies might hire one person whose skills span all three cloud competencies. For CIO Frank Modruson, with cloud:

> The traditional operational roles will shrink in number, move increasingly to the supplier, and cover more scale. What you call technical fixing, there will always be a need for a bit of that, for example, dealing with the joins between different provider services and technologies, having know-how of in-house systems.[28]

While IaaS and Saas require some new skills, moving to PaaS requires much tighter integration with software development and application life-cycle management to realize maximum benefits. IT departments have to redesign applications with PaaS in mind and the deployment model is largely driven by how the service provider offers its service. PaaS will almost certainly require a greater level of retraining and skills. And 'technical fixing' also has to take on a more business-focused mind-set than before. As one PaaS supplier commented:

Clients need to be willing to configure the network and design applications in a different way, perhaps use different-size servers and not just see cloud from a technical point of view, but get the balance right on how much it costs me to re-engineer versus the benefits and cost savings from a cloud solution ... and often it's the business benefit in terms of elasticity and time to market, not cost savings, that are the driving factors.[29]

Stephanie Lester of Glasshouse told us:

The cloud model of rent and virtualization means that you will still need technical expertise, especially about your own systems and cloud 'fit' but, [in]sofar as technical, 'doing,' work migrates to the supplier, or becomes automated, you will need less headcount in this area.

The **contract facilitator** is crucial for lubricating the relationship between supplier(s) and the business users, not least by ensuring that problems and conflicts are seen to be resolved fairly and promptly within what are usually long-term relationships. It is an action-orientated capability. Interestingly, the need for this role is rarely spotted straight away when outsourcing. Instead, the capability tends to grow in response to ongoing issues, for which it emerges as an adequate response, such as:

- Users may demand too much and incur excessive charges

- The business user asks for 'one-stop' shopping

- The supplier demands it

- Multiple supplier services need co-ordinating

- Easier monitoring of usage and services is required.

In the cloud context, contract facilitators construct services from third-party offerings. They also front differences in ways of operating brought in by cloud. Neil Thomas of Cable and Wireless offers one example:

We have debates with customers where they insist on a mutually agreed time for planned outages. Normally, that's what you do on a dedicated platform, but in a shared platform, if no customers mutually agree, you never end up being allowed an outage, or there is a high overhead … that's an example of where we and the customer have had to learn together. Those people you describe as contract facilitators also worry about security and faults, because it's a shared platform; also billing systems.[30]

The **relationship builder** has an integrating, operational role, facilitating the wider dialogue and establishing understanding, trust, and cooperation amongst business users and technology/cloud specialists. Relationship builders develop users' understanding of technology and cloud and its potential for their lines of business. They help users and specialists to work together, help to identify business requirements, ensure user ownership, and build user satisfaction with technology and cloud services. With cloud comes a further emphasis in this role on business analysis and requirement identification: 'The one role that has got the most to gain out of cloud inside the customer organization is [that of] the business analyst with a technical appreciation.'[31]

All our respondents stressed that cloud required more business-facing skills than ever before and, as in the case of the relationship builder role, also meant the release of human resources from more mundane technical work to fulfill vital business-facing activities.

CLIENT RETAINED CAPABILITIES: SUMMARY

In table 7.1 we bring together these capabilities, expressed as roles and skills. The nine roles all demand high performers who can develop into a high-performance team. In contrast to the more traditional skills found in IT functions, there needs to be a much greater emphasis on **business skills and business orientation** in nearly all roles. While the exceptions used to be the technical fixer and to some extent the technical architect roles, we have found these two roles needing an increasing amount of business understanding and relationship building. There is a significantly increased requirement for **'soft' skills** across all roles and this is accelerated by cloud, the exception being the contract monitor role. The major shift we have been observing in organizations such as Esso, ICI, DuPont, Commonwealth

TABLE 7.1 | **The Nine Core Back-Office Capabilities as Roles**

Manager Role	New Cloud Challenge	Time Horizon	Description	Skills profile
Leader	Cloud staffing Cloud business strategy Technology function redesign Cloud project oversight	*Present / Future*	Integrates the technology-cloud effort with business purpose and activity	Business – high Interpersonal – high Technical – medium
Business Systems Thinker	Cloud fit and timing Business-cloud projects Relationships with business execs.	*Future*	Ensures that technology-cloud capabilities are envisioned in every business process	Business – high Interpersonal – medium Technical – medium
Relationship Builder	Cloud operational business leverage Business education	*Present*	Gets the business constructively engaged in operational technology-cloud issues	Business – medium Interpersonal – high Technical – high
Architecture Planner and Designer	Cloud strategy Technology-business alignment Systems integration Cloud project planning New security/data issues	*Future*	Creates the coherent blueprint for a technical platform that responds to present and future needs	Business – low/medium Interpersonal – medium Technical – high

(continued on page 142)

Manager Role	New Cloud Challenge	Time Horizon	Description	Skills profile
Technical Fixer	Apposite Iaas, Saas, Paas skills Broader technical skills base 'Fixing' role in cloud projects	*Present*	Rapidly trouble-shoots problems which are being disowned by others across the technical supply chain	Business – low Interpersonal – low/medium Technical – high
Informed Buyer	Cloud market knowledge Matching business demand with cloud supply Cloud supplier management	*Present/ Future*	Manages the technology-cloud sourcing strategy to meet the needs of the business	Business – high Interpersonal – high Technical – medium
Contract Facilitator	Cloud service development and integration Cloud product manager Service delivery	*Present*	Ensures the success of existing contracts for external technology-cloud services	Business – medium Interpersonal – high Technical – medium
Contract Monitor	Cloud SLAs Regulatory implications Cloud security issues	*Present/ Future*	Protects the business's contractual position present and future	Business – medium Interpersonal – medium Technical – medium
Vendor Developer	Developing cloud suppliers Maturing cloud relationships Securing future innovation and value added from cloud deployment	*Future*	Identifies the potential added value from technology-cloud service suppliers	Business – high Interpersonal – medium/high Technical – medium

Bank, Lloyds of London, BP, Procter and Gamble, and GE is toward fewer personnel, but of very high quality. We are seeing cloud accelerating these developments. On **technical skills**, the shift in house, again accelerated by cloud, has been towards less 'doing' and more conceptual technical activity.

The mix of business, technical, and interpersonal skills will vary by role. Looking at the technology function, the informed buyer needs strong communication and negotiation skills, strong knowledge of the outsourcing market, and high business skills but only medium knowledge of technologies. The technical fixer, on the other hand, will have very high technical skills and good knowledge of business systems but, unlike every other role, needs only medium interpersonal skills. The relationship builder will need high interpersonal skills, medium knowledge of the business, and high technical skills. Each capability needs to be fulfilled by a distinctive mix of technical, business, and interpersonal skills and needs high performers who can work as a coordinated team across the capabilities.

We also tabulate our research findings on the new challenges cloud brings to each of these roles. Table 7.1 points to further skills and problem-solving capabilities needing to be developed for each role where cloud deployment begins to figure significantly on the technology and business agendas. Cloud requires all nine retained capabilities, but also requires a shift in emphasis in how these are applied. This shift is represented in figure 7.4, which shows that cloud adoption and deployment renders four capabilities particularly crucial for the in-house technology function as a whole. We label these the 'business savvy,' 'architect,' 'sourcing specialist,' and 'business innovator' capabilities or attributes. These capabilities were stressed by all our interviewees. In practice these capabilities have needed to grow as the outsourcing market has expanded. Now cloud requires a further adaptation and strengthening of these capabilities. We found that cloud in particular requires business savvy and strategic sourcing and architecture capabilities to a much higher degree than found in more traditional, and even other outsourced, IT functions. Meanwhile, our parallel research into innovation found that the business innovator role within the in-house function is key to securing the collaborative innovation – between the technology function, the business, and suppliers – needed to optimize the business potential of cloud.[32] One CIO suggested how his role might develop with cloud:

For the CIO, information is going to be more important, [as is] becoming more intimately familiar with business processes – ... indeed, running some of the back-office stuff. The business visionary is a potential evolution ... it will vary by industry and company.[33]

FIGURE 7.4 | **The Emerging Technology Function: Cloud Highlights Four Roles**

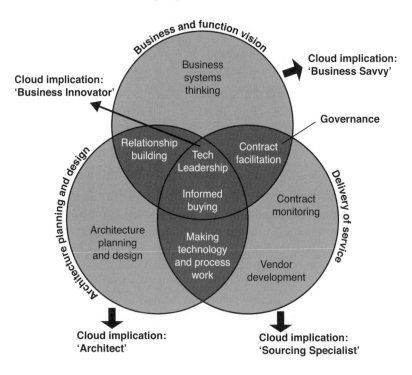

The shifts in the operating model we are anticipating pose significant challenges that need to be addressed for progress to be made. Table 7.1 points to a range of challenges and the managerial responsibilities for dealing with them. But the research consistently surfaced five key concerns across our respondents.

The Human Resource Challenge. In practice, recruitment and retention of the small, high-quality group we have described has always been a major human resource challenge. Cloud has just made it that much harder – cloud skills were running at a 20–40 percent premium throughout 2011–2014 and the skills shortages have indeed slowed client organizations in their ability to adopt cloud technologies, especially where they also have to compete with suppliers. Two solutions are upskilling and hiring. As one multinational oil company executive commented: 'You've got to be able to upskill your organization and to have a human resource policy which provides such training to people in your organization.' The logistics manager at a major retailer said: 'To be honest, we had to recruit a few people.' Once suitable people have been hired, you will need to:

- pay them at a level within striking distance of that provided by alternative employers
- provide them consistently with the level of challenge they look for in the job
- develop a career path for them.

We have already seen hybrid staff being developed in-house. For example, Xerox, Dupont, WW Grainger, and Johnson & Johnson offer job rotation paths and flexible career paths to retain their core people. Cloud adds further reasons for this.

The 'Change-in-Ethos' Challenge. The issues with more traditional IT functions and the character of cloud as a disruptive innovation is caught in the following observation by Jim Rivera of SalesForce. com:

> IT has been largely responsible for keeping systems up and running, and the statistics are [that] anywhere from 60 percent to 80 percent of what they focus on is really geared towards just keeping the lights on – keeping things going and not on adding more business value. The problem is that the business changes quickly: business managers have their demands and IT simply cannot get the stuff (power and resources to meet new requirements). Of course, there needs to be strong governance to make sure what people are doing is consistent in terms of architecture and security and that people are not getting into the types of business-critical systems that only IT should

be touching. However, IT doesn't have to do everything any more. With cloud, IT can get out of the way of the business, be no longer a roadblock for certain types of systems, which the business can handle with oversight from IT.[34]

Other providers talked of needing to be much sharper on service metrics, transparency, and corrective action enabled by automation. Speed also means that much greater operational readiness is needed with cloud on the part of suppliers. This passes over to client staff, not least because of internal pressure from business units to perform faster.[35]

Such changes present new opportunities for IT professionals, if they are only willing to take them:

> The cloud, whether it be private, public, [or] hybrid, is creating positive opportunities for IT professionals. I say to my IT people: you're going to have many more business conversations; you're going to be having more service catalogue conversations. You're talking about solutions, you're not talking about applications and stacks and the things that have traditionally been the IT lingua franca. If you are a systems administrator and you're looking at converged infrastructure today, systems, storage, network, and security people will be calling at your door. Cloud requires a breadth of skills. Or you can become a cloud architect or specialize as a cloud professional. Alternatively, if you want to specialize, for example as a systems person, opportunities continue because now you have to go deeper into the skill set from a technology point of view and you're no longer provisioning for one application stack, you're provisioning for the enterprise or for the cloud. So, whether you want to go into the business side of things or you want to do go deeper into technology or you want to go wider with technology, cloud brings you some incredible new opportunities as an IT professional.[36]

The Project Management Challenge. Project management needs to be an *organizational* core capability and not the preserve of one business function. Therefore, it does not appear explicitly in figure 7.3. Candidates for the project manager role are most likely to be found amongst relationship builders and technology fixers, but, clearly, business systems thinkers, leaders, architects, and informed buyers must have very active roles in projects with a strong technology/

cloud component. As one BH Billiton senior executive told us: 'we outsourced too much project management capability in our first deal, and even if you have somebody doing projects for you, you can never give up project sponsorship, ownership and accountability.'[37]

In practice, we have seen the technology function rebuild some of its project management capability in the face of large-scale outsourcing, especially where IT-enabled business transformation was on the agenda. Large business projects dependent on cloud components will need the same hyperactive involvement of the 'technology' roles outlined above, as well as supplier resources, but also the business needs to show maturity in allocating business sponsors, champions, and full-time business user managers to the project team and take responsibility for outcomes.

However, cloud may well have to start small and quick at first, and this may well accelerate an existing trend towards prototyping and agile and fast delivery of business benefits. According to Tim Barker of SalesForce.com:[38] 'In terms of process skill, agile development, scrum methodology – the kinds of things that IT organizations are already moving towards – I see cloud computing putting this on a fast track.'

With cloud, the lines between development, testing, and deployment are likely to blur even more. Matthew Coates of Accenture, indeed, sees agile development and centers of excellence as natural start points for cloud initiatives within the technology function. On this view, in-house learning on cloud would occur on a series of small '80/20' projects (focusing on the 20 percent of the system/service that gives 80 percent of the benefits) with quick business 'wins.' This would build, over time, into a strong in-house cloud knowledge and cloud 'fixing' capabilities. If this is so, and our research supports the viability of this agile development model,[39] then it means a shift in the ways of working not just for technology staff, but also for business managers and operational staff.

The Innovation Challenge. The technology function model we have detailed is designed to deal with dynamic business contexts and is, amongst its other tasks, designed for innovating. Leaders, business systems thinkers, and architects look after future business innovations and their technical underpinnings; the informed buyer and the vendor developer innovate in relationships and what can be got from the external services market; technical fixers, relationship builders, and contract facilitators achieve micro-innovations in operational issues. However, as we established in chapter 6 and will reiterate in chapter 8, organizations still need to make major shifts if they are to harness major innovations from technology/cloud service suppliers. Following on from chapter 3, where we spoke of creativity from a service perspective, our own work shows that four fundamental practices underpin effective collaborative innovation and the deeper the collaboration the more organizations can deliver not just IT-operational, but also business process and strategic innovations.[40]

Leading shapes and conditions – in fact sets up – the collaborative ethos and environment. Business and technology leaders signal through commitments, incentives, and risk mitigation the joint exploitation of opportunities. These need to be imbedded in forms of **contracting** that specify how risks and rewards provide incentives for innovation, collaboration and high performance to achieve common goals. At the same time, **organizing** for innovation requires more co-managed governance structures and greater multifunctional team working across the collaborating organizations. Technical work requiring the application of existing specialist know-how and techniques can be outsourced relatively safely, assuming competent specialists can be hired. But as more work becomes 'adaptive'[41] – as reflected in moves to agile cloud development mentioned above – more multiple stakeholders need to be engaged with defining the problem and working together on arriving at and implementing a solution. Team working now requires the ability to collaborate within a client organization, between client and supplier, and between suppliers in multi-supplier environments. Organizing for collaboration also means assigning responsibility for delivering results. These three shifts in leading, contracting, and organizing enable the collective delivery of high performance, innovation, and superior business outcomes. But **performance** is only possible where high personal, competence-based, and motivational trust has been generated amongst the parties. High trust is a key element and shaper of successful collaboration, which requires the client–supplier relationship to be open, based on learning, adaptive, flexible, and interdependent. Performing as trusted partners is a key component for collaborative innovation. Although studies have noted that there is no such thing as instant trust in outsourcing, it can be built over time through demonstrable performance.

The 'Evolution-with-cloud' Challenge. Technology functions have been evolving over the last two decades and figure 7.5 captures the phases they tend to go through. After an initial period of uncontrolled and increasingly costly and dysfunctional IT proliferation (e.g. no synergies or economies of scale), a 'delivery' phase of developing internal capability and control ensues. At this stage, the IT executive needs to focus on building the reality of technical and service compe-tence, while ensuring that business managers get a correct perception of improvements in IT performance. Building IT know-how and capability is vital during this stage. Particularly important here are contract facilitation, architectural planning, and technical fixing capa-bilities. Given the learning needed and the lack of skills in managing external suppliers, buying-in of external resources as needed is the

FIGURE 7.5 ▎**Back-Office Evolution: From Technology to Cloud and Digital Business**

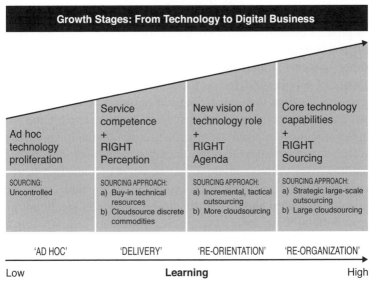

Growth Stages: From Technology to Digital Business			
Ad hoc technology proliferation	Service competence + RIGHT Perception	New vision of technology role + RIGHT Agenda	Core technology capabilities + RIGHT Sourcing
SOURCING: Uncontrolled	SOURCING APPROACH: a) Buy-in technical resources b) Cloudsource discrete commodities	SOURCING APPROACH: a) Incremental, tactical outsourcing b) More cloudsourcing	SOURCING APPROACH: a) Strategic large-scale outsourcing b) Large cloudsourcing
'AD HOC'	'DELIVERY'	'RE-ORIENTATION'	'RE-ORGANIZATION'
Low		Learning	High

Source: adapted from Willcocks, Cullen and Craig (2011) *The Outsourcing Enterprise* (Palgrave).

better sourcing approach. With the delivery phase accomplished and providing a reliable platform, a 'reorientation' phase sees the business units needing to become more pro-active in leveraging technology strategically for business purpose, while the technology staff need to become more business-focused. The CIO, with the help of senior business executives, will need to provide active leadership to achieve these objectives. Relationship building, business systems thinking, and contract monitoring need particular attention and development in this phase. The lack of internal capability to manage large-scale outsourcing points to incremental use of the external IT (and cloud) services markets.

With 'delivery' and 'reorientation' accomplished, the organization can then embark on 'reorganization.' With IT and business closely aligned and business managers mature in their ability to fulfill their roles in leveraging IT for strategic purpose, including on innovation and change projects, many IT roles can be devolved to the business units. Meanwhile, the IT function can complete its move to a high-performing core capabilities model. Large-scale outsourcing (and cloud sourcing) becomes much less risky and the strategic payoffs more likely.

This phase model provides good 'stop, think, act' ammunition because it has several large implications for cloud, and cloud supplier, adoption. As we have seen with IT outsourcing (ITO) and business process outsourcing (BPO), a maturing ability with one type of service (ITO) rarely translates into the same level of competence with another, however similar (BPO). There is also the issue of the relative maturity of suppliers to deliver the specific technology and service. Figure 7.5 suggests that managers need to pinpoint their maturity as a technology function and business. They can then use the model to pinpoint the most appropriate cloudsourcing approach. Our present research suggests that, with a few exceptions, in-house will be early to middle in the delivery phase. If so, the client organization needs to revisit building in-house capability over the three phases, in the role sequence suggested above, but this time specifically for cloud. This begins with building service competence for cloud. This is where the centers of excellence concept fits:

> The centers of excellence idea is that you pull in from across your IT organization the skilled individuals and give them some slack and scale to deliver whatever you need in cloud. ... then that will grow and then

you will start to think strategically about how your IT organization is going to change and how governance needs to change in your business and IT organization. (Matthew Coates, Accenture)

At the delivery stage, it is viable to outsource to the cloud what we call 'discrete commodities.' Cloud examples include data storage, email, and indeed the media is full of such examples. But cloud learning is key, so buying in resources from suppliers and consulting firms to work on issues and projects the internal group manages is an important capability-building process. Our research suggests that the massive pressure from the business to deliver on cloud's potential should be resisted, until both the technology function and the business units are well into the cloud re-orientation phase. The business potential of cloud is delivered when internal cloud capabilities map onto the re-organization phase. At that stage, the CIO is likely to be a business innovator, with the role of chief technology officer or architect being enhanced to manage the strategic technical capability of the organization. CIO Sanjay Mirchandani gives insight into this evolution process from an internal EMC perspective:

> The business pressure on a CIO today is not 'Can this be done?'; it's 'How fast we can we get this done?' The compression in expectation is phenomenal. … I think most companies of our size will go through similar stages: the low-hanging fruit, the stuff IT owns, R&D, QA systems, test systems, and then you move into mission-critical business [and] critical business supporting systems and then you can get more ambitious and say, 'Okay, how can I provide most of the stuff in a self-service model, remembering that the bulk of the users in a hi-tech company like EMC are technical?' Plus or minus, I think this is the journey that most companies will take.[42]

CONCLUSION

Against the building momentum on cloud we have heard many practitioner voices sounding cautionary notes. For example:

> Large organizations are not going to speedily move their IT estate to software-as-a-service solutions because they have so much legacy background.

And in supply chain- and customer-facing organizations their IT systems have become very complicated, highly automated, and close knit … you cannot just grab a bit of it and put it out to the cloud.[43]

Very few things are going to be 100 percent cloud. Like any wave of computing, it doesn't replace the others; it goes on top.'[44]

One CIO, Frank Modruson, suggested that consumers will move faster to the newer technologies, followed by SMEs: '[As f]or large organizations, we'll talk about it for a while longer, then it will show up faster than we realize … not completely, not exactly the way we might anticipate and with some inertia.'[45]

IaaS may be a better stepping stone allowing organizations to take early advantage of cloud services. People without IT legacy may well go straight to the cloud, while SMEs are moving more swiftly into SaaS. But whatever the emerging pattern of take-up and speed, cloud represents a potential crossing point from one type of organization to quite another. Technology has been and continues to be a huge burden on organizations. Our research for this book found time and again that it takes a huge amount of effort to make technology work. Technology has, to a considerable extent, blinded people to what the real purpose of the technology function was. The more technology gets moved out of the way – into the cloud and/or supplier – the more the technology function can focus upon the real job, which is how to exploit for business purpose the capability that the technologies happen to make available. Primarily, this will lie in a combination of service (as we pointed out in chapter 3), information, management, business analytics, IT-enabled business innovation, and digital business. In this chapter we have provided a management road map for this journey, which, our research suggests, is feasible and which it would be enormously wasteful to miss.

CHAPTER 8

Cloud Futures: Changing the Form of Organization

INTRODUCTION

The previous chapter discussed developing the retained organization, suggesting ways forward for managing, harnessing, and capitalizing on cloud computing. What was not addressed, however, was whether in practice wholesale new forms of organization will emerge, harnessing cloud computing and challenging incumbents and existing players in their marketplaces. An influential paper by Erik Brynjolfsson and colleagues at MIT written in 2010 hinted that we cannot consider cloud purely in relation to old organizational forms: 'Computing is still in the midst of an explosion of innovation and co-invention. Those that simply replace corporate resources with cloud computing, while changing nothing else, are doomed to miss the full benefits of the new technology.'[1] This chapter considers the extent to which the benefits of cloud computing may reshape organizations themselves. The chapter leaves behind comparisons with existing data center and outsourcing arrangements, focusing instead on the potentially disruptive innovation cloud computing is likely to cause over the longer term.

At its heart the introduction of cloud computing shifts the way that business applications are delivered within the enterprise. Whereas previously they were held within the organization, with cloud computing they are located 'elsewhere' and accessed via the Internet (traditionally represented as a cloud in computer network diagrams[2]).

On this basis, cloud computing is often represented as in figure 8.1, suggesting that the organization remains static (a box) and accesses computing services from the Internet (represented as the cloud). This 'computer science' view overplays the technical architecture of the network and subsequently underplays the determinism this arrangement has on the organization. The implication is that an organization remains unaffected by this system – it is simply outsourcing its IT capability.

FIGURE 8.1 ▎ **The Traditional View of Cloud Computing**

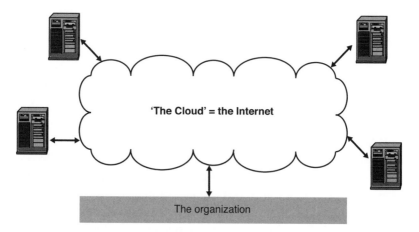

Yet thinking further about the organization in the diagram, it becomes clear that this view is problematic. An organization, at its most basic level, is a messy mix of people, technology, and practices (i.e. ways of doing things). Representing organizations as a box separate from technology underplays the complexity of this 'mess.' While in the past the factory gates might have clearly defined the boundary for this 'box,' for most organizations today this is a poor representation. Taking organizations as a mix of technology, people, and practices suggests that changes in the technological arrangements fundamentally alter what the organization is. For some industries this is obvious (for example, television was completely changed by the invention of video tape and, later, digital production, and similarly telecommunications by the mobile telephone). For others it is more subtle.

We therefore need to think carefully about how organizations might be changed by cloud computing. In undertaking such an analysis we consider two alternative theoretical perspectives – technological determinism and social constructionism,[3] which will help us isolate and understand the change that may occur.

Technological determinism is the view that organizations are directly changed by the introduction of new technology. Technology determines the path the organization will take, and we should understand technology in order to understand its potential impact on the organization. While few would adopt the phrase, this assumption is widely held: consider most corporate purchasing decisions for IT, in which it is argued that the IT *will* improve things.

Social constructionism is a more subtle way of understanding the potential of cloud computing. It is based on the observation that what technology is *in its use*, is not inherent to the technology itself but entwined with the social and political context in which it is introduced. While a new technology might have attributes that its designers intended to be used in specific ways, it is only *in use* by a group of people that its actual form and function arrive. The use of SMS messages on mobile phones might be an example of this – they were designed as debugging tools, which its designers did not consider important, but in society, in particular among the group of European young people unable to afford phone call charges, they emerged as the dominant use for the mobile phone.[4] Indeed, these young people *interpreted* the mobile as a device for SMS rather than as a type of telephone (as the designers might have intended). At this point, obviously, designers, observing the social construction of the SMS-focused mobile telephone, began to design these devices to reflect this change – the SMS was no longer relegated to a lowly position within menus, and mobile keyboards were redesigned for 'texting.' The technology was thus led by its use and, in particular, by how it was socially constructed in use. These two sides of the analysis thus form a whole in which we examine the potential impact of cloud computing on enterprises.

Drawing upon these two perspectives simultaneously, within the remainder of this chapter we open out our analysis to consider the macro impact cloud computing might have on public and private enterprises. The chapter contrasts how cloud computing might change the organizational form through strategic decisions under the control of the chief executive's team and based on a technological determinism perspective, with a social constructionist perspective exploring how cloud can change the organization whatever the chief executive might initiate. In particular, we isolate six ways that cloud computing can change organizations. These are:

- The organization is changed through increased collaboration with stakeholders

- The organization is changed through the adoption of new forms of IT capability within the organization

- The organization is changed as the socially constructed boundary between work and home is blurred

- The IT department is reinterpreted as a result of cloud computing, altering the strategic direction of the organization

- The organization is changed by the actions of external parties harnessing cloud computing

- The organization is changed through the integration of IT systems with the wider value network.

The six changes together enable a new form of organization to emerge; when the organization is a business entity, we call it a 'cloud corporation.' The chapter thus concludes by bringing together the technologically deterministic and socially constructed analyses to define what we mean by a cloud corporation.

SIX WAYS CLOUD WILL CHANGE THE ORGANIZATION

1 The organization is changed through increased collaboration with stakeholders

Prior to cloud computing the general assumption of corporate IT was that it would (for the most part) remain within an organizational firewall. For the employee this firewall acted as the factory gates described above, demarcating the activity that occurred within the organization ('work') from activity that occurred outside the organization (non-work). Similarly, for the IT department the firewall marked the border of the organization and needed to be strictly maintained and secured. While for many organizations the physical factory gates had gone and employees could work from multiple locations and collaborate with stakeholders outside the office (e.g. at a coffeehouse, business conference, or client's office), this electronic firewall continued to act as the 'gates,' inhibiting electronic collaboration and mobile working and demarcating work done 'within' the organization.

Introducing cloud computing involves moving computing outside this firewall, in effect dismantling the firewall and enabling much richer collaboration with various stakeholders. This is not to discount the significant security implications of cloud (see chapter 4), but rather to highlight that such security decisions can be made on an application-by-application basis, rather than as a blanket assumption.

Consider, for example, the salesman meeting a customer over coffee. At present it is often the salesman's decision which internal documents he can share with customers – often through e-mail or printouts used for such meetings. Cloud computing might enable him to actually share the live documents from within the organization's document repository, ensuring that the customer remains up to date and perhaps even allowing them to engage in a conversation with the reports' author as the report is developed further. In a similar example, McAfee[5] recounts how global contractor Balfour Beatty used cloud services to allow the instant sharing of photos, blueprints, and documents with a range of stakeholders, including customers, inspectors, contractors, etc., without having to make complex security changes to a standard firewall.

Such sharing blurs the demarcation between the organization and the stakeholder – with points of controlled collaboration (rather than secrecy) marking the organization's boundary. The organization's edge thus becomes more amorphous and less distinct, allowing the organization to capitalize on the expertise of these stakeholders directly and to improve communication with those stakeholders.

Over time, one can imagine a complex web of relationships emerging as organizations increasingly collaborate on specific information functions. The organization's boundary is less distinct as these information flows change. Furthermore, a class of employees may emerge whose role sits increasingly between organizations, mediating between them as they negotiate their increasingly interconnected relationships to mutual benefit.

This impact is perhaps most profound through the impact of social media on organizations. Far from being reserved for consumer interaction, these cloud-based services have become central to both internal communications and external customer relations for many enterprises. Indeed, McKinsey consultants believe that social media (or the social matrix, as they described it) are 'becoming a ... key piece of organizational infrastructure that links and engages employees, customers and suppliers as never before.'[6] While many organizations currently rely on e-mail as their communication platforms, others, for example Atos (an IT services supplier), have pledged to entirely replace these with social-networking platforms in a desire to improve productivity.

Within organizations, social media are a natural extension to knowledge management systems, which focused on developing a sense of community and collaboration among employees.[7] They allow employees to share information, follow the actions of others, and develop communities of practice.[8] However, where they are based on cloud computing, they can extend beyond the organizational boundary to allow collaboration with stakeholders and customers. Media companies, retailers, and brand-based companies have already harnessed social media in developing their PR and marketing activity. For example, Walmart exploits social media to identify weekly promotions and TV producer RTL to fine tune television plots based on feedback.

One of the concerns of the corporate use of social media, however, is that these cloud-based services for organizations are very similar to personal social-networking services (they may even be the same). This may cause confusion for individuals wrestling to understand their relationship with the organization and the appropriate behavior toward it. As technology such as cloud blurs the boundary of organizations, it is beholden upon employees to maintain this boundary in their social media interaction – and the media are full of stories where employees have failed in this task, to the detriment of their company's brand.

2 The organization is changed through the adoption of new forms of IT capability within the organization

Another example of the blurring of the organizational boundary can be seen in the harnessing of cloud-computing services to develop new forms of information services for use within the organization. For example, using Dropbox to support department file-sharing among the employees of an SME, or integrating Google Maps to enhance the information services of the logistics department. While these may be small innovations in themselves, when combined they can lead to significant changes in the way a business operates and develops. In chapter 6, Avon (the cosmetics company) provided an interesting example of this blurring as cloud services were harnessed to reshape its internal processes. Let us look at it in more detail, as Avon shows what can happen when corporations collaborate using emerging standards to achieve integration of cloud services.

As a leading global beauty company with more than 100,000 sales leaders and millions of representatives worldwide, Avon runs regular campaigns, but reports on these were typically received too late to affect current sales activity. A single standardized platform and reporting function was needed to support global campaigns, but these needed to interact seamlessly with existing technologies and Internet portals. Avon therefore evolved onto a SalesForce.com platform that was integrated with Avon's own data-warehousing platform. Successful pilots and deployments were run out in 2009–2010 across more than ten countries. There is now a twice-daily information flow from order transactions through the data warehouse to the SalesForce.com portal, supported by easy-to-use interfaces customized to be consistent with the Avon look and feel. There is also seamless integration with Avon's Web portal, with single sign-on, making it easy for sales leaders to access all the information they need in one place. Mobile access was planned and is being enacted. Business performance has also been enhanced in a number of ways. Sales leaders can act quickly on exception-driven information, maximize their earnings, and drive Avon's revenue growth. Standard business processes and performance metrics help control and efficiency worldwide. The easy-to-use system attracts recruits and increases retention levels.

Avon goes further in blurring its organizational boundary. It exploits a Facebook application to allow its sales leaders to socially network. As Jim Rivera of SalesForce.com described:

> Avon did a fascinating thing where they built a Facebook application on [the SalesForce] platform and on the Facebook platform and … just plugged in external applications … They built this custom application to help manage their network of Avon ladies within Facebook. So now, as an employee of Avon, as an Avon Lady, all I do is sign into Facebook. You get all the promotions coming to you. You're understanding what the new products are, what things you should be pushing and then, within the same application, you turn around and you start to push that out into your network. And it's amazing. So they've actually used that as their portal for their sales people in Facebook.

Here, Avon's sales and marketing business processes extend into Facebook and through that into the social networks of their customers. Their processes have moved outside the traditional organizational boundary to create amorphous collaborations, through sales leaders, with customers and their social networks.

Another example of the harnessing of cloud computing is presented by Newgrove. Newgrove specializes in providing easy-to-use geospatial business intelligence dashboards to large enterprises, enabling them to make better decisions in near real time. Businesses come to Newgrove to gain better understanding of their own business. By providing them with certain corporate information (e.g. the location and business traffic of a retailer's stores, whether digital or physical), Newgrove harnesses its proprietary software (running on a PaaS – Microsoft Azure) to present information for decision-making on a Google Maps interface. The company's staff can then make decisions by looking at the information presented on a map via any device connected to the Internet. The value of Newgrove's service is in enabling the integration of huge amounts of information – potentially from different suppliers – thus developing a cloud-based business that provides valuable information services. The employees using the service are likely unaware that it is external to the organization's other systems.

Like many other cloud companies, Newgrove's business is integrating ('mashing up,' as it is known) the cloud services of others

to add value. Newgrove is thus reliant on the services of others –
and, as the technical director explained, 'you've got to make sure
you are picking your service providers very, very carefully.' Indeed,
Newgrove spends considerable time developing relationships with
its cloud suppliers – while acknowledging that it cannot change the
service levels or offering of the large cloud computing suppliers upon
which its services rely:

> It's a standard SLA and it works across the world in all [the suppliers'] data
> centers. They are not going to change it, or they're certainly not going to
> change it for anything less than £100,000 in legal fees … It's take it or leave
> it, which is quite nice in some ways because, you know, you don't have to
> worry about it. It's not a decision to be made … We can't offer a better
> SLA than the SLA that we're getting from them. We simply pass on the SLA
> to our clients. (Senior executive, Newgrove, interviewed May 25, 2013.)

It is, however, this mashing-up of others' services that allows a small
company with a dozen developers to provide a robust and easy-to-use
geospatial information service to blue-chip clients globally.

3 The organization is changed as the socially constructed boundary between work and home is blurred

We now consider cloud computing's impact on employment itself
and on the social construction of the organization for its employees.

As organizational IT leaves the confines of the corporate firewall,
it becomes easier to access from outside organizational offices. This
is particularly risky around the phenomenon of 'bring-your-own
devices' (BYOD), where IT departments are under pressure to accept
employees' use of their own mobile phones, tablets, and laptops,
which are shared between both work-life and home-life activities.
These devices can then be used for a range of enterprise and consumer
cloud services to be used for work – some provided by the employer,
others signed up for by the individual (the so called 'buy-your-own
device'). Using their own tablet PC will perhaps, for these people,
suggest that their organization is a more amorphous phenomenon, less
defined and precise. The activity of work is defined more by what is

done than by specific technological artefacts or arrangements. Where entering the factory gates might have previously defined the point at which the citizen became an employee, with BYOD it is the employee who must interpret which activity is as employee and which is as citizen. The employee must, as they pick up their device, interpret whether they are 'at work' or 'at leisure.' This defines where, when, and how the boundary of the organization is managed and controlled. The organization itself is socially constructed in the act of working. This may prove particularly problematic as employees find it difficult to define the important barrier between social and work lives when the technologies used for both are similar or even the same.

Customers of corporations can become similarly confused. Where traditionally a company might be judged by the luxury of its premises, the smartness of its stationery, and the uniform of its employees, cloud computing allows organizations of all types (including the nefarious) to appear similar. Websites, online payments, video-conferencing systems, customer relationship management, advanced telephone services are all available to anyone with an Internet connection and a credit card.

However, as one example of the possibilities already being made real, consider the development of what Kaganer et al. have called 'the human cloud.'[9] The authors cite a small media company, Rief Media, run out of Newport Beach, U.S.A., and Aegon, a life insurance multinational. Rief Media has a 14-person workforce scattered around the world, all independent contractors hired through an online service called oDesk. Aegon has an on-demand workforce of 300 licensed virtual agents managed through online intermediary LiveOps. These are not Aegon employees but they are scheduled for inbound and outbound calling through LiveOps' routing software. The human cloud, as described by the researchers, is centered on an online middleman who engages a pool of virtual workers who can be tapped on demand to provide a wide range of services to any interested buyer. Jobs as at 2013 typically involved content generation, sales and marketing, and design and optimization, but 2013 industry reports cited 15 other work categories being performed including research and development, translation, idea generation, Internet search and business analytics, and customer support. The authors counted some 100 active platforms in 2012, up from 40 in 2011. Clearly, while the notion of a flexible contracted workforce is not new, cloud greatly accelerates the possibilities.

4 The IT department is reinterpreted as a result of cloud computing, altering the strategic direction of the organization

Perhaps the most significant reinterpretation of computing may happen to the computing department itself. We met this before (in chapter 7), but it is an issue worth revisiting. Nicholas Carr influentially argued that:

> In the long run the IT department is unlikely to survive, at least not in its familiar form. It will have little left to do once the bulk of business computing shifts out of private data-centres and into 'the cloud'. Business units and even individual employees will be able to control the processing of information directly, without the legions of technical specialists.[10]

While chapter 7 addressed the issue of skills and retained capability (challenging Carr's assumptions), it is the change such a view brings to the social construction of the IT department itself that we discuss here.

The general management assumption of cloud seems to chime with Carr's sentiment, and cloud computing is thus interpreted as signaling the death knell for IT departments (or at least much of their skill). The IT department is thus interpreted as having much to fear from cloud and, on this scenario, for them to support cloud would be, as one interviewee put it, 'like turkeys voting for Christmas.' This is problematic, as it reinterprets the role of IT within the organization and challenges its involvement in the strategic direction IT takes. If IT is assumed to have a vested interest in challenging cloud, then its analysis of the pros and cons is likely to be somewhat biased. Furthermore, many senior executives, aware of the huge cost IT often represents to organizations, will likely interpret cloud computing as something of even greater benefit. These forces together may lead to an overly positive analysis of cloud at boardroom level. The IT department is thus increasingly socially constructed as a disabler rather than enabler of IT innovation. Indeed, it is this exact sentiment that one famous cloud computing SaaS vendor tapped into in advertising 'No software'[11] and suggesting its staff should circumvent the IT director.

The problem with this social construction of IT is that one of the significant roles of IT departments is to manage the strategic direction of IT within the whole organization. The more they are isolated (or seen to be isolated) from that strategy the harder it is for them to adopt (and be seen to adopt) a rational, overarching view, and the easier it is for each separate part of the organization to adopt its own IT strategy – perhaps by harnessing SaaS specifically targeted at its domain. An organization could quickly become challenged by the disparate cloud computing adoptions across the organization – particularly as signing up for many of these SaaS services requires little more than a credit card. For this reason, the social construction of the IT department and the social construction of the IT strategy are important and should be carefully managed. Nicholas Carr may have unwittingly (or perhaps deliberately) played to the wish lists of the senior executives of corporations and, by offering the vision of the 'hollowed-out' IT department, created the circumstances in which they socially constructed this as the IT future. Our own work and Matthew Coates's comments in the Preface suggest that this would be a simplistic and dangerous interpretation to place on the future direction of IT functions.

5 The organization is changed by the actions of external parties harnessing cloud computing

All the above discussion focused on how internal decisions to adopt cloud computing could alter the organization either deterministically (through the changes it wrought) or through its social construction of other aspects of the organization. Yet even for organizations that avoid the adoption of cloud computing, its impact can be felt and they too can face change despite the adoption of cloud being ostensibly outside their perceived citadel. These final two sections therefore consider how cloud-computing adoption outside the organization can deterministically alter the organization itself. We then consider the impact of (and inhibitors to) this change. We begin by considering how an organization can be directly changed by its stakeholders' adoption of cloud computing technology. This is perhaps most obviously demonstrated by the case of Sukey.org.

In January 2011, the streets of London echoed to the sound of students campaigning against the imposition of tuition fees. Tens of thousands poured into the streets to make their voices heard and the police, desperate to avoid the vandalism and violence of a protest in November the year before, attempted to use a 'kettling' technique.

Kettling involves the police confining the demonstrators into a small area such as a square. Once they are trapped, the police simply wait – containing the demonstrators until they are tired and hungry and just want to go home. The police's ability to kettle students thus requires coordination in encircling the demonstrators – for which they rely on sophisticated (and expensive) communications infrastructure involving radios, control centers, and helicopters (within their organizational firewall).

But at this protest, some of the students had installed a smartphone application called 'Sukey,' created by integrating (mashing up) a number of cloud-based services.[12] Why Sukey.org? The app's name comes from an English nursery rhyme:

Polly put the kettle on,
Polly put the kettle on,
Polly put the kettle on,
We'll all have tea.

Sukey take it off again,
Sukey take it off again,
Sukey take it off again,
They've all gone away.
(as recounted in Charles Dickens' *Barnaby Rudge*)

Sukey.org used social media to allow those on the ground to report the movements of protestors and police through Twitter and other social networks. These reports were then catalogued on a Google Map accessible by protestors using their smartphones. The application (built quickly by a small number of students) harnessed cloud computing and the mobile phone infrastructure to provide the protestors with a sophisticated information system similar to that of the police. This system was believed to limit the ability of the police to kettle the protestors – as they quickly moved through side streets to avoid the police cordons.

This example shows how the police force was challenged and its abilities constrained by a small group harnessing the 'cloud' despite the police's investment in advanced information and communications technology. This shows that the availability of cloud computing deterministically altered what it is to police a demonstration, despite the fact that the police had not changed their own infrastructure. It shows how organizational boundaries can become blurred as a consequence of outside action. Consider how such blurring has already occurred, for example with Kodak and digital photography, HMV (a U.K. music retail company) and Apple's iTunes, Blockbuster video rental and online movie rental and download, and in the book industry with Amazon's Kindle, and others.

6 The organization is changed through the integration of IT systems with the wider value network

Perhaps the most significant change we anticipate cloud computing bringing will be the detailed workflow collaboration that can emerge to create business processes spanning multiple organizations through cloud services. In this way, the value networks that exist between organizations (for example as a cleaning company adds value to a hotel chain in ensuring that its rooms are clean, or a logistics company adds value to a retailer by enabling online sales). However, for many companies such value-addition is limited by the inability to integrate IT systems effectively.

However, why couldn't air crash investigators have limited collaborative access to the simulation systems of airline manufacturers to aid their investigations, facilitated by the locating of such systems in the cloud? Could pharmaceutical companies manufacture more effective and profitable drugs if they were able to share limited parts of their databases with other stakeholders in the manufacturing process easily – or even with doctors and prescribers? While such integration has been possible with existing systems, it has required complex technical arrangements to connect through the firewalls of partners – often at considerable cost. Cloud computing opens up the possibility of such collaboration and makes it easier to achieve (increasing both opportunity and risk).

Understanding the likely impact of cloud computing on value networks demands understanding of how technology can change organizations and redesign industries. We can see examples of such changes in history. In his influential book *The Box* Marc Levinson recounts the history of the shipping container, detailing how the shipping industry's innovation transformed the way raw materials were carried.[13] Prior to 'containerization,' ships carried break-bulk cargo that was man-handled through complex port facilities with inefficient repackaging at each stage. Containerization, through standardizing the way cargo was packaged and controlled, transformed global supply chains for products – allowing the world to be, to use Thomas Friedman's metaphor, 'flattened.'[14] The cost of goods was driven down by a simple, standardized, and organized process of shipping that allowed new practices to emerge and blurred the boundaries of the organizations involved (as they were able to easily collaborate – for example, a haulage company could easily pick up loads from a shipping company).

If based on a similar standardization, cloud computing could offer a similar advantage for information to that which the shipping container offered for transported goods – allowing a standardized and organized approach to IT that extends beyond the enterprise and drastically reduces friction in the global information supply chain in the way containerization reduced friction in the physical supply chain.

At the time of writing, cloud computing reflects the early stages of a similar transition, with the existence of both old and new forms of 'shipping lines' – services separated by incompatible standards. We anticipate that in the future cloud computing will evolve to provide standardized interfaces[15] between applications, which will allow a digital workflow to be constructed that transcends organizational boundaries and thus enable new forms of organizing to emerge, to the benefit of all. This standardization would be driven by cloud facilitating smaller software companies to compete. This will see the large enterprise software space (dominated by existing suppliers) being challenged by the careful integration of smaller 'apps' from smaller software houses capitalizing on cloud for their delivery.

Standardization would also benefit the financial models of these smaller software businesses.

Such standardization, however, requires a significant amount of work. Most cloud computing offerings in 2013 are far from standardized, as the current incumbents seek to ensure that their systems become the standard. At present and without accepted standards, companies must choose between different cloud providers without an easy way to transition between them. We envisage, however, a significant growth in cloud computing demand, which will create an installed base and drive standards adoption. It is at this point that we envisage cloud computing forming the collaborative infrastructure to integrate IT workflows in the same way that the shipping container allowed global logistics to integrate manufacturing workflows and create the just-in-time manufacturing revolution observed in the last 30 years.

Just as the existing client/server PC infrastructure provided the 'new plumbing' for organizations in the 1990s, so we envisage cloud computing providing a new plumbing between organizations in the future. Understanding how and when this will happen, however, requires understanding how IT standards generally emerge. This is the topic of the next section.

THE NEW CLOUD DRIVE: STANDARDS FOR INFRASTRUCTURE

Cloud computing, if widely adopted, will provide the basic IT infrastructure upon which the enterprise relies – with all other IT (laptops, tablets, Internet access) as commodity items. Such infrastructure must be enabling, opening possibilities for new activities rather than simply automating existing activity. Such cloud infrastructure must also be shared with a large community of users capitalizing upon its existence. Providing a pre-installed base forms a core part of the value of infrastructure.[16] Such cloud infrastructure requires integration into individual elements through standardized interfaces and an openness such that there are no limits to the number of users, vendors, and stakeholders who may use it.

A significant amount of research has been undertaken on how IT standards for such infrastructure emerge. If cloud computing is to form the core IT infrastructure of future organizations, then it is vital that we understand how cloud standards might emerge. The economics of standards are, according to Hanseth, 'increasing returns and positive feedback, network externalities, path dependency and installed base':[17]

- **Increasing returns and positive feedback:** The greater the number of people who use a cloud computing service, the more value they gain. This creates a positive feedback loop whereby the greater the number of people who adopt a standard cloud service, the more likely the standard will be adopted by other people.

- **Network externalities:** The value of the cloud standard depends upon the number of people who have adopted that standard.

- **Path dependency:** A cloud standard is based on its historical development, and past events can have a large impact on its future development. For example, the demand for mechanical typewriters that do not jam dictated the placement of the keys on the standard QWERTY computer keyboard. Following the same logic, the decisions being made now about the adoption of cloud may have long-lasting ramifications.

- **Installed base:** As a standard emerges, so does an installed base of users who have adopted the emerging standard. These users face lock-in due to the switching costs incurred if they rejected the standard at this point.

As cloud standards emerge, achieving a balance between locking in existing users (and thus maintaining the installed base) and opening up the standard to draw in other users (and thus increasing the installed base) that will be the key to success. During this period, new users are desperately trying to identify the likely successful cloud standards. Hanseth describes the importance of what he terms 'blind giants' in such standardization effort.[18] These are huge organizations and governments whose early-adoption decisions have significant implications for the standards trajectory due to their scale, but who are 'blind,' as they must make decisions about adoption when the information about the standard is lacking (i.e. prior to its adoption by other such large organizations).

For cloud computing, this process of standardization is already under way and organizations that are going to capitalize on the future with cloud must follow the standardization process carefully. In particular, the adoption of cloud computing by governments will be significant.

A CLOUD WITHOUT STANDARDS – A RETURN TO THE 1980S?

To understand the likely impact of such standardization we can look back at how existing IT standards emerged. In particular, we can look at the lessons learned from the PC since the 1980s (see chapter 1).

For Vint Cerf,[19] the father of the Internet, cloud computing represents a return to the days of the mainframe, when service bureaus rented their machines by the hour to companies, who used them for payroll and other similar tasks. Such comparisons focus on the architectural similarities between centralized mainframes and cloud computing – cheaply connecting to an expensive resource 'as a service' through a network. But cloud is more about the provision of lower cost computing. A better analogy than the mainframe, then, is the introduction of the humble micro-computer and the revolution it brought to corporate computing in the early 1980s.

When micro-computers were launched, many companies were using mini or mainframe computers, which were cumbersome and expensive and needed specialist IT staff to manage them.[20] Like cloud computing today, when compared with these existing computers the new micros offered ease of use, low cost, and apparently low risk, which appealed to business executives seeking to cut costs, or unable to afford minis or mainframes.[21] Usage exploded and in the period from the launch of the IBM PC in 1981 to 1984 the proportion of companies using PCs increased dramatically from 8 percent to nearly 100 percent as the value and potential of the micro became apparent.[22] Again, as with the cloud,[23] micro-computers were marketed directly to business executives rather than IT staff and were accompanied by a narrative that they would enable companies to dispense with heavy mainframes and the IT department for many tasks – doing them quicker and more effectively. Surveys from that time suggested accessibility, speed of implementation, response time, independence, and self-development were the major advantages of the PC over the mainframe[24] – easily recognizable in the hyperbole surrounding cloud services today. Indeed, Nicholas Carr's 2005 pronouncement of the end of corporate IT[25] would probably have resonated equally well in the early 1980s, when the micro looked set to replace the need for corporate IT. Indeed, in 1980 over half the companies in a sample taken by Guimaraes and Ramaujam claimed no IT department involvement in the acquisition of PCs.[26] But problems emerged from the wholesale uncontrolled adoption of the micro and by 1984 only 2 percent of those sampled did not involve the IT department in PC acquisition. The proliferation of PCs meant that in 1980 as many as 32 percent of IT managers were unable to estimate the proportion of PCs within their company and few could provide any useful support for those who had purchased them.[27]

Micros ultimately proved cheap individually but expensive en masse[28] as their use exploded and new applications for them were discovered. In addition to the increased use, IT professionals worried about lack of documentation (and thus poor opportunity for maintenance), poor data management strategies, and security issues.[29] New applications proved incompatible with others – what has been called 'the time-bomb of incompatibility' – and different system platforms (e.g. CP/M, UNIX, MS-DOS, OS/2, Atari, Apple …) led to redundancy and communication difficulties between services and to the failure of many apparently unstoppable software providers – household names at the time, such as Lotus, Digital-Research, WordStar, VisiCalc, and dBase.[30]

Ultimately, it was the IT department that brought sense to these machines and began to connect them together for useful work using compatible applications – with the emergence of companies such as Novell and Microsoft to bring order to the chaos.[31]

Lessons can be drawn from this history for cloud computing. Clearly, the strategic involvement of IT services departments is required. Such involvement should focus not on the current cost-saving benefits of the cloud, but on the strategic management of the potentially escalating use of cloud services within the firm. IT services must get involved in the narrative surrounding the cloud – ensuring that their message is neither overly negative (and thus making it appear that they have a vested interest in the status quo) nor overly optimistic, as potential problems exist. Either way, the lessons of the micro-computer are relevant again today. Indeed, Keen and Woodman argued in 1984 that companies needed the following four strategies for the micro:

1. Coordination rather than control of the introduction.

2. Focusing on the longer-term technical architecture for the company's overall computing resources, with personal computers as one component.

3. Defining codes for good practice that adapt the proven disciplines of the IT industry into the new context.

4. Emphasis on systematic business justification, even of the 'soft and unquantifiable benefits that are often a major incentive for and payoff of using personal computers.'[32]

It would be wise for companies contemplating a move to the cloud to consider this advice carefully – while, of course, replacing 'personal computer' with 'cloud computing' throughout.

CLOUD COMPUTING BLURS THE BOUNDARY OF THE ORGANIZATION

The six forms of change above suggest that organizations are changed by cloud computing to become more flexible, fluid, and open-ended – particularly at their boundaries. They become more collaborative as cloud computing enables services that break down the boundaries between employees, other organizations, collaborators, and even regulators. As Jim Harris, CIO of Accenture, told us: 'These technologies are enabling companies to do things they never could have imagined before. It changes the financial model of the company. It changes the talent model. It changes just about everything.'

Understanding cloud computing is thus about understanding how the boundary of the organization is altered by changes in the IT arrangements employed. The examples suggest a blurring of boundaries as IT systems integrate and connect organizations together and as employees' work becomes less precisely defined. We have coined the term the 'cloud corporation' to highlight that cloud computing is not about the Internet (see figure 8.1) but rather concerns the way the organization itself can become increasingly 'clouded,' internally and externally, as its boundaries become more amorphous (figure 8.2).

Figure 8.2 ▎ **Blurring the Boundary of the Organization through Cloud Computing**

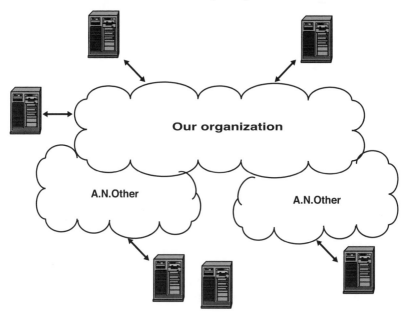

CONCLUSION: THE CLOUD CORPORATION

This chapter has demonstrated how cloud computing can blur the boundaries of organizations and has discussed the potential of standardized information exchange formats to increase the collaboration between organizations. We define the cloud corporation as a natural consequence of these forces.

First, the corporation itself is cloud-like, with ill-defined boundaries. Its technical infrastructure is provided by cloud access devices (simple commodity laptops, tablets, smartphones, printers, etc. – potentially BYOD), each connected to the Internet. As Carr rightly pointed out in 2008, configuring these devices will not require legions of IT specialists, as their role will be simply to interface with services provided from the cloud.[33]

Recall figure 6.3 and let us recap briefly on the constitution and functioning of a cloud corporation. The actual work of the organization will be mediated through business processes provided as a service, which consist of the integrating of large numbers of cloud service components (e.g. storage, resource planning, communications) that provide the information services and are mashed up to produce businesses-processes-as-a-service (BPaaS). These can involve multiple organizations and thus enable the integration of organizations described above. Once in place, the amorphous nature of such BPaaS would allow third parties to be directly integrated within them – accountants, suppliers, regulators, for example. For most organizations, such a change would improve their processes, free IT staff to focus on business strategy, and allow a much easier relationship with suppliers of services. Such a change is an evolution rather than a revolution – what have been termed 'incremental innovations' (see chapter 6) on the existing outsourcing path, albeit with certain 'architectural innovations' that improve processes and technologically advance the organization's business.

For most organizations, the entire interface with the cloud will be through the service components. Such service components themselves rely upon a complex stack of services from other cloud providers who specialize in providing the services needed to develop the cloud service components. At the very bottom of the stack is the hardware and networking upon which the services rely.

These changes will not affect all parts of an enterprise equally. Organizations face the challenge of both responding to new innovations like cloud computing and continuing to exploit their existing business models. As discussed in chapter 6, organizations need to be 'ambidextrous' – that is, they need to balance the diametrically opposed demands of adaptability and alignment.[34] They need to adapt nimbly, harnessing and exploiting the innovative potential of cloud whilst continuing to leverage their existing business models and approaches. This is a hard balancing act and the previous chapter outlined the demands on and remodeling of the skills of IT executives charged with continuing to invest in existing practices while also innovating new practices that may have the potential to limit their role. For, as John Seely Brown reminds us,[35] Nicholas Carr's 2003 pronouncement that 'IT doesn't matter'[36] ignored the fact that each new computing capability creates new possibilities and options that can be exploited for corporate and market – and, indeed, societal – advantage. Carr's 2003 vision was a static one – a sort of 'end of computing' that seems now as out of date as Fukuyama's prediction in 1992 of the 'end of history.'[37] It will be recalled that Fukuyama argued that the universalization of Western liberal democracy signaled the end point of humanity's socio-cultural evolution and the final form of human government. Carr has continually predicted the end of corporate computing and indeed sees the 'big switch' to the Internet, and subsequently cloud, as a further opportunity to accelerate the commodification of corporate IT as a service. But this is 1) to seriously underplay the basis of business competition, where differentiation and mass customization rather than just standardization are perennially key; 2) to seriously misunderstand cloud technologies as an open-ended, ever developing source of differentiation and mass customization; 3) to greatly underestimate the role of learning and building the capability to both implement and exploit these advanced technologies to achieve competitive advantage; and 4) to significantly misjudge the complexity and accelerating development of these technologies and the need for technical specialists in client as well as service organizations – to understand technological trajectories, advise senior business executives, identify the business potential of new technological advances, and manage and leverage their ICT/cloud service suppliers. To add a further point, it also ignores the bigger picture and how cloud will fit with other technologies in the move to creating cloud corporations – and this is the subject of our final chapter.

CHAPTER 9

Conclusion: The Bigger Picture

INTRODUCTION

This final chapter builds upon chapter 8 to look to the future and considers the impact cloud computing is likely to have on society and the economy. In 2007, nobody imagined using a data center on the other side of the world to send a text message or book a calendar appointment. Yet, well before 2013, Apple Siri and Google Now were exploiting cloud computing to provide these services. Here we discuss the social and technological implications of cloud, looking at its potential impact on smart cities, communication, and business. Within this we also note the emergence of other technology trends such as super-low-cost computing (for example, the $10 computer-on-a-chip) and additive manufacturing and explore their potential in shaping the commercial landscape when linked with cloud computing. Essentially, the chapter addresses the question: If computing is in the cloud – what next?

But first, as in chapter 1, we need to give the future of cloud a bigger context. Computing, in its various forms, has proved a disruptive innovation for many industries, including, just as a few examples, photography, music, telephony, and financial services. Cloud computing, as an innovation in computing, is likely to enable similar new forms of disruption. However, what might these be? The McKinsey Global Institute report we mentioned in chapter 1 listed 12 technologies that are anticipated to have significant global implications, of which cloud computing is one. However, of the other 11 we identify 5 that, we believe, have close associations with cloud computing innovation and will be intimately connected with the development of cloud. First, here, we will look at the full list of 12 disruptive technologies; then we will consider in more detail the potential impact of these five innovations and their relationship with cloud computing.

THE BIGGER PICTURE 2014–2025

To give cloud a bigger context, then, a useful starting point is a thoughtful examination by McKinsey Global Institute of the key disruptive technologies for the 2013–2025 period.[1] The study assessed technologies on four main criteria, namely:

- Whether the technology is rapidly advancing or experiencing breakthroughs

- Whether the potential scope of its impact is broad

- Whether economic value could be significantly affected

- Whether its economic impact is potentially disruptive.

On these criteria, the McKinsey Global Institute analysis identified 12 disruptive technologies with the potential, between them, to impact on billions of consumers, hundreds of millions of workers, and trillions of millions of dollars of economic activity across industries. What are these?

- **Mobile Internet access:** increasingly inexpensive and mobile computing devices plus Internet connectivity

- **Automation of knowledge work:** intelligent software systems to perform knowledge work involving unstructured tasks and subtle judgments

- **Internet of things:** networks of low-cost sensors and actuators to collect data, monitor, make decisions, and optimize processes

- **Cloud technology:** hardware and software resources delivered over the Internet or network, often as a service

- **Advanced robotics:** robots with enhanced dexterity, intelligence, and senses to automate tasks or augment humans

- **Autonomous and near-autonomous vehicles:** vehicles navigating and operating with no or reduced human involvement

- **Next-generation genomics:** fast, low-cost gene sequencing, advanced big data analytics, and synthetic biology

- **Energy storage:** devices or systems that store energy for later use, including batteries

- **3D printing:** additive manufacturing techniques to create objects by printing layers of material based on digital models

- **Advanced materials:** with superior characteristics and functionality e.g. strength, weight, conductivity

- **Advanced oil and gas exploration and recovery:** exploration and recovery techniques making unconventional oil and gas extraction economical

- **Renewable energy:** electricity generation for renewable sources with less harmful climate impact

This is an interesting list of technologies with huge potential – indeed, a book could be written about each of them. The report makes a number of observations, with which we can largely agree. ICT is going to be pervasive. Combinations of technologies could multiply impact. Consumers could win big, especially in the long run – something that Moschella supported (see chapter 1). The nature of work will change and millions of people will need new skills – we addressed the corporate implications for changes in the skills base in chapter 7. The future for innovators and entrepreneurs looks bright – though we found in chapter 6 that business innovations will take longer to come through than many have been suggesting. Technology impacts will differ between advanced and developing economies. Benefits of technologies may not be evenly distributed (see chapter 4). The link between hype and potential is not clear – something this book has focused on analyzing and clarifying. Scientific discovery and innovation will surprise us (see chapters 2, 3, and 6, which suggested possible directions). There will be troubling challenges (see also chapters 3, 4, and 5). For example, cloud computing and mobile Internet access could raise quality and productivity in education, health care, and public services. But their benefits are accompanied by rising concerns over security and privacy breaches (something we addressed in chapter 5) and other major challenges (see chapter 4).

What particularly interests us here are *the technologies that are likely to operate in combination with cloud and with each other* to create massive impacts on individuals, organizations, and business, economic, and social life. These are mobile Internet access, the automation of knowledge work, big data, the Internet of things, robotics, and digital fabrication.

MOBILE INTERNET

The mobile phone has become a ubiquitous part of modern life. Even in remote parts of Africa its impact is felt. Alongside keys and money, it is an object considered essential for modern life.[2] However, in the last five years the mobile phone has changed its form considerably, such that the term 'phone,' with its link to sound, seems anachronistic. Hannah, the five-year-old daughter of one of the authors, recently asked her father, 'Why do some phones only do talking? And why do some have a wire?' For her a phone is a magical mobile device for watching films on when stuck in a traffic jam, for taking pictures, and for playing games – talking is secondary.

The integration of the Internet into these smartphones (and similar connected devices such as e-books, GPS navigation systems, hand-held games consoles, and tablet PCs) changes their form and function.[3] They become highly addictive cloud computing connections – 37 percent of adults and a striking 60 percent of teenagers who use smartphones describe themselves as 'highly addicted.'[4]

Significantly, a smartphone is sold incomplete. Its function, meaning, and usage require the installation of 'apps' that harness both the local processing capacity of the phone and cloud computing services. These apps align the device to the usage desired by the user – creating a device that draws the user into interaction with it. One person's smartphone is thus an inherently different device from those of their neighbors. It is not simply 'personalized,' but rather completed by the installation of its apps. Such smartphones are platforms[5] upon which cloud computing sits, platforms that the McKinsey report estimates will have an economic impact worth between $3.7 trillion and $10.8 trillion by 2025.[6]

The key lesson for cloud computing, then, is that these may become the dominant cloud access devices for the cloud corporation's services. One bank we researched in 2013 had already adopted a policy described by its chief operating officer as 'everything possible mobile.' Mobile technologies are injecting cloud computing into social and work practices from which they were previously excluded. Social practices such as meeting friends, checking the weather, booking a taxi, and taking a picture have already been revolutionized to involve cloud computing. Similarly, adding apps to a worker's smartphone can turn it into a corporate CRM device, a stock-checking service, or a staff oversight device and can enable new, more nomadic and mobile, forms of work life.[7]

As new mobile Internet devices emerge, so we envisage new social and work practices evolving – and new cloud computing services being required to service them. Consider, for example, 'Google glass,' which introduces an Internet connection, camera, microphone, speaker, and screen into a pair of glasses. Organizations will 'complete' these incomplete cloud-access devices in different ways. Their use may become required by delivery drivers to video the acceptance of parcels and provide real-time proof of delivery to customers, or to ensure that shop assistants do not steal (or support the theft of) goods or money. Services may be developed to help tour guides remember information. All these mobile Internet devices afford their users portability, connectability, openness (to add applications), and identifiability (to identify people and their location)[8] and thus add a sense of place to the nomadic lifestyle. It will, however, be cloud computing that turns these affordances into new services that will change our organizational and social lives.

Today, mobile Internet access is reshaping organizations, even as we write, by allowing workers increasing mobility and flexibility. As we move forward, cloud computing will be central to whatever 'the mobile Internet' becomes and, with it, whatever work and social practices become. Finally, it is worth remembering that digital Internet penetration is still low (by Western standards) in India and China. These huge markets are likely to be opened up by cheap smartphones – bringing with them apps that create new markets. For example, in

Bangladesh, the Dutch-Bangla Bank Limited (DBBL) gained over 1 million mobile-payment subscribers in its first ten months of operation.

AUTOMATION OF KNOWLEDGE WORK: THE ROLE OF BIG DATA

Traditionally, a significant part of knowledge work was the inference of causality from a limited data set such that decisions could be made. Data was expensive to acquire and required careful knowledge work to exploit. More recently, data have been in abundance – particularly as the Internet and sensors have been providing new sources of data for organizational decision-making. However, until recently, the storage and processing of very large quantities of data could only be achieved by purchasing very large numbers of computer processors. Often only universities, research institutes, and large organizations were able to dedicate the resources needed for such analysis. Through its pay-as-you-go economic model, however, cloud computing allows any organization, or indeed individual, to rent such capacity when needed and at relatively low cost. This offers the opportunity for organizations of all sizes to capitalize upon data and find profitable ways to exploit data they may previously have ignored.

This ability to access the capacity to process data is coupled with a preponderance of opportunities for capturing data through the proliferation of sensors and data-capture devices and through the explosion of data produced by consumers on the Internet. This deluge of data should not be underestimated. In 2013, it was estimated that the amount of stored information in the world was 1200 exabytes (an exabyte is 1 billion gigabytes), 98 percent of this in digital form; if printed in book form, it would make a 52-layer covering of the entire surface of the United States.[9] Google processes around 24 petabytes of data a day. Previously, the technology and skills required to undertake such processing would be limited to huge organizations. However, providing data analysis as a service through cloud computing allows this form of big data analysis to be available to any organization.

Here, we should specify what big data might mean. IBM defined two types of data: 'data in motion' and 'data at rest.' Most of the discussion about big data has focused on data at rest (data which is stored on a hard drive) and it is the processing of large quantities of data at rest that has been the focus of cloud computing debates. Here, cloud computing provides the bulk-processing capacity to sift through hard disks awash with data. Data in motion (the analysis of real-time streams of data coming from devices) has been less considered. However, as sensors and data-capture devices such as the Google Glass or smartphones provide more real-time data, so a number of organizations will begin to capitalize on data in motion. Consider, for example, cloud services such as real-time voice translation services, real-time dictation services, real-time visualization business processes, and logistics. But of course data in motion presents complexities in terms of timing and data volatility.

The desire with big data is to seek to discover correlations within the data that can lead to improved strategic decision-making, whether or not the causality is understood. Like data warehousing before it, big data is about discovering previously unknown patterns within business. One simple example from our research is a supermarket chain discovering a correlation between diaper sales and beer sales on a Friday evening, caused by fathers collecting diapers on the way home from work and deciding to buy beer as well. Supermarkets are full of such relationships being discovered through the power of modern, technology-enabled data analysis. Once known, such information allows – and can direct in detail – supermarket promotions and the targeting of advertising. While supermarkets and large Internet companies have been doing this type of analysis for a number of years, it is the opportunity for different types of organization to have access to such analysis that will allow new forms of businesses to emerge which capitalize on such analysis. It is also the coupling of cloud-computing data analysis resources with new data sources such as the Internet of things (discussed below) that will lead to a profusion of new applications: for example, real-time modeling of traffic flows coupled with communication to GPS systems within vehicles and indeed with self-driving cars. Analysis in real-time using cloud computing may drastically improve traffic flows while allowing emergency services to redirect traffic out of their path and away from potential problems. In the next section we discuss the Internet of things and how computational capacity, sensors, and output devices can be integrated into products to make them smart.

THE INTERNET OF THINGS AND ROBOTICS

Until recently, humans formed the central computing component of our existence. Most machines were controlled by humans pushing pedals, buttons, and levers. As Werner von Braun famously said in the 1960s: 'Man is the best computer we can put aboard a spacecraft and the only one that can be mass produced with unskilled labor.'[10] Only in the last two decades have computers begun to mediate humans' relationship with technology in devices such as televisions, microwaves, and automobiles. These high-value items justify the previously high costs of the processors within.

Today a Raspberry Pi computer retails for about $25.[11] It comes on a single circuit board without a case but, when connected to a TV or monitor, it will run a huge range of applications from web browsers with high-definition video through to 3D video games. At the heart of this machine is a $10 BroadCom2835 chip, which runs the entire machine (the rest of the Raspberry Pi is essentially its connections). This chip, and others like it that are often even cheaper, provide extremely cheap, high-performance processing – for example in video cameras or smartphones. It is chips like these that can be embedded cheaply in other technology to allow them to be connected to the Internet through ubiquitous wi-fi or 4G networking. Indeed, we are rapidly approaching the point where for a few cents we can embed Internet computing into products and devices of all varieties. For example, FedEx provides customers with 'SenseAware' devices – about the size of a mobile phone – which can be placed in packages to monitor location, temperature, light, humidity, pressure, and more – allowing customers to continuously monitor their packages and ensure the ambient conditions are correct for precious biological or electronics products.[12]

Devices enabled in this way can then talk to cloud-based services, providing data and receiving instruction. Enabling a wide range of devices to communicate through the Internet has given rise to the term 'the Internet of things.' It is these devices that will provide the data for big-data analysis and that will demand cloud computing services. The Internet of things is thus not a new concept, but is rather about the collapse in price and subsequent profusion of computing within the world (or rather, the affluent world).

Consider, for example, the washing machine, which has hardly changed in 30 years. It consists of a drum, motor, heating element, water valves, and a rudimentary computing system to coordinate its operation. In the early days, this computing was done with an electromechanical timer (which rotated slowly and physically clicked switches as it turned); today it is accomplished by a simple computer processor connected to various switches and a rudimentary display. This simple computer is specialized for the operation of that particular machine and cannot be updated or changed. Improve and Internet-enable this computer processor and the washing machine can quickly dispense with its buttons and dials – and their associated cost – instead allowing users to interact with it through a Webs interface and wi-fi. A user's smartphone becomes the interface with the washing machine, and the washing machine becomes a platform – capable of having new applications devised using the same basic hardware. For example, an application can arrange to turn the machine on when energy prices are most competitive, thus reducing user energy costs – or, if we demand more immediate washing, the application can turn the heating element off for a few minutes at energy peak times to avoid high prices (and reduce dependence on fossil fuel used for such peak times). An application can connect the washing machine with a service center – ensuring that it is serviced when parts report malfunction. We could go further: the machine could regulate its program based on the detergent variety purchased; a camera could spot the errant red sock in with the white sheets, stopping the program until it is removed; the machine could also remain connected to its supplier, feeding back information on its reliability and enabling better future design. Finally, the information from usage patterns could be coupled with purchasing data to consider where to target marketing and advertising effectively (and perhaps to report to parents that their son or daughter isn't doing their washing!).

All this may seem fairly simple, if useful. However, it is when these Internet-enabled devices are connected together that the possibilities explode. Companies are exploring the possibility of embedding such sensors and computers in the fabric of our cities. New applications will then be enabled, when these devices are connected to cloud-based services. For example, why shouldn't the lights in a car park communicate both with the cars and with their owners' smartphones so that when I walk into a car park the light over my car begins to flash. Why does a light switch have to be physically wired to a light by expensive copper cable, which is also expensive to install? If the light bulb was Internet-enabled, the switch could be located anywhere and run for years using a simple battery to power the on/off messages it would send over the Internet to the bulb. Its use could be monitored (for example to check that an elderly relative got up in the morning) and changed (for example to turn on more lights as they are needed in a room).

Consider now an automatic coffee machine whose users, hankering after an espresso to get them through a boring conference, may be kept unaware that the infrastructure is monitoring their choices to influence global coffee production as much as to ensure that the coffee is sufficiently hot.[13] They may become annoyed to discover that their coffee is stronger or weaker than colleagues' as gender profiling based on image recognition decides the 'right' coffee for them. They may be horrified that the device ceases to work at the very moment of need because of a fault in contract payments within the accounts department. Clearly, such connectivity will have its demons as well as its angels.

Similarly, companies involved in providing the coffee and milk for such machines might become enrolled in this so-called reconfiguration of coffee service and this could reconfigure the knowledge asymmetries within the existing market. Suddenly, an engineering company that previously made plastic and metal coffee machines is now in a position to better understand coffee demand than coffee growers or retailers. The machine itself could negotiate automatically on local markets for its milk provision, or compare material prices with similar machines in other markets and even alter prices of coffee for consumers based on local demand. Through the embedding of cloud computing within a coffee machine the knowledge flows of the coffee market shift.

You may think such examples far fetched, but of course all this has happened already to the market for music. This market is increasingly controlled by a purveyor of what are, in practice, 'sophisticated walkmen' (remember the Sony Walkman?) based on a cloud service. Think also of e-books – increasingly controlled by online retailers selling e-book readers. Now imagine the emergence of the smart city with huge numbers of devices from street lights to refrigerators connected to the cloud. How will the inhabitant of such smart cities understand what they are interacting with – the quasi-objects they used to consider objects? How will such objects afford their informational uses alongside their more usual functions? At the center of this reconfiguration of material objects is a computer system residing in the cloud and aggregating information. It is the aggregation of data flowing from devices that may be central to the lessons of the cloud for smart cities. But why restrict our thinking just to smart cities? On an even bigger scale, one can see that big data is central to, and bound in with, the future of cloud.

DIGITAL FABRICATION

At the Urban Age's Electric City conference in December 2012, Lord Anthony Giddens stated that he felt digital fabrication constituted a new industrial revolution. Digital fabrication, 3D printing, and additive manufacturing are all titles for a new approach to the construction of objects. Traditional objects are made either with a mold (e.g. plastic toys), which must be produced prior to the manufacturing process, or by subtracting material from a solid (e.g. machining and drilling metal blocks to make aircraft parts).

In contrast, 3D printing works by building the artefact layer by layer in a printing-type process. A print head (much like an inkjet printer head, but instead of ejecting ink it ejects metal or plastic resin) moves in three dimensions, slowly 'printing' layer after layer to build up the object. Such 3D printers are relatively simple devices. Apart from the head, the main components are similar to those of an inkjet printer, and they could easily become a household item. Furthermore, the process can scale: items the size of a car are already produced this way[14] and researchers are experimenting with printing buildings using a moving gantry crane to print concrete.[15]

Using additive manufacturing, the same printer can print different objects without any change other than its software instructions and with practically no wasted material.[16] This would enable production of single items and the personalization of the items produced. As MIT's Neil Gershenfeld has argued: 'the killer app in digital fabrication, as in computing, is personalization, producing products for a market of one person.'

This technology is significant in a debate on the future of cloud computing, as existing manufacturing of technology requires large organizations with extensive resources for innovation. Cloud computing, as we have discussed, allows innovation in digital products to be undertaken without such large organizational forms. Additive manufacturing extends such innovation to physical products by challenging the traditional economies of scale available due to the high fixed costs of manufacturing. By decoupling the demand for large, complex production facilities, innovation can become a personal and individual activity – as demonstrated by the growth of the Maker movement.[17] Furthermore, cloud computing allows 3D modeling systems and CAD software to be used on a pay-as-you-go basis, further supporting the small enterprise.

Digital fabrication allows us to 'think globally and fabricate locally.'[18] Peter Basiliere, research director at Gartner, the analyst company, commented: '3D printing is a technology accelerating to mainstream adoption. The hype leads many people to think the technology is some years away, when it is available now and is affordable to most organizations.' In three years' time, a high-quality 3D printer could cost less than $2,000. Indeed, already by 2013 Boeing was printing 200 parts for 10 of its aircraft platforms and 3D printers were routinely used in the production of dental appliances and hearing aid earpieces.[19] For Chris Andersen, digital fabrication is the foundation of a new industrial revolution and part of a bigger picture where the last ten years (2002–2012) 'have been about discovering new ways to create, invent and work together on the Web. The next ten years will be about applying those lessons to the real world.'[20] If the Internet has revolutionized the way corporations sell in the 21st century, cloud is now poised to transform the way we manufacture, with huge implications for manufacturing services everywhere.

There is, however, a downside to allowing individuals and small enterprises such tools for manufacture. Cody Wilson, a 24-year old law student, has worked to design and distribute online simple 3D printers with instructions for creating the lower receiver component of the AR-15 rifle.[21] This part is significant, as it is the only component that requires legal approval to produce, all the other parts being freely available on the open market. Printing this part enables the building of a working AR-15 without legal registration[22] and the component has already been proved to work (albeit for a small number of rounds[23]). There are similarly worrying automatic 3D scanners (similar to those available in the Xbox Kinect games console) coupled with 3D printers that may allow individuals to copy physical artefacts such as objets d'art as easily as people 'ripped' CDs to an MP3.

Cloud computing is integral to the likely development of such printing technology. First, SaaS services allow users to experiment and share 3D models (e.g. thingiverse.com), and second, SaaS services are emerging to allow individuals and companies to design artefacts from within the browser. Thus 3D printers can lower the barriers for entry when competing on the design and manufacture of certain objects and products. This levels the playing field for the design and manufacture of objects capable of being printed by 3D printers.

CONCLUSION

As always, the future remains unknowable. Cloud computing is but one shift in the nature of computing. However, in severing the requirement for a physical computer, in shifting the economic models for how computing is procured, and in moving computing out of organizational boundaries, it may prove to have profound consequences.

Thus far, the debate on cloud computing has been dominated by technological issues and has been founded upon comparisons with existing equivalent IT resources in terms of cost, security, and so on. This book's aim has been to challenge such technology-centric perspectives, supplanting them with a richer perspective including the managerial and social implications of cloud. For us cloud is about a reduction in the friction of information flows within and between organizations and individuals and a reduction in the friction of commissioning (and decommissioning) IT-based services. The implication of such a reduction of friction, though, is an increase in the speed of change and innovation. Businesses are facing considerably more pressure than ever before to maintain the pace of innovation in their corporate information systems to keep up with the new competitiveness enabled by the cloud. This will demand new and improved skills, capabilities, and management practices. This book provides informed insight into, as well as a vantage point on, the road ahead. We offer it as a useful roadmap to help business leaders through the strategic challenges they are inevitably going to encounter as they move their organizations toward becoming cloud corporations.

Notes and References

INTRODUCTION

1 The annual gathering of IAOP – the global standard-setting organization and advocate for the outsourcing profession with more than 120,000 members and affiliates worldwide.
2 www.horsesforsources.com/research-services.
3 The HfS blog can be found at www.horsesforsources.com.

PREFACE

1 Harris, J. and Alter, A. (2010) *Six Questions Every Executive Should Ask About Cloud Computing*. Boston, MA, Accenture Institute for High Performance.
2 www.accenture.com/us-en/technology/technologylabs/Pages/insight-accenture-technology-vision-2012.aspx.
3 Accenture (2013) *Accenture Technology Vision, 2013*. London, Accenture.

CHAPTER 1

1 Moschella, D. (1997) *Waves Of Power: Dynamics Of Global Technology Leadership 1964–2010*. New York, Amacom.
2 Strassmann, P. (1997). *The Squandered Computer*. New Canaan, Information Economics Press.
3 See Willcocks, L. and Graeser, V. (2001) 'Delivering IT and E-Business Value'. *Computer Weekly*.
4 Strassmann, op. cit.
5 Dec, K. (1996) *Client/Server: Fiscal Benefits and Justification*. Gartner Group Symposium, Lake Buena Vista, Florida.
6 Strassmann, op. cit.
7 Willcocks, L. and Lester, S. (eds) (1999) *Beyond The IT Productivity Paradox*. Chichester, Wiley.
8 Willcocks, L. and Lacity, M. (2012) *The New IT Outsourcing Landscape: From Innovation To Cloud Services*. London, Palgrave.
9 Dertouzos, M. (1997) *What Will Be: How The New World Of Information Will Change Our Lives*. New York, HarperEdge. See also Hagel, J. and Armstrong, A. (1997). *Net Gain: Expanding Markets Through Virtual Communities*. Boston, Harvard Business School Press.
10 Willcocks and Graeser, op. cit.

11 Willcocks and Lester, op. cit.

12 Moschella, op. cit.

13 Manyika, J. Chui, M. Bughin, J., Dobbs, P., Bisson, P. and Marrs, A. (2013) *Disruptive Technologies: Advances that Will Transform Life, Business and The Global Economy*. New York, McKinsey Global Institute.

14 Accenture (2013) *Accenture Technology Vision, 2013*. London, Accenture.

15 See Keane, B. Sabadra, A. and Diamond, M. (2013) *Cloud Transforming IT Services*. USA, Deutsche Bank Markets Research.

16 See later chapters of this book. Also Luftman, J., Zadeh, H., Derksen, B. et al. (2013) 'Key Information Technology and Management Issues 2012–13: An International Study.' *Journal of Information Technology*, 28, 4, forthcoming. Here business intelligence is ranked number one most influential technology internationally, with cloud computing ranked number two.

17 See Lacity, M. and Willcocks, L. (2013) 'Cloud Services Forecast: Rain and Shine.' *Pulse Magazine*, May/June: 2–6. The survey sample of 133 delegates captured a range of firm sizes as measured by number of employees worldwide. The average size of firm for customer respondents was 50,751 employees, for provider firms 32,494 employees and advisory firms was 4201 employees. The size ranged from a very small advisory firm with only three employees to a very large client firm with over 300,000 employees.

18 Willcocks, L., Venters, W. and Whitley, E. (2013) 'Cloud Computing as Innovation: Studying Diffusion.' Proceedings of the Seventh Global Sourcing Workshop. March 11–14, Val d'Isere, France.

19 Enterprise Cloud Adoption Survey Results, Everest Group, August 2012, available at www.everestgrp.com

20 See Lacity, M., Reynolds, P., Khan, S. and Willcocks, L. (2013) 'Outsourcing Cloud Services: The Great Equalizer for SMEs?' Proceedings of the Fourth International Conference on the Outsourcing of Information Services. Mannheim, Germany, June 10–11, 2013.

21 Ibid.

22 Everest Group (2013) *Enterprise Cloud Adoption Survey – 2013*. Dallas, Everest Group.

CHAPTER 2

1 SNA is IBM's proprietary networking architecture. Created in 1974 it is a complete *protocol stack* for interconnecting *computers* and their resources. SNA describes the protocol and is, in itself, not actually a program. The implementation of SNA takes the form of various communications packages, most notably Virtual Telecommunications Access Method (VTAM), which is the mainframe package for SNA communications. SNA is still used extensively in banks and other financial transaction networks, as well as in many government agencies.

2 Kleinrock, L. (2005) 'A Vision for the Internet.' *ST Journal of Research* 2(1): 4–5. See also Cafaro, M. and Aloisio, G. (2011) *Grids, Clouds and Virtualization.* London, Springer: 1–22.

3 Berman, F. and Hey, T. (2004) 'The Scientific Imperative.' In: Foster, I. and Kesselman, C. (eds) *The Grid 2: Blueprint for a New Computing Infrastructure.* North Holland, Elsevier: 13–23.

4 Owens, D. (2009) 'Securing Elasticity in the Cloud.' *Communications of the ACM*: 53(6): 48–51. See also Durkee, D. (2010) 'Why Cloud Computing Will Never Be Free.' *Communications of the ACM*, 53(5): 62–69.

5 Kern, T., Willcocks, L. P. and Lacity, M. C. (2002) 'Application Service Provision: Risk Assessment and Mitigation.' *MIS Quarterly Executive*, 1(2): 113–26.
Kern, T., Willcocks, L. and Lacity, M. (2006) 'Applications Service Provision to Netsourcing: A Risk Mitigation Framework.' In: L. Willcocks and M. Lacity (eds) *Global Sourcing of Business and IT Services.* Basingstoke, Palgrave Macmillan: 256–74.

6 Susarla, A., Barua, A. and Whinston, A. B. (2003) 'Understanding the Service Component of Application Service Provision: Empirical Analysis of Satisfaction with ASP Services.' *MIS Quarterly*, 27(1): 91–123.

7 Blum, A. (2012) *Tubes: Behind the Scenes at the Internet.* London, Viking.

8 Zhang, Q., Cheng, L. and Boutaba, R. (2010) 'Cloud Computing: State-of-the-art and Research Challenges.' *Journal of Internet Service Applications*, 1: 7–18.

9 Commodity hardware is based on open standards (usually based on IBM PC architectures with Intel's x86 instruction set) purchased from generic suppliers. Though this is lower in performance than specialized servers (such as those from IBM or Sun Microsystems), by using large numbers of servers such limitations can be overcome. Killalea, T. (2008) 'Meet the Virts: Virtualisation Technology Isn't New, but It Has Matured a Lot over the Past 30 Years.' *ACM Queue*, 6(1): 14–18.

10 Cusumano, M. (2010) 'Cloud Computing and SaaS as New Computing Platforms.' *Communications of the ACM*, 53(4): 27–9. See also Cafaro, M. and Aloisio: 1–22.

11 Mell, P. and Grance, T. (2011) *The NIST Definition of Cloud Computing.* U.S. Department of Commerce, National Institute of Standards and Technology.

12 Boss, G., Malladi, P., Quan, D., Legregni, L. and Hall, H. (2007) 'Cloud Computing.' In: *IBM Technical Report: High Performance On Demand Solutions (HiPODS).* London, IBM.

13 Cubitt, S., Hassan, R. and Volkmer, I. (2011) 'Does Cloud Computing Have a Silver Lining?' *Media Culture & Society*, 33(1): 149–58. See also Iyer, B. and Henderson, J. (2010) 'Preparing for the Future: Understanding the Seven Capabilities of Cloud Computing.' *MIS Quarterly Executive*, 9(2): 117–31.

14 A version of this definition was first introduced in Willcocks, L., Venters, W. and Whitley, E. (2011) *Cloud and the Future of Business: From Costs to Innovation: Part 1: Promise,* London, Accenture.

15 Armbrust, M., Griffith, R., Joseph, A. D., Katz, R., Konwinski, A., Lee, G., Patterson, D., Rabkin, A., Stoica, I. and Zaharia M. (2010) 'A View of Cloud Computing.' *Communications of the ACM*, 53–8(4): 50–8.

16 Cubitt, Hassan, and Volkmer, op. cit.: 149–58. McKendrick, J. (2011) 'Cloud Computing's Hidden "Green" Benefits.' *Forbes*, June: 63–6.

17 Greenpeace (2010) *Make IT Green: Cloud Computing and its Contribution to Climate Change*. London, Greenpeace International.

18 West, J. and Goldenberg, S. (2012) 'Apple Defends Green Credentials of Cloud Computing Services.' *The Guardian*. London, July 16.

19 See Armbrust, M., Fox, A., Griffith, R., Joseph, A., Katz, R., Konwinski, A., Lee, G., Patterson, D., Rabkin, A., Stoica, I. and Zaharia, M. (2009) *Above the Clouds: A Berkeley View of Cloud Computing*. UC Berkeley Reliable Adaptive Distributed Systems Laboratory for an extensive discussion of the technical issues of cloud computing that lead to such cost savings.

20 Gray, J. (2008) 'Distributed computing economics.' *Queue*, 6(3): 63–8.

21 This framework was originally published in the following academic research paper: Venters, W. and Whitley, E. (2012) 'A Critical Review of Cloud Computing: Researching Desires and Realities.' *Journal of Information Technology*, 27(3): 179–97.

22 Brynjolfsson, E., Hofmann, P. and Jordan, J. (2010) 'Economic and Business Dimensions of Cloud Computing and Electricity: Beyond the Utility Model.' *Communications of the ACM*, 53(5): 32–4.

23 Halpert, B. (2011) *Auditing Cloud Computing: A Security and Privacy Guide*. Hoboken, NJ, Wiley.

24 Krutz, R. L. and Vines, R. D. (2010) *Cloud Security: A Comprehensive Guide to Secure Cloud Computing*. Indianapolis, IN, Wiley.
McAfee, A. (2011) 'What Every CEO Needs to Know About the Cloud'. *Harvard Business Review*, 89(11): 124–32.

25 Merz, M. (2006) 'Embedding Digital Infrastructure in Epistemic Culture'. In: Hine, C. (ed.) *New Infrastructures for Knowledge Production: Understanding E-Science*. Hershey, PA, Information Science Publishing: 99–119.

26 Nelson, M. R. (2009) 'The Cloud, the Crowd and Public Policy'. *Issues in Science and Technology*, 25(4): 71–6.

27 Owens, op. cit.: 48–51.

28 Anthes, op. cit. 'Security in the Cloud.' *Communications of the ACM*, 53(11): 16–20.

29 Durkee, op. cit.: 62–69.

30 For example, Krutz and Vines, op. cit.

31 Stated during a lecture at the LSE. See Ballmer, S. (2010) 'Seizing the Opportunity of the Cloud: The Next Wave of Business Growth.' In: *Remarks by Steve Ballmer, Chief Executive Officer*. London, London School of Economics.

32 For example, Hickey, A. (2011) 'Amazon's Not Alone: 10 Notable Cloud Outages in the Last Year.' *CRN.com, United Business Media*, April 29.

33 Marston, S., Li, Z., Bandyopadhyay, S., Zhang, J. and Ghalsasi, A. (2011) 'Cloud Computing – The Business Perspective.' *Decision Support Systems*, 51(1): 176–89.

34 Kern, Willcocks, and Lacity, op. cit.: 113–26.

35 Yoo, C. S. (2011) 'Cloud Computing: Architectural and Policy Implications.' *Review of Industrial Organization*, 38(4): 405–21.

36 This also confirms the work of Durkee and Hamilton and is as suggested by Metz. See Durkee, op. cit.: 62–9. See also Hamilton, J. (2008) *Internet-scale Service Efficiency. Large-scale Distributed Systems and Middleware (LADIS)*. New York, ACM;

Metz, C. (2012) 'Mavericks Invent Future Internet Where Cisco Is Meaningless.' *Wired*, October: 53–5.

37 World Economic Forum (2010) *Exploring the Future of Cloud Computing: Riding the Next Wave of Technology-driven Transformation*. Geneva, World Economic Forum.

38 See, for example, Armbrust, Griffith, Joseph, Katz, Konwinski, Lee, Patterson, Rabkin, Stoica and Zaharia, op. cit.: 50–8. Also Marston, Li, Bandyopadhyay, Zhang, and Ghalsasi, op. cit.: 176–89; Zhang, Cheng, and Boutaba, op. cit.: 7–18.

39 Zhang, Q., Cheng, L. and Boutaba, R. (2010): 7–18.

40 Alan Turing's definition of a 'universal Turing machine' was a thought experiment to design a machine capable of computing any computable sequence. It was argued to be one of the foundational ideas of modern computing. It is the simplest computing model powerful enough to calculate all possible functions which can be calculated – given a near infinite time and near infinite memory. The idea is used here to denote the idea of a near infinite computing capability.

41 Weinhardt, C., Anandasivam, A., Blau, B., Borissov, N., Meinl, T., Michalk, W. and Stößer, J. (2009) 'Cloud Computing – A Classification, Business Models and Research Directions.' *Business & Information Systems Engineering*, 1(5): 391–9.

42 Iyer, B. and Henderson, J. (2010) 'Preparing for the Future: Understanding the Seven Capabilities of Cloud Computing.' *MIS Quarterly Executive*, 9(2): 117–31.

43 Youseff, L., Butrico, M. and Da Silva, D. (2008) 'Toward a Unified Ontology of Cloud Computing.' *Proceedings of the Grid Computing Environments Workshop, 2008 (GCE '08)*. Austin, TX, Institute of Electrical and Electronics Engineers (IEEE): 125–37.

44 Weinhardt, Anandasivam, Blau, Borissov, Meinl, Michalk and Stößer, op. cit.: 391–9. See also Youseff, Butrico, and Da Silva, op. cit.

45 Smith, R. (2005) *Grid Computing: A Brief Technology Analysis*. CTO Network Library. See also Foster, I., Zhao, Y., Raicu, I. and Lu, S. (2008) 'Cloud Computing and Grid Computing 360-Degree Compared.' *Grid Computing Environments Workshop, 2008 (GCE '08)*. Austin, TX, Institute of Electrical and Electronics Engineers (IEEE): 60–9. See also Cafaro and Aloisio, op. cit.: 1–22.

46 Popek, G. and Goldberg, R. (1974) 'Formal Requirements for Virtualizable Third-generation Architectures.' *Communications of the ACM*, 17(7): 412–21 provides details of early virtualization approaches.

47 Killalea, op. cit.: 14–18.

48 Boss, Malladi, Quan, Legregni and Hall, op. cit.

49 Owens, op. cit.: 48–51.

50 Creeger, M. (2009) 'CTO Roundtable: Cloud Computing.' *Communications of the ACM*, 52(8): 50–6. See also Armbrust, Fox, Griffith, Joseph, Katz, Konwinski, Lee, Patterson, Rabkin, Stoica and Zaharia, op. cit.

51 Espadas, J., Molina, A., Jiménez, G., Molina, M., Ramírez, R. and Concha, D. (2011) 'Tenant-based Resource Allocation Model for Scaling Software-as-a-Service Applications over Cloud Computing Infrastructures.' *Future Generation Computer Systems*, 3: 156–68.

52 Rochwerger, B., Breitgand, D., Levy, E., Galis, A., Nagin, K., Llorente, I. M., Montero, R., Wolfsthal, Y., Elmroth, E. and Caceres, J. (2009) 'The Reservoir Model and

Architecture for Open Federated Cloud Computing.' *IBM Journal of Research and Development*, 53(4): 1–11.

53 Ballmer, op. cit.

54 Moore, G. E. (1965) 'Cramming More Components onto Integrated Circuits.' *Electronics*, 38(8): 114–17.

55 www.businessinsider.com/best-larry-ellison-quotes-2013-4?op=1#ixzz2XJZUY6pP.

CHAPTER 3

1 The typology of innovations comes from Willcocks, L., Cullen, S. and Craig, A. (2011) *The Outsourcing Enterprise: From Cost Management to Collaborative Innovation*. London, Palgrave. See also chapter 6.

2 Out of recognition of this, the BPO pure player Xchanging established itself in its first contracts in 2001 at BAE Systems and the London Insurance Market with seven competencies, one of which was service. Studies of the key competencies of outsourcing suppliers frequently list customer development as core, with service suffused through several others. See Lacity, M. and Willcocks, L. (2009) *Information Systems and Outsourcing: Studies in Theory and Practice*, London, Palgrave, for more details of these examples.

3 See Willcocks, L. and Lacity, M. (2009) *The Practice of Outsourcing: From Information Systems to BPO and Offshoring*, London, Palgrave; Willcocks, Cullen and Craig, op. cit. for summaries and illustrative examples. Also Cullen, S. and Willcocks, L. (2003) *Intelligent IT Outsourcing* (Oxford: ComputerWeeklyHeinemann).

4 RightNow (2010) *Customer Experience Impact Report*. New York, RightNow/Harris. This report was conducted online within the United States by Harris Interactive for RightNow Technologies between September 11 and 15, 2009, among 2295 U.S. adults aged 18 years or older. Results were weighted as needed for age, sex, race/ethnicity, education, region, and household income. www.RightNow.com.

5 Interview with Wolfgang Faisst of SAP, November 2010. Quoted in Willcocks, L., Venters, W. and Whitley, E. (2012) *Cloud and The Future of Business 3 – Impacts*. London, Accenture/Outsourcing Unit.

6 SERVQUAL is a well researched, longstanding, simple, and useful model for qualitatively exploring and assessing customers' service experiences and has been used widely by service delivery organizations. It is an efficient model for identifying the gap between perceived and expected service and is the most complete attempt to conceptualize and measure service quality for use across industries. A detailed assessment appears in Pitt, L., Watson, R. and Kavan, C. (1995) 'Service Quality – A Measure of Information Systems Effectiveness.' *MIS Quarterly*, 19(2): 56–67.

7 Figures from IDC (2009) 'IDC's New IT Cloud Services Forecast: 2009–2013.' http://blogs.idc.com/ie/?p=543, and from twitter.com/raconteur media (2010) 'Raconteur on Enterprise Cloud Computing', July 20. See also Harris, J. and Nunn, S. (2010) 'Agile IT – Reinventing the Enterprise.' *Outlook*, October 2: 40–7. There are various estimates relating to cloud and much depends on what is counted as cloud. IBM,

for example, has launched 11 cloud computing labs worldwide and in 2009 the company expected the market to grow from $47 billion in 2008 to $126 billion in 2012. Others have suggested a market revenue size of $150 billion by 2014.

8 See Greenhalgh, T., Glenn, R., MacFarlane, F., Bate, P. and Kyriakidou, O. (2004) 'Diffusion of Innovation in Service Organizations: Systematic Review and Recommendations.' *The Milbank Quarterly*, 82(4): 581–629; Rogers, E. (1985) *Diffusion of Innovations*. New York, Free Press.

9 See *Economist* (2013) 'Ascending to the Cloud.' June 29.

10 Integrated development environments are the tools and workbenches used by developers to aid the development of applications.

11 See Hey, T. and Trefethen, A. (2008) 'E-Science, Cyberinfrastructure and Scholarly Communication.' In: G. Olson, A. Zimmerman, and N. Bos (eds) *Scientific Collaboration on the Internet*, Cambridge, MIT Press: 15–31; *Economist* (2010) 'The Data Deluge.' February 25.

12 MapReduce is a means of integrating vast clusters of data beyond the capability of SQL. It is based on clustering of data and thus suited to cloud infrastructures – like those in Google's data centers. http://labs.google.com/papers/mapreduce.html.

13 For example, Jumpbox.com provides complete, downloadable, virtualized servers based on open source products. Traditionally, if you wanted to install software like SugarCRM (an open source CRM product) you would need to install Linux, MySQL and various application packages and undertake a large amount of configuration. With Jumpbox the whole application stack can be downloaded – either to a local server or direct to Amazon Elastic Compute Cloud.

14 Vargo, S. and Lusch, R. (2004) 'Evolving to a New Dominant Logic for Marketing.' *The Journal of Marketing*, 68(1): 1–17.

15 Vargo and Lusch, op. cit.: 5.

16 That is, it can be understood only in terms of the relationship between the customer and the provider of goods such as cloud services.

17 Grönroos, C. (2008) 'Service Logic Revisited: Who Creates Value? And Who Co-creates?' *European Business Review*, 20(4): 304.

18 Iyer, B. and Henderson, J. (2010) 'Preparing for the Future: Understanding the Seven Capabilities of Cloud Computing.' *MIS Quarterly Executive*, 9(2): 117–31.

19 Durkee, D. (2010) 'Why Cloud Computing Will Never Be Free.' *Communications of the ACM*, 53(5): 62–9.

20 Vargo and Lusch, op. cit.: 2.

21 Maude, F. (2011) 'ICT Strategy: Strategic Implementation Plan to Deliver Savings of Over a Billion Pounds.' *Cabinet Office*. Archived at www.cabinetoffice.gov.uk/news/ict-strategy-strategic-implementation-plan-deliver-savings-over-billion-pounds.

22 Kautz, K., Madsen, S. and Norbjerg, J. (2007) 'Persistent Problems and Practices in Information Systems Development.' *Information Systems Journal*, 17(3): 217–39.

23 Owens, D. (2009) 'Securing Elasticity in the Cloud.' *Communications of the ACM*, 53(6): 48–51.

24 Christensen, C. M. (1997) *The Innovator's Dilemma: When New Technologies Cause Great Firms to Fail*. Cambridge, MA, Harvard Business Press.

25 Ciborra, C. U. (1996) 'The Platform Organization: Recombining Strategies, Structures and Surprises.' *Organization Science*, 7(2): 103–18.
26 Porter, M. E. (1980) *Competitive Strategy*. New York, The Free Press; Hammer, M. and Champy, J. (1993) *Reengineering the Corporation: A Manifesto for Business Revolution*. New York, Harper Business.
27 Mathiassen, L. and Pries-Heje, J. (2006) 'Business Agility and Diffusion of Information Technology.' *European Journal of Information Systems*, 15(2): 116–19.
28 Mircea, M., Ghilic, B. and Stoica, M. (2011) 'Combining Business Intelligence with Cloud Computing to Deliver Agility in Actual Economy.' *Economic Computation and Economic Cybernetics Studies and Research*, 45(1): 39–54.
29 Brynjolfsson, E., Hofmann, P. and Jordan, J. (2010) 'Economic and Business Dimensions of Cloud Computing and Electricity: Beyond the Utility Model.' *Communications of the ACM*, 53(5): 32.
30 Leimeister, S., Böhm, M., Riedl, C. and Krcmar, H. (2010) 'The Business Perspective of Cloud Computing: Actors, Roles and Value Networks.' In: T. Alexande, M. Turpin and J. van Deventer (eds) *18th European Conference on Information Systems*, Pretoria, South Africa: 1861–73.
31 Friedman, T. (2005) *The World is Flat: A Brief History of the Globalized World in the 21st Century*. London: Allen Lane.
32 Weinhardt, C., Anandasivam, A., Blau, B., Borissov, N., Meinl, T., Michalk, W. and Stößer, J. (2009) 'Cloud Computing – A Classification, Business Models and Research Directions.' *Business & Information Systems Engineering*, 1(5): 391–9.
33 Whitley, E. A. and Willcocks, L. P. (2011) 'Achieving Step-change in Outsourcing Maturity: Toward Collaborative Innovation.' *MIS Quarterly Executive*, 10(3): 95–109.
34 Ibid.
35 Mircea, Ghilic and Stoica, op. cit.
36 See Smith, D. (2010) *Exploring Innovation*. London, McGraw Hill.

CHAPTER 4

1 See Willcocks, L., Venters, W. and Whitley, E. (2010) 'Glimpsing the Future through the Cloud: From Cost to Innovation,' Presentation at the Cloud Business Summit, London, November 30. For more details see also www.HfSresearch.com and www.outsourcingunit.org.
2 When Gene Amdahl created IBM clones that were 'plug-compatible' with IBM's legendary 360 and 370 series , but through the use of large-scale circuit integration were superior, IBM responded with aggressive sales tactics, which its opponents called FUD (fear, uncertainty, and doubt). In particular, IBM suggested that they were about to release better machines in the very near future – successfully persuading customers to hold off purchasing Amdahl mainframes. For a detailed description see Henderson (2009) *The Encyclopaedia of Computer Science and Technology*. New York, Infobase Publishing. Facts On File: 10.

3 Based on later research findings, this is different from our first formulation, which had Equivalence, Abstraction, Automation, and Tailoring. See Willcocks, L., Venters, W. and Whitley, E. (2011) *Cloud and the Future of Business, Paper 1 – The Promise*. London, Accenture/LSE.

4 One might also note that a firm's financial assets invariably sit in a cloud off premises – at their banking service provider's – exhibiting an apparently high level of confidence.

5 E.g. www.emis-online.com/emis-hosting-services.

6 Distributed Denial of Service – the flooding of a server with requests from a widely distributed set of computers beyond the level it can cope with. In order to undertake such an attack, control is needed of a large number of computers – and thus malware that provides such access is often used. The distributed nature of such attacks makes them very hard to respond to. One major concern for cloud providers is the potential misuse of their services to aid such an attack (http://en.wikipedia.org/wiki/Denial-of-service_attack). One respondent commented on brand hacking: 'I've had people attempt to crack – hack into – web-based solutions and cloud-based solutions … but in the same way they would have done had it been on our servers. They are trying to hack the client, not the solution … The big thing is, people hack brands or hack applications regardless of what the infrastructure is underneath.' (Steve Furbinger – RAPP, quoted in Willcocks, L. Venters, W. and Whitley, E. (2011) *Cloud and the Future of Business, Paper 2 – Challenges*. London, Accenture/Outsourcing Unit.

7 Killalea, T. (2008) 'Meet the Virts: Virtualization Technology Isn't New, but It Has Matured a Lot Over the Past 30 Years.' *ACM Queue*, 6(1): 14–18.

8 Quote from David Leyland, a senior executive with cloud supplier Glasshouse. Quoted in Willcocks, Venters and Whitley (2011) Paper 1.

9 Microsoft CEO Steve Ballmer gave this speech at the London School of Economics and Political Science on October 5, 2010 – *Seizing the Opportunity of the Cloud: The Next Wave of Business Growth*. On www.lse.ac.uk – see 'media and events.'

10 Healey, M. (2010) 'How Cloud Computing Changes IT Outsourcing.' *Information Week*, June 15: 45–7.

11 Brynjolfsson, E., Hofmann, P. and Jordon, J. (2010) 'Economic and Business Dimensions Cloud Computing and Electricity: Beyond the Utility Model.' *Communications of the ACM*, 53(5): 32–4.

12 Services such as Akamai focus on accelerating access to Web resources using route-optimization technologies, caching, compression, and pre-fetching of data. Akamai maintains tens of thousands of network servers globally, which monitor Internet traffic and use this information to optimize data routes. www.akamai.com.

13 As one example: 'every customer is on the same service level agreement in SalesForce in terms of [the fact that] they can't, you can't buy your way to … a higher level of service availability, for example. And our view of that was that it's really a principle of our architecture. So what we, you know, every technology, whether they are AIG or [a] one person start-up, gets the same level of service.' (Tim Barker, SalesForce.com, quoted in Willcocks, Venters and Whitley (2011) Paper 2).

14 Jimmy Harris, Accenture. Interview November 2010. Quoted in Willcocks, Venters, and Whitley (2011) Paper 2.

15 Amazon offers a 10 percent discount if they fail to reach 99.95 percent up-time (http:// aws.amazon.com/ec2-sla/). 3Tera has a greater focus on enterprise clients and its virtual, private data-center offering provides a discount of 10 percent of monthly service fees for availability between 99.999 percent and 99.900 percent and 25 percent of monthly service fees for less than 99.9 percent (http:// blog.3tera. com/computing/175/). For many businesses such discounts are irrelevant compared with the business cost of service downtime – particularly as IaaS is cheap compared with maintaining existing infrastructure – hence the discount is small.

16 The IT Infrastructure Library is a standardized 'best-practice' approach to IT service management (www.itil-officialsite.com/home/home.asp).

17 Interview with Greg Bybee of VMware, November 2010. See Willcocks, Venters and Whitley (2011) Paper 2.

18 Heiden, G. Van der (2010) 'The Status of the Application Services and SaaS Market in Europe.' *Gartner Outsourcing & IT Services Summit*. London, Gartner. See also Sethi, A. and Aries, O. (2010) 'The End of Outsourcing (As We Know It).' *Business Week*, August 10, online viewpoint.

19 A point also made in Killalea, op. cit.

20 Dave Leyland, business development executive of Glasshouse, August 2010. Quoted in Willcocks, Venters and Whitley (2011) Paper 3.

21 Interview with Steve Furbinger of RAPP, October 2010. Quoted in Willcocks, Venters and Whitley (2011) Paper 2.

22 Excerpt from an interview with Hong Choing of Microsoft in December 2010. Quoted in Willcocks, Venters and Whitley (2011) Paper 2.

23 Interview with Bruce Carlos, April 18, 2013.

24 See Carr, N. (2009) *The Big Switch*. Boston, MA, Harvard Business Press: 5. See also Carr, N. (2005) 'The End of Corporate Computing.' *MIT Sloan Management Review*, 46(3): 67–73.

25 Cornford, T. (2003) 'Information Systems and New Technologies: Taking Shape in Use.' In: C. Avgerou (ed.) *Information Systems and the Economics of Innovation*. Cheltenham, Edward Elgar Publishing: 162–77.

26 See, for example, Keen, P. G. W. and Woodman, L. (1984) 'What To Do with All Those Micros: First Make Them Part of the Team.' *Harvard Business Review*, 62(5): 142–50. Those with longer memories will recall predictions of the demise of the internal IT department throughout the 1980s, to be replaced by software packages and business unit computing. The rise of IT outsourcing from the late 1980s was also regularly predicted to lead to the end of the IT department.

27 See Willcocks, Venters and Whitley (2010) *Glimpsing the Future*.

28 See Lee, D. (1986) 'Usage Patterns and Sources of Assistance for Personal Computer Users.' *MIS Quarterly*, 10(4): 313–25.

29 See Benioff, M. and Adler, C. (2009) *Behind the Cloud – The Untold Story of How SalesForce.com Went from Idea to Billion-dollar Company and Revolutionized an Industry*. San Francisco, CA, Jossey-Bass.

30 Interview with Robin Daniels of SalesForce.com, November 2010. Quoted in Willcocks, Venters and Whitley (2011) Paper 2.

31 E.g. trust.salesforce.com or http://status.aws.amazon.com/.

32 See Etro, F. (2009) 'The Economic Impact of Cloud Computing on Business Creation, Employment and Output in Europe.' *Review of Business and Economics*, 54(2): 179–91.

33 See Willcocks, L. and Lacity, M. (2009) *The Practice of Outsourcing: From Information Systems to BPO and Offshoring*. London, Palgrave, especially chapters 1 and 2.

34 Quoted in personal correspondence, April 24, 2013, as part of our (so far anonymized) 2013/14 round of research interviews.

35 Mooney, J., Ross, J. and Phipps, J. (2012) 'Embrace the Inevitable: Six Imperatives to Prepare Your Company for Cloud Computing.' *CISR Research Briefing*, 12(10, October).

36 Ibid.

37 Willcocks, L. Reynolds, P., Thorogood, A. and Schlagwein, D. (2013) 'Cloud Computing as Innovation: Slow Trains Coming?' Public Seminar, Sydney Accenture offices, April 23.

38 See Reynolds, P., Lacity, M. and Willcocks, L. (2014) *Cloud Strategizing: Building The Future Starting Today*. LSE Outsourcing Unit Working Paper, February. London, LSE.

39 Armbrust, M., Fox, A., Griffith, R., Joseph, A. D., Katz, R., Konwinski, A., Lee, G., Patterson, D., Rabkin, A., Stoica, I. and Zaharia, M. (2010) 'A View of Cloud Computing.' *Communications of the ACM*, 53(4): 50–8.

40 We thank Mike Hanley of PA Consulting for coining this phrase in conversation with us in January 2011.

CHAPTER 5

1 Information Commissioner's Office (2013) *Key Definitions for the Data Protection Act*. Archived at www.ico.org.uk/for_organizations/data_protection/the_guide/key_definitions.

2 Ibid.

3 Information Commissioner's Office (2012) *Outsourcing: A Guide for Small and Medium-sized Businesses*. Archived at www.ico.org.uk/for_organizations/data_protection/the_guide/~/media/documents/library/Data_Protection/Detailed_specialist_guides/outsourcing_guide_for_smes.ashx.

4 Ibid.

5 See the discussion in Article 29 Data protection working party (London, Information Commissioner's Office, 2010) about the distinction between data controller and data processor.

6 Davies, S. (2013) 'Sweden's Data Protection Authority Bans Google Cloud Services over Privacy Concerns' (13 June). Archived at www.privacysurgeon.org/blog/incision/swedens-data-protection-authority-bans-google-apps/.

7 Ibid.

8 Davies, S. (2012) 'Why Norway's Rigorous Stance on Cloud Computing Highlights the Primacy of Strong Privacy Policies' (13 June). Archived at www.privacysurgeon. org/blog/incision/why-norways-rigorous-stance-on-cloud-computing-highlights-the-crucial-importance-of-strong-privacy-policies/.

9 European Commission (2012) *Digital Agenda: New Strategy to Drive European Business and Government Productivity Via Cloud Computing* (27 September). Archived at http://europa.eu/rapid/press-release_IP-12-1025_en.htm.

10 Kroes, N. (2013) 'How we're boosting trust in the cloud, post-PRISM.' Archived at http://blogs.ec.europa.eu/neelie-kroes/cloud-contract-term/.

11 Ibid.

12 International Working Group on Data Protection in Telecommunications (2012) 'Sopot memorandum.' Working paper on cloud computing – Privacy and data protection issues (April 24).

13 European Parliament (2012) *Fighting Cyber Crime and Protecting Privacy in the Cloud.* Directorate General for Internal Policies; Policy Department C: Citizens' Rights and Constitutional Affairs (October). Archived at www.europarl.europa.eu/committees/en/studiesdownload.html?languageDocument=EN&file=79050.

14 International Working Group on Data Protection in Telecommunications, op. cit.

15 Ibid.

16 Ibid.

17 Information Commissioner's Office (2012) *Guidance on the Use of Cloud Computing* (February 10). Information Commissioner's Office (2012) *Outsourcing.*

18 European Parliament, op. cit.

19 Ibid.

20 Ibid.

21 Ibid.

22 *Prism* (2013) *The Guardian* (June 7). Archived at www.guardian.co.uk/world/prism.

23 European Commission, op. cit.

24 Information Commissioner's Office (2008) *Privacy by Design.* Archived at www. ico.org.uk/for_organizations/data_protection/topic_guides/~/media/documents/pdb_report_html/PRIVACY_BY_DESIGN_REPORT_V2.ashx.

25 See, for example, JISC (2010) *Identity Management Toolkit* (June 30). Archived at www.jisc.ac.uk/whatwedo/programmes/aim/idmtoolkit.aspx.

26 Kern, T., Willcocks, L. P. and van Heck, E. (2002) 'The Winner's Curse in IT Outsourcing: Strategies for Avoiding Relational Trauma'. *California Management Review*, 44(2): 47–69.

27 See, for example, Wang, R. (2011) 'Monday's Musings: Lessons Learned From Amazon's Cloud Outage' (April 25). Archived at www.forbes.com/sites/ciocentral/2011/04/25/mondays-musings-lessons-learned-from-amazons-cloud-outage/.

28 Anthes, G. (2010) 'Security in the Cloud.' *Communications of the ACM*, 53(11): 16–18.

CHAPTER 6

1 See Naughton, J. (1999) *A Brief History of The Future. The Origins of the Internet.* London, Phoenix. See also Naughton, J. (2008) 'Thanks, Gutenberg – But We're Too Pressed for Time to Read.' *The Observer,* January 27, p. 12 Business section.

2 As just one example see ECISM (2009) *Future Internet 2020: Visions of an Industry Expert Group.* Brussels, EC Information Society and Media.

3 Freeman, C. and Louca, F. (2001) *As Time Goes By: From Industrial Revolution To Information Revolution.* Oxford, Oxford University Press.

4 Hagel, J. and Seeley Brown, J. (2010) *Cloud Computing – Storms on the Horizon.* Boston, MA, Deloitte Center for the Edge.

5 Willcocks, L. P., Cullen, S. and Craig, A. (2011) *The Outsourcing Enterprise.* Basingstoke, Palgrave Macmillan.

6 Retana, G. F., Forman, C., Narasimhan, S., Niculescu, M. F. and Wu, D. J. (2012) 'Technical Support and IT Capacity Demand: Evidence from the Cloud.' *Thirty-third International Conference on Information Systems,* Orlando, FL.

7 Xue, M. and Harker, P.T. (2002) 'Customer Efficiency.' *Journal of Service Research,* 4(4): 253–67. Also Xue, M., Hitt, L. M., and Harker, P.T. (2007) 'Customer Efficiency, Channel Usage and Firm Performance in Retail Banking.' *Manufacturing and Service Operations Management,* 9(4): 535–58.

8 Greenhalgh, T., Glenn, R., MacFarlane, F., Bate, P., and Kyriakidou, O. (2004) 'Diffusion of Innovation in Service Organizations: Systematic Review and Recommendations.' *Milbank Quarterly,* 82(4): 581–629.

9 Venters, W. and Whitley, E. A. (2012) 'A Critical Review of Cloud Computing: Researching Desires and Realities.' *Journal of Information Technology,* 27(3): 179–97.

10 Whitley, E. A. and Willcocks, L. P. (2011) 'Achieving Step-change in Outsourcing Maturity: Toward Collaborative Innovation.' *MIS Quarterly Executive,* 10(3): 95–109.

11 Ibid.

12 Greenhalgh, Glenn, MacFarlane, Bate, and Kyriakidou, op. cit.

13 See also Lacity, M. and Willcocks, L. (2012) *Advanced Outsourcing Practice: Rethinking ITO, BPO and Cloud Services.* London, Palgrave.

14 A recent paper shows that information technology innovations often move in packs and this seems to be the case with cloud. It is the interactions between base technology innovations, technology service innovations and technology process innovations that made Internet computing, and will make cloud, a disruptive, radical IT innovation. See Carlo, J., Lyytinen, K., and Rose, G. (2011) 'Internet Computing as a Disruptive Technology: The Role of Strong Order Effects.' *Information Systems Journal,* 21: 91–122.

15 Some research sees the cloud disruptive sequence being 1. new delivery models, 2. technology disruption, 3. restructuring the IT industry and 4. disruption of other industries. See Hagel and Seeley Brown, op. cit. We see technological disruption being cumulative and ongoing. Clearly cloud does introduce new delivery models, which we see as maturing over time. Here, we are particularly interested in how these delivery models will need to grow the service dimension and produce business services. Undoubtedly there is already disruption of the IT supply industry, as

documented in our previous paper. In this chapter we focus on how businesses and government agencies will innovate in their practices, structures, processes, and market offerings.

16 Interview with Jimmy Harris, Accenture, November 2010. Quoted in Willcocks, L., Venters, W. and Whitley, E. (2011) *Cloud and the Future of Business 4 – Innovation.* London, Accenture/Outsourcing Unit.

17 Interview with Steve Beck, December 2010.

18 Barzilai-Nahon, K. and Mason, R. M. (2010) 'How Executives Perceive the Net Generation.' *Information, Communication and Society*, 13(3): 396–418.

19 Interview with Tim Barker, SalesForce.com, November 2010. Quoted in Willcocks, Venters and Whitley, op. cit.

20 Interview with Mike Dino DiPetrollo, November 2010. Quoted in Willcocks, Venters and Whitley, op. cit.

21 See Willcocks, L. Petherbridge, P. and Olson, N. (2003) *Making IT Count: Strategy, Delivery and Infrastructure*, London, Palgrave, for a detailed assessment of how IT is managed and the typical problems IT functions face.

22 Interview with Tim Barker, SalesForce.com, op. cit.

23 Interview with Jim Spooner, November 2010. Quoted in Willcocks, Venters and Whitley, op. cit.

24 Ibid.

25 One famous case is of a pharmaceutical company that paid for capability with a credit card and got the results of the analysis sooner and cheaper than via a formal, in-house request to computing resources.

26 Interview with Jimmy Harris, op. cit.

27 Interview with David Leyland, Glasshouse, July 2010. Quoted in Willcocks, Venters and Whitley, op. cit.

28 Interview with Jimmy Harris, op. cit.

29 Ibid.

30 Ibid.

31 Interview with Steve Furminger, December 2010. Quoted in Willcocks, Venters and Whitley, op. cit.

32 Interview with Kevin Lees, November 2010. Quoted in Willcocks, Venters and Whitley, op. cit.

33 Interview with Jim Rivera, SalesForce.com, November 2010. Quoted in Willcocks, Venters and Whitley, op. cit.

34 Interview with Russell Marsh, December 2010. Quoted in Willcocks, Venters and Whitley, op. cit.

35 Interview with Stephanie Lester, Glasshouse, November 2012. Quoted in Willcocks, L. and Lacity, M. (2012) *The Emerging IT Outsourcing Landscape: From Innovation to Cloud Services*. London, Palgrave.

36 Interview with Jimmy Harris, op cit.

37 See O'Reilly III, C. and Tushman, M. (2004) 'The Ambidextrous Organization.' *Harvard Business Review*, 82(4): 74–81.

38 Brown, J. S. (2003) 'Does IT Matter? Letter to the Editor.' *Harvard Business Review*, (July): 109–12.

39 Interview with Jim Rivera, op. cit.

40 Britton, D., P. Clark, et al. (2004) 'A Grid for Particle Physics – From Testbed to Production.' *GridPP*, www.Gridpp.ac.uk. See also Berman, F. and Hey, T. (2004) 'The Scientific Imperative.' In: I. Foster and C. Kesselman (eds) *The Grid 2*. San Francisco, CA, Morgan Kaufmann.

41 Zheng, Y., Venters, W. and Cornford, T. (2011) 'Agility, Paradox and Organizational Improvisation: The Development of a Particle Physics Grid.' *Information Systems Journal*, 21(4): 303–33.

42 For more information on our research on the innovative management practices of particle physicists at CERN see www.pegasus.lse.ac.uk – a five-year research study of their Grid Development. Pegasus is funded by the UK EPSRC research council – Grant no. EP/D049954/1.

43 Traweek, S. (1988) *Beamtimes and Lifetimes: The World of High Energy Physics*. Cambridge, MA, Harvard University Press; Knorr-Cetina, K. (1999) *Epistemic Cultures: How the Sciences Make Knowledge*. Cambridge, MA, Harvard University Press.

44 The examples are anonymous as at September 2013 as we were still researching the cases and seeking permissions. However, the Fortune 500 companies include two global retailers and the SMEs include a cloud-based business in the art industry. Relevant working papers can be accessed at www.outsourcingunit.org as they are published.

CHAPTER 7

1 See Willcocks, L. Venters, W. and Whitley, E. (2011) *Cloud and the Future of Business 1 – Promise*. London, Accenture/LSE Outsourcing Unit.

2 Interview with Jimmy Harris of Accenture, October 2010. Quoted in Willcocks, L. Venters, W. and Whitley, E. (2011) *Cloud and the Future of Business 5 – Management*. London, Accenture/LSE Outsourcing Unit.

3 Simon May of Microsoft, quoted in Sherriff, L. (2011) 'What the Future Holds.' *Cloud Business*, July 19.

4 Chuck Hollis, EMC Chief Technology Officer, speaking at the EMC Inform conference, summer 2011 (www.crn.com.au/News/260029,exclusive-emcs-chuck-hollis-on-big-data-and-the-private-cloud.aspx). According to the study 1.8 zettabytes of data will be created and replicated in 2011 and that figure will have risen to 35 zettabytes by 2020, equating to a 1000 percent increase in server images in that period. Figures from IDC's Digital Universe study 'Extracting Value from Chaos,' IDC (2011). The study also suggests that by 2020, about a third of all data will either live in, or pass through, the cloud.

5 For further insight into constructive management responses to this massive data explosion – through data platforms and business analytics – see Nanterme, N. and Campbell, K. (2011) *Accenture Technology Vision 2011*. London, Accenture.

6 Horses for Sources and LSE Outsourcing Unit survey of cloud computing, November 2010.

7 See Overby, S. (2011) 'CIOs Lack Adequate Cloud Computing Knowledge.' *CIO Magazine*, August 1, 2011. She reports on a survey of providers and advisors by KPMG Sourcing Advisory.

8 Interview with Matthew Coates in discussion with Andrew and John Hindle of Accenture, September 16, 2011. Quoted in Willcocks, Venters and Whitley (2011) *Cloud and the Future of Business 5*.

9 See Willcocks, L., Cullen, S. and Craig, A. (2011) *The Outsourcing Enterprise: From Cost Management to Collaborative Innovation*, London, Palgrave, for the most recent detailed account of this history and a description of the retained core capabilities needed by clients to run IT and back-office functions.

10 This research is distilled in several recent publications. See Lacity, M. and Willcocks, L. (2009) *Information Systems and Outsourcing: Studies in Theory and Practice*. London, Palgrave; Willcocks, Cullen, and Craig, op. cit.; Willcocks, L. and Lacity, M. (2012) *The New Outsourcing Landscape: From IT to Cloud Services*. London, Palgrave; Lacity, M. and Willcocks, L. (2012) *Advanced Outsourcing Practice: Rethinking ITO, BPO and Cloud Services*. London, Palgrave.

11 See Willcocks, L., Venters, W. and Whitley, E. (2011) *Cloud and the Future of Business 2 – Challenges*. London, Accenture, LSE Outsourcing Unit. Also Willcocks, L., Venters, W. and Whitley, E. (2011) *Cloud and the Future of Business 4 – Innovation*. London, Accenture, LSE Outsourcing Unit.

12 Our research in 2000–2002 documented developments in application services provision that were, in retrospect, the prototype for the emerging cloud landscape, but that at the time lacked the further necessary developments and convergence in technology, large-scale supplier investment, and multiple large client take-up. See Kern, T., Lacity, M. and Willcocks, L. (2002) *Netsourcing: Renting Business Applications and Services over a Network*. New Jersey, Prentice Hall.

13 We use the term 'technology function' rather than the more normal 'IT function' to capture the convergence of technologies taking place, the development of cloud computing, and the role of technologists in the increasing digitization of business. The function's role is shifting, reflected in the changing status of the CIO. This, we are finding, does not stand for 'career is over' (perhaps 'concept is over'?) but the work is changing, with a possible division going to occur between those who keep the current technology base optimal – the chief technology officer – and those who focus on strategy, business, information, and innovation. Already in our model the informed buying capability has been developing to relieve the CIO of responsibility for managing the external supply side.

14 In our survey of 347 buyers across industry sectors, between 64 and 80 percent of buyers said that they were going to increase their outsourcing moderately or significantly in the next year (Survey by LSE Outsourcing Unit and Horses For Sources, July 2011; see www.horsesforsources.com/research-services and www.outsourcing unit.org).

15 In this chapter we focus on management of the technology function, which is central to cloud deployment. However, the retained capabilities model we detail also applies, with minor adjustments, to IT- and cloud-enabled business back-office and other functions such as human resources, procurement, accounting and finance,

and sales. The supporting case research appears in Willcocks, L. and Lacity, M. (2006) *Global Sourcing of Business and IT Services*, London, Palgrave, chapters 3, 6, 7, 8. See also Lacity, M. and Willcocks, L. (2011) 'Business Process Outsourcing Studies: A Critical Review and Future Research Directions.' *Journal of Information Technology*, 26(4): 1–38.

16 See Willcocks, Cullen and Craig, op. cit. chapter 1.

17 Interview with Matthew Coates, op. cit.

18 Quoted in Willcocks and Lacity, op. cit.

19 Interview with Matthew Coates, op. cit.

20 This research is from Willcocks and Lacity, op. cit.

21 We saw a bank and a manufacturer give away their architects, assuming that the task of architecture planning was technical and therefore one for the suppliers. Three years into outsourcing found each of them rebuilding this capability, because they could not understand, let alone talk with and influence the suppliers about, how to address existing and fresh demand through a new technology platform with better economics. See Willcocks and Lacity, op. cit., chapter 7.

22 Quoted in Hall, S. (2011) 'Cloud Architect: Triple Play of Skills.' *CIO.com* and *Infoworld* April 5.

23 David Linthicum of Microsoft in 'Why the Shortage of Cloud Architects Will Lead to Bad Clouds.' *Computerworld*, July 28, 2011.

24 Interview with Hong Chiong of Microsoft, October 2010. Quoted in Willcocks, Venters and Whitley, op. cit.

25 Interview with Oscar Trimboli, Partner & Channels Director at Polycom, on April 23, 2013.

26 See Poston, R., Kettinger, W. and Simon, J. (2009) 'Managing the Vendor Set: Achieving Best Price and Quality Service in IT Outsourcing.' *MISQ Executive*, 8(2): 45–58. These authors draw lessons from how one multinational organization managed its vendor set in the outsourcing of software development and testing activities. They conclude that client managers who outsource to vendors need to establish the appropriate balance between building strong collaborative relationships and encouraging market competition among a set of three or more vendors to ensure best price and service quality.

27 Taken from case research in Willcocks and Lacity, op. cit., chapter 7.

28 Interview with Frank Modruson, CIO of Accenture, July 2011. He gave the example of Accenture's own recruitment and selection process. Accenture is highly reliant on talent, but the secret sauce is who you attract, select, and hire and this is not embedded in the technology and software. As a result, the organization has been a SaaS center for recruiting for six years. Quoted in Willcocks, Venters and Whitley, (2011) *Cloud and the Future of Business 5.*

29 Interview with Neil Thomas, Cable and Wireless, September 16, 2011. Quoted in Willcocks, Venters and Whitley, (2011) *Cloud and the Future of Business 5.*

30 Ibid.

31 Interview with Tim Barker of SalesForce.com, November 2010. Quoted in Willcocks, Venters and Whitley, (2011), *Cloud and the Future of Business 5.*

32 See Willcocks, Cullen and Craig, op. cit., chapter 5 for a detailed analysis with case examples.

33 Frank Modruson, op. cit.

34 Interview with Jim Rivera of SalesForce.com, October 2010. Quoted in Willcocks, Venters and Whitley, (2011), *Cloud and the Future of Business 5*.

35 Interviews with Kevin Lees of VMware and Jim Spooner of Glasshouse, November 2010. Quoted in Willcocks, Venters and Whitley, (2011), *Cloud and the Future of Business 5*.

36 Interview with Sanjay Mirchandini, EMC, December 2010. Chuck Hollis, Chief Technology Officer of EMC, elaborates on this by suggesting three relatively new roles: cloud architects, process re-engineers, and business enablers. The other key cloud-related roles include cloud service managers, cloud capacity planners, cloud infrastructure administrators, cloud security architects, and cloud governance, risk, and compliance managers. Our own model embraces these roles, using a different vocabulary, and assumes a higher degree of cloud outsourcing than at EMC. Quoted in Willcocks, Venters and Whitley, (2011), *Cloud and the Future of Business 5*.

37 Quote from outsourcing research in Willcocks, Cullen and Craig, op. cit.

38 Interview with Tim Barker, op. cit.

39 See Willcocks, L., Petherbridge, P. and Olson, N. (2003) *Making IT Count: Strategy, Delivery, Infrastructure*. Oxford, Butterworth, chapter 8. Also Willcocks, Cullen and Craig, op. cit.

40 See Whitley, E. and Willcocks, L. (2011) 'Achieving Maturity in Outsourcing Capability: Towards Collaborative Innovation.' *MISQ Executive*, 10(3), 95–107.

41 Heifetz, R. A. (1994) *Leadership without Easy Answers*. Cambridge, MA, The Belknap Press of Harvard University Press.

42 Interview with Sanjay Mirchandani, op. cit.

43 Interview with Neil Thomas, op. cit.

44 Fraser Kyne, technology specialist, Citrix: 'cloud signifies skills change for IT Pros, Citrix says.' Downloaded from *Forbes*, June 30, 2011.

45 Interview with Frank Modruson, op. cit. In very large organizations, he saw e-mail, infrastructure, and stand-alone or isolated systems moving to the cloud quite quickly, and the more deeply integrated systems such as ERP moving on a much longer time frame because of complex requirements and difficulties in finding cloud providers operating at the right scale.

CHAPTER 8

1 Brynjolfsson, E., Hofmann, P. and Jordan J. (2010) 'Economic and Business Dimensions of Cloud Computing and Electricity: Beyond the Utility Model.' *Communications of the ACM*, 53(5): 32–4.

2 Indeed, some argue that the term cloud computing emerged because of the use of the cloud to represent the Internet in such networking diagrams. See Regalado, A. (2011) 'Who Coined "Cloud Computing"?' *Technology Review*, 3: 140–8.

3 These perspectives are widely known within the study of technology adoption. Examples in the literature are: Bijker, W. (1995) *Of Bicycles, Bakelites and Bulbs; Toward a Theory of Sociotechnical Change.* Cambridge, MA: MIT Press; Bijker, W., Hughes, T. and Pinch, T. (eds) (1987) *The Social Construction of Technological Systems: New Directions in the Sociology and History of Technology.* Cambridge, MA, MIT Press.

4 See Agar, J. (2013) *Constant Touch: A Global History of the Mobile Phone.* London: Icon Books.

5 McAfee, A. (2011) 'What Every CEO Needs to Know About the Cloud.' *Harvard Business Review,* 89 (11, November): 124–30.

6 Bughin, J., Chui, M. and Manyika, J. (2013) 'Ten IT-enabled Business Trends for the Decade Ahead.' *McKinsey Quarterly,* May: 1–13.

7 Venters, W. (2010) 'Knowledge Management Technology-in-practice: A Social Constructionist Analysis of the Introduction and Use of Knowledge Management Systems.' *Knowledge Management Research and Practice,* 8: 161–72.

8 Venters, W. and Wood, B. (2007) 'Degenerative Structures that Inhibit the Emergence of Communities of Practice: A Case Study of Knowledge Management in the British Council.' *Information Systems Journal,* 17(4): 349–68.
Venters, W. (2006) 'The Use of Technology within Knowledge Management: A Review.' *Journal of Intelligent Systems,* 15(1–4): 329–56.

9 Kaganer, E., Carmel, E., Hirschheim, R. and Olsen, T. (2013) 'Managing The Human Cloud.' *MIT Sloan Management Review,* 54(2, Winter): 23–32.

10 Carr, N. (2008) *The Big Switch: Rewiring the World, from Edison to Google.* New York, W. W. Norton.

11 Mark Benioff of SalesForce.com famously sold his software direct to sales departments and suggested that IT departments were getting in the way of the innovations cloud computing might bring. See Benioff, M. and Adler, C. (2009) *Behind the Cloud – The Untold Story of How SalesForce.com Went from Idea to Billion-dollar Company and Revolutionized an Industry.* San Francisco, CA, Jossey-Bass.

12 'Sukey take it off again.' *The Economist,* January 28 2011.

13 Levinson, M. (2006) *The Box: How the Shipping Container Made the World Smaller and the World Economy Bigger.* Princeton, NJ, Princeton University Press.

14 Friedman, T. (2005) *The World is Flat: A Brief History of the Globalized World in the 21st Century.* London, Allen Lane.

15 For example, the increasingly influential Apache CloudStack offers a standardized open-source cloud-based IaaS service that allows services to be ported between different cloud providers.

16 Hanseth, O. and Braa, K. (2000) 'Who's in Control: Designers, Managers – or Technology? Infrastructures at Norsk Hydro.' In: C. Ciborra (ed.) *From Control to Drift.* Oxford University Press: 125–47.

17 Hanseth, O. (2000) 'The Economics of Standards.' Ibid: 56–70.

18 Ibid.

19 www.lifehacker.com.au/2011/02/when-cloud-computing-looks-like-a-return-to-mainframe.

20 Ceruzzi, P. (2002) *A History of Modern Computing.* Cambridge, MA, MIT Press.

21 Keen, P. G. W. and Woodman, L. (1984) 'What to Do with All Those Micros: First Make Them Part of the Team.' *Harvard Business Review*, 62(5): 142–50.

22 Guimaraes, T. and Ramanujam, V. (1986) 'Personal Computing Trends and Problems: An Empirical Study.' *MIS Quarterly*, 10(2): 179–87.

23 Benioff and Adler, op. cit.

24 Lee, D. (1986) 'Usage Patterns and Sources of Assistance for Personal Computer Users.' *MIS Quarterly*, 10(4): 313–25.

25 Carr, N. (2005) 'The End of Corporate Computing.' *MIT Sloan Management Review*, 46(3): 67–73.

26 Guimaraes and Ramanujam, (1986) op. cit.: 179–87.

27 Guimaraes, T. and Ramanujam, V. (1986) op. cit.

28 Keen, and Woodman, op. cit.

29 Benson, D. (1983) 'A Field Study of End User Computing: Findings and Issues.' *MIS Quarterly*, 7(4): 35–45.

30 Campbell-Kelly, M. (2003) *From Airline Reservations to Sonic the Hedgehog: A History of the Software Industry*. Cambridge, MA, MIT Press.

31 Ibid.

32 Keen and Woodman, op. cit.

33 Carr (2008), *The Big Switch*.

34 O'Reilly III, C. and Tushman, M. (2004) 'The Ambidextrous Organization.' *Harvard Business Review*, 82(4): 74–81.

35 Brown, J. S. (2003) 'Does IT Matter? Letter to the Editor.' *Harvard Business Review*, July: 109–12.

36 Carr, N. (2003) 'IT Doesn't Matter.' *Harvard Business Review*, May: 41–9.

37 Fukuyama, F. (1992) *The End of History and the Last Man*. New York, Free Press.

CHAPTER 9

1 Manyika, J., Chui, M., Bughin, J., Dobbs, P., Bisson, P. and Marrs, A. (2013) *Disruptive Technologies: Advances that Will Transform Life, Business and the Global Economy*. New York, McKinsey Global Institute.

2 Jan Chipchase (2007) Nokia – Ted Talk, www.ted.com/talks/jan_chipchase_on_our_mobile_phones.html.

3 Kallinikos, J., Aaltonen, A. and Marton A. (2013) 'The Ambivalent Ontology of Digital Artifacts.' *Management Information Systems Quarterly*, 37(2): 357–70.

4 'Schumpeter "Slaves to the smartphone"' (2012) *The Economist*, March 10. www.economist.com/node/21549904.

5 Gawer, A. and Cusumano, M. (2002) *Platform Leadership*. Boston, MA, Harvard Business School Press.

6 This value is based on improved service delivery, productivity improvements, value from Internet use, and new usage. Manyika, Chui, Bughin, Bisson and Marrs, op. cit.

7 Sorensen, C. (2011) *Enterprise Mobility: Tiny Technology with Global Impact on work*. Basingstoke, Palgrave Macmillan.

8 Ibid.

9 This example is taken from Mayer-Schonberger, V. and Cukier, K. (2013) *Big Data: A Revolution That Will Transform How We Live, Work and Think*. London, John Murray, which provides a detailed overview of the theory of big data and in particular its focus on seeking correlation in data without demanding the need or expectation to understand causality.

10 www.quotes.net/quote/34580.

11 These computers were developed to provide cheap hobby and educational computing for children. By 2013, over a million had been sold. See www.raspberrypi.org.

12 McKinsey Global Institute report, May 2013: 1–52.

13 The example is taken from Pritchard, S. (2012) 'Mobile Comms: Coffee and TV.' In: *IT Pro*, May 4. London: Dennis Publishing.

14 For example, for the 2012 film *Skyfall*, one of James Bond's Aston Martins was printed in this way.

15 See Behrokh Khoshnevis from University of Southern California (see TEDx talk: www.youtube.com/watch?v=JdbJP8Gxqog).

16 This point is significant because with subtractive manufacturing the subtracted material is wasted. Furthermore, the design of subtractively manufactured components often contains wasted material. For example, it is impossible to hollow out a part without leaving a hole (necessary to get the waste material out) to be covered. Many components therefore contain lots of unnecessary material. Aeroplane manufacturers are looking at additive manufacturing to produce metal parts that are hollow where no load is being carried but do not contain holes or joins.

17 As exemplified in publications such as http://makezine.com.

18 http://fablabadelaide.org.au/what-is-a-fab-lab.

19 Manyika, Chui, Bughin, Bisson and Marrs, op. cit.

20 Anderson, C. (2012) *Makers: The New Industrial Revolution*. New York, Random House Business Books.

21 They were, however, removed from the hosting site soon after the 2013 Newtown Connecticut massacre, when 20 children and 6 adults were killed by a similar weapon.

22 Indeed, a group called 'Defense Distributed' intends to create an entirely 3D-printable gun. http://defensedistributed.com.

23 www.forbes.com/sites/andygreenberg/2012/12/19/3d-printing-startup-makerbot-cracks-down-on-printable-gun-designs.

INDEX

Printed and bound by CPI Group (UK) Ltd, Croydon, CR0 4YY